Chutzpah Marketing

Simple Low Cost Secrets to Building Your Business Fortune

Philip Copitch, Ph.D.
Marketing Maven

Written and illustrated by Philip Copitch, Ph.D.
Printed in the United States of America.

HERE TO SERVE YOU:

Hutzpah Press titles are available in quantity discounts for promotions, premiums and fund raisers.

Our titles can be custom imprinted with your company name and information.

FOR FURTHER INFORMATION
PLEASE CONTACT:

HUTZPAH PRESS
PO BOX 400
IGO CA 96047-0400

Please contact:
Geri Copitch, Sr. Editor
Geri@CopitchInc.com

Dr. Phil's web site:
www.CopitchInc.com

DEDICATION

Special thanks goes to my bride of over 20 years—Geri, an amazing person who warms the hearts of all who know her and the only one I know who can put up with me.

Thank you for encouraging my behavior.

Philip Copitch, Ph.D.

Tell me, I forget.

Show me, I remember.

Involve me, I understand.

Chutzpah Table of Contents

7. Advertising Part D: Your Office, Store, and Vehicles Are Chutzpah Marketing Tools 160

8. Your phone and email are chutzpah marketing tools 211

LIST OF SIDEBAR SYMBOLS

The Chutzpah Light Bulb icon represents an audacious idea.

The Shooting Star icon represents a low cost brilliant action. These stories are inspirational and often worth copying.

The Chutzpah Bomb icon represents a huge pile of mistake. Avoid at all costs! Learn from another's mistake.

Frequently asked questions concerning marketing, asked to Dr. Copitch at seminars and presentations.

INTRODUCTION

Hopefully you are asking, "What is Chutzpah Marketing?"

First, what is chutzpah? It is boldness coupled with supreme self-confidence. An old Yiddish joke illustrates the power of chutzpah:

> A man murders his mother and father. Then he throws himself on the mercy of the court because he's an orphan.

Now that's chutzpah!

Chutzpah marketing is business boldness coupled with supreme self-confidence. It is the art of doing something right, fairly, and with value.

Business is said to be cutthroat, but that is not what I am teaching. I am talking about being basically lazy and getting a lot done. I want you to do what works, and skip the aggravation of wasted effort. A chutzpah marketer doesn't waste time or money. She works hard and plays hard while loving it all. She has clear goals and follows them. She looks at her options and makes only well informed decisions. Once a decision is made she does not second-guess herself. She is confident that she did her homework and is now following a sound course of action. A chutzpah marketer can make a decision. She is task oriented and prides herself on task completion.

A chutzpah marketer won't spend a dime if 9¢ will do. But, she is not cheap. She is value oriented. When making purchases she is value conscious. She is future oriented and sees that she is investing in her business, not merely spending money.

A chutzpah marketer is ethical. She carefully abides by the ethical standards of her profession. The ethical standards are incorporated into the very foundation of her business plan.

Please let me tell you a story.

Uncle Sol had a tough life. It started in northern Europe. His family was encouraged to move by the Cossacks. This took the family to central Europe. In time, he and his family were invited to relocate by the Nazis. They spent everything they had to get to America in 1942.

Uncle Sol found himself in New York City with no job, no money, and a distinctively thick Yiddish accent.

Uncle Sol had always been a salesman. So, he went to the biggest store in town and tried to put in an employment application.

"This turned out not to be so easy," Sol told his friend Moesha.

"So, how did you get the job?" Moesha asked.

"Vell I went to the head of the employment department and I said, 'I know you don't know me from Moses, but I'm a really good salesman.'"

"The boss man was not so impressed with me so I said, 'Look, you must have a department that isn't making its money for you, give me a chance. I'll work for free for a month. If at the end of the month, you don't like my work, you say, 'Sol, sorry but it didn't work out.' And I go. No hard feelings. You didn't pay me a penny. What do you have to lose? But, if I make you <u>lots</u> of money, you pay me, and I keep making you lots of money.'"

"The boss thought it over a bit and said to me, 'The fishing department is the worst department in the store. Can you sell fishing equipment?'"

"Can I <u>sell</u> fishing equipment?" I told the boss. "Can a fish swim?"

Over the next two weeks the sales in the fishing department went up steadily. By the third week, the boss man was so curious about how Uncle Sol was achieving such numbers, he went down to investigate. He hid behind a display case and listened.

"Vell, that is a pretty good hook," Uncle Sol told a middle-aged man. "But I don't think it is right for you. It's pretty good, but this bronze tip hook over here, it only costs 11 cents a box more, but it can really hold a fish."

"I'll take it," the man said.

"What do you fish with?" Uncle Sol asked.

"A bamboo pole…"

"A bamboo pole!" Uncle Sol said as he took the brass tipped hooks from the man. "You don't need these. With your pole, why bother… you couldn't land a big fish with an old bamboo pole."

"Really? But I want them," the man said as he took back his brass tipped hooks from Uncle Sol.

"You need a Flexi Bow 17Xr5. It's pricey, but with those hooks…"

The man took hold of the rod.

"Where do you fish from?" Uncle Sol inquired.

"Down at Staten bea…"

Uncle Sol grabbed back the fishing pole. "From the beach! You don't need the Flexi Bow to fish from shore… Who fishes from dirt?"

The man snatched back his fishing pole. "I want to use <u>this</u> pole!"

"But for that pole you're going to need to be out where the big fish live. That pole is for people who want to catch the big fish. You'll need the Wave Crasher xz1000."

All this time the boss man was listening intensely. He had never seen such a skilled salesman.

At closing the boss man went to see Uncle Sol.

"You have the job," he said as he shook Uncle Sol's hand. "I saw you sell the Wave Crasher xz1000 today, the most expensive item in the department. I still can't believe it, a customer came in for a fishing hook, and you sold him a boat! Amazing!"

"A fishing hook, no, no, no, he no come in for a fishing hook," Uncle Sol said.

"Really, but I saw…"

"No one comes into this store for fishing hooks. We're in the basement, no one knows we're even here. So I have to go upstairs and get them." Uncle Sol said.

"Upstairs?"

"Sure, upstairs. I went up to the pharmacy department and this nice man was buying some lady monthly products so I said to him. 'I see you're no having any fun this weekend, do you fish?'"

Uncle Sol had Chutzpah: business boldness coupled with supreme self-confidence.

> The best way to predict your future is to create it.
>
> Peter Druckert

Are you allowed to build a business and make an impressive living? Are you allowed to afford amazing vacations, retirement plans, and a second home?

The simple answer is yes!

So let's get started on getting you lots more paying customers that talk highly of your work and subsequently get you even more paying customers.

A note on terminology

Throughout this text I will switch between male and female pronouns. This represents my experience in the business world. I have worked with a lot of men and woman business owners.

I will use words like: customer, consumer, buyer, purchaser, patron, subscriber, or shopper interchangeably.

I expect my readers to be from a wide variety of businesses. Thus, the shopkeeper may be more comfortable with the word *customer*, while the lawyer may be used to the word *client*. When talking about a potential customer or client I often use the word *prospect* meaning: *a person regarded as a potential customer or subscriber to something.*

> The more I know about business, the more I'm convinced that it is conducted in homes and churches far more than in office buildings.
>
> Laura Moncur, Merriton

"Well Hobson, that's the rough concept for the new business plan. Why don't you muck out the fine details and have it on my desk by 9 A.M. Monday."

1. TALK TO, NOT AT, YOUR CUSTOMERS

Throughout this book, in many different ways, we are going to discuss motivating a customer to pick your company over every other company in your community. In some cases, due to the Internet, you may well be competing with companies all over the world. Business is a highly competitive endeavor, and the goal of your marketing program is to get the customer to pick you.

There are a lot of other voices yelling "pick me," all in direct competition with you for the money in your potential customer's pocket. Most of these other voices have more money and name recognition than you presently have. So, how do you compete for the minds of your prospects? The answer is, your marketing must talk to your prospect, solving a want that she has when she has it. You must use chutzpah marketing!

Before I explain how to talk to your customer, let me take a moment to define chutzpah marketing.

Chutzpah marketing is everything and anything you do to get the customer to pick you, keep picking you, and to tell their friends and family that they should pick you!

Anything and everything? Yep, anything and everything! From print advertising to customer service; from signage to clean restrooms; from welcoming smiles to clear return policies. Chutzpah marketers embrace the customer from first contact until after the product or service is all used up or completed. I agree completely with L.L. Bean who said, "No sale is really complete until the product is worn out, and the customer is satisfied."

Chutzpah marketers strive to enthuse customers at every contact point. Basic contacts run the gambit, including each time the customer enters the store, calls on the phone, enjoys the product or service, or tells others of their experience with the chutzpah business, are major events for the chutzpah marketer. A chutzpah marketer's goal is to have their customer be filled with avid enjoyment whenever they interact or think about your business.

Luckily for us, most businesses treat their customers as if they are the enemy, or at least a nuisance. So a little chutzpah marketing goes a long way, and a lot of chutzpah marketing takes your company to outstanding heights.

To pull this chutzpah enthusiasm together we are going to need to know how your company fits into the the minds of your customers.

The psychology of your customer's mind

The human mind has the ability to keep track of six or seven things at one time. This could be numbers, such as a phone number, or a list of seven items to pick up at the store.

Local phone numbers are typically seven digits long, 123-4567. They tend to be pretty easy for most people to learn. Once you add the area code, you get ten digits e.g. (202)456-1414. Most people have a tough time remembering ten digits. In order to master this we kind of cheat. We categorize the numbers into memorable packages of seven digits or less. For example, the area code for Washington, D.C. is 202. So, if I told you that the number for the White House Switchboard is 456-1414, you could put the two pieces of information together and pretty easily memorize the phone number for the White House Switchboard 202-456-1414.

There has been a lot of research done to prove that humans do well remembering seven things at a time. By grouping items together, we can easily expand our basic skill past seven items.

In marketing lingo, getting things to stick in a customer's mind is called branding or positioning. Throughout this book I am going to show you how to get your company's offerings positioned in your customer's mind so that you will have a customer for life. In addition to becoming a customer for life, this same customer will talk glowingly about your company, thus sending more customers your way. All this on a shoestring budget.

Branding

In the cereal aisle Wheaties has taught you that it is the "Breakfast of Champions". Cheerios has taught you that they are the "heart healthy" cereal. Kix has branded themselves as the "mom approved" cereal. What position does your company hold in the mind of the community? For some of you it may be that the community doesn't know you exist (yet!). For others, you are an established business with little growth potential until you evolve your branding.

Your company's positioning needs to be a choice made by you. It is how you have taught others to think of you (or not think of you).

When people shop they shop in categories. The consumer's mind is too full to keep all information readily available. So, consumers place things into categories. Examples of categories are:

Expensive shoe stores	Inexpensive shoe stores
Dirty restaurants	Clean restaurants
Sit down restaurants	Fast food
Friendly tire store	Unfriendly tire store
Large cheese selection	Basic cheese selection

The categories are developed by consumers based on their personality and their experiences. So, the same grocery store can be in different categories for different people. My wife and I have different categories for the grocery store we shop at the most:

My Beloved Wife	Dr. Phil
Convenient	On the way home
Friendly employees	Talkative employees

My Beloved Wife	Dr. Phil
Great vegetable selection. Clean, consistently good quality	Overpriced

We have our categories built from our experiences. Although we do a lot of shopping there, we go way across town to the less expensive, larger store that neither of us really likes.

The two stores understand us too. One advertises, *Lowest Prices In Town*, while the other proclaims, *Friendliest Store in Town*.

The categories are the stores' attributes, their positions in our minds. If they want to stay in our minds they need to live up to their attributes. If you look at my categories you will see that the "friendliest store in town" attribute is often a bother to me. I don't care for the small talk. I wouldn't mind if they had an express line specifically for No Chitchat. I want to get in and out of the store. The friendly chitchat with every customer adds up to slow moving lines for me.

If a store opened up right next-door to the friendly store, one that was exactly the same, but with a no chitchat checkout, I would choose that store on most days.

In the marketplace, business are in competition with each other. They are categorized in the minds of your potential customers and these categories, branding, is how the customer limits their choices. Have you ever wondered why the mega companies like Coke and Pepsi even bother to advertise? They're sold everywhere. Everyone already knows about them. The reason they constantly advertise is to stay in the minds of their customers. They each spend millions for a category position in our minds.

William J. McEwen in his book[1], **Married To The Brand, Why Consumers Bond With Brands For Life**, explains that, "Brands serve a greater purpose—not just for the marketer, but for the consumer, too." He continues:

> Brands identify, define, and express the experience of using the particular products and services with which customers connect. Brands are partners in the dating game, the entities with which individual consumers sometimes form important, reciprocal, and even loving relationships.

---

1 Copyright 2005, Gallup Organization

Chutzpah branding in the real world

What we need to focus on is the benefit to the customer. Let's say you're in the plumbing business or the deli business—so you sell a kitchen sink repair or

> **A business exists to create a customer**
>
> Peter F. Drucker

a pastrami on rye. What did the customer receive? More succinctly, what <u>value</u> did the customer receive?

A customer will only buy your commodities, products, services, or skills if he perceives a benefit to himself that is greater than the cost to his wallet. Customers buy because of perceived value, not because of your skill, item price, or wicked good looks. The sale and all subsequent sales are about the customer. Is the customer getting <u>their needs met</u>.

What businesses like to sell	What customers like to buy, what they value
Toaster ovens	Melted cheese on bread anytime I want it… or maybe a Pop-Tart.
Wills and trusts	A way to get my kids to go to college and finally make something out of themselves without having to hear what my sisters think I should do with my money!
Hamburgers	A cool quiet place to sit down for just a minute and feed the kids, so I can get them to soccer practice by 5.
Pizza	Food that relieves me from having to cook or clean up much.

A chutzpah marketer focuses on the needs of the customer. Too often businesses focus on their needs, forgetting that without repeat customers they are doomed.

For example, the business' versus the customer's view point:

Business' point of view	Customer's point of view
We need to sell $1800 during lunch today.	Easy to get to, cheap lunch that makes me think I'm eating kind of OK—just in case the wife asks. I have to grab a sandwich and get gas during lunch or I'll be late picking up the kids at school.
I need 6 service calls today	I need my sink unclogged by 3 PM, so I can get the kids from school. Who can I trust, because I don't know what they do under the sink, and I'm pretty sure they all overcharge.

New FTC Rulings

According to the Federal Trade Commission (http://business.ftc.gov):

The FTC's Bureau of Consumer Protection enforces laws that protect consumers against unfair or deceptive practices. The Business Center gives you and your business tools to understand and comply with the law. Regardless of the size of your organization or the industry you're in, knowing — and fulfilling — your compliance responsibilities is smart, sound business.

The guidance documents in the Business Center are your link to the law. Browse by topic - Advertising & Marketing, Credit & Finance, Privacy & Security - or by industry, to find what you need to know.

The legal resources section of the Business Center is where you'll find more in-depth, legal information - like case highlights, advisory opinions, staff letters, and rules the FTC enforces. You'll also find staff reports and FTC workshops.

The multimedia gallery offers short videos and podcasts that explain your compliance responsibilities.

The materials in the Business Center don't have any copyright restrictions, so you can share them with your employees, your colleagues and your community.

I highly recommend reading the FTC rules. You are legally obligated to follow them.

The following may be of most interest:
- Advertising and Marketing
  (http://business.ftc.gov/advertising-and-marketing)
- Federal Trade Commission 16 CFR Part 255 (Guides Concerning the Use of Endorsements and Testimonials in Advertising
- Online Advertising and Marketing
  (http://business.ftc.gov/advertising-and-marketing/online-advertising-and-marketing)
- Selected Industries (http://business.ftc.gov/selected-industries)
- Advertising FAQ's: A Guide for Small Business [PDF] (Advertising FAQ's: A Guide for Small Business | BCP Business Center)

The following is excerpted from the FTC's: **Advertising FAQ's: A Guide for Small Business.**

What truth-in-advertising rules apply to advertisers?
Under the Federal Trade Commission Act: Advertising must be truthful and non-deceptive; Advertisers must have evidence to back up their claims; and Advertisements cannot be unfair.

Additional laws apply to ads for specialized products like consumer leases, credit, 900 telephone numbers, and products sold through mail order or telephone sales. And every state has consumer protection laws that govern ads running in that state.

What makes an advertisement deceptive?
According to the FTC's Deception Policy Statement, an ad is deceptive if it contains a statement - or omits information - that:
Is likely to mislead consumers acting reasonably under the circumstances; and

Is "material" - that is, important to a consumer's decision to buy or use the product.

What makes an advertisement unfair?

According to the <u>Federal Trade Commission Act</u> and the FTC's <u>Unfairness Policy Statement</u>, an ad or business practice is unfair if:

It causes or is likely to cause substantial consumer injury which a consumer could not reasonably avoid; and

It is not outweighed by the benefit to consumers.

How does the FTC determine if an ad is deceptive?

A typical inquiry follows these steps:

The FTC looks at the ad from the point of view of the "reasonable consumer" - the typical person looking at the ad. Rather than focusing on certain words, the FTC looks at the ad in context - words, phrases, and pictures - to determine what it conveys to consumers.

The FTC looks at both "express" and "implied" claims. An express claim is literally made in the ad. For example, "ABC Mouthwash prevents colds" is an express claim that the product will prevent colds. An implied claim is one made indirectly or by inference. "ABC Mouthwash kills the germs that cause colds" contains an implied claim that the product will prevent colds. Although the ad doesn't literally say that the product prevents colds, it would be reasonable for a consumer to conclude from the statement "kills the germs that cause colds" that the product will prevent colds. Under the law, advertisers must have proof to back up express <u>and</u> implied claims that consumers take from an ad.

The FTC looks at what the ad does not say - that is, if the failure to include information leaves consumers with a misimpression about the product. For example, if a company advertised a collection of books, the ad would be deceptive if it did not disclose that consumers actually would receive abridged versions of the books.

The FTC looks at whether the claim would be "material" - that is, important to a consumer's decision to buy or use the product. Examples of material claims are representations about a product's performance, features, safety, price, or effectiveness.

The FTC looks at whether the advertiser has sufficient evidence to support the claims in the ad. The law requires that advertisers have proof before the ad runs.

BigRed's as a brand

BigRed's Burgers is the newest burger joint in Fiction, California, a community of 100,000 people. Let's evaluate BigRed's to see how this business is positioned in the friendly town of Fiction.

Minnie and Big Red both retired from county employment a few years ago. Their dream was to move from the big city and open an old fashion hamburger shack like the one they fondly remember from their youth. They wanted to supplement their retirement income by grilling burgers and making friends. Their menu was simple: large portions of burgers, fries, onion rings, soft drinks, and ice cream shakes, for a fair price. They figured that they would be making money hand over fist.

After two years in business, the business was making just enough to stay open, but they hadn't yet repaid themselves for the startup funds. On a positive note, both Minnie and Big Red loved going to work and they had made some good friends in their newly adopted town.

BigRed's competition

I asked Minnie and Big Red to fill out the following 2 question form:

1. Name the business competition in your area:

_____
_____
_____
_____
_____
_____

_____
_____
_____
_____
_____
_____
_____
_____
_____

2. Place them in the following graph:

Fast Food

Sit Down
(wait staff)

Not Busy   Busy

Burger restaurants in Fiction, CA.

They completed the form as follows:

1. Name the business competition in your area:

McDonald's, Burger King, Wendy's, Carl's Jr., In-N-Out Burger, Red Robin, Marie Callender's, and Denny's.

2. Place them in the following graph:

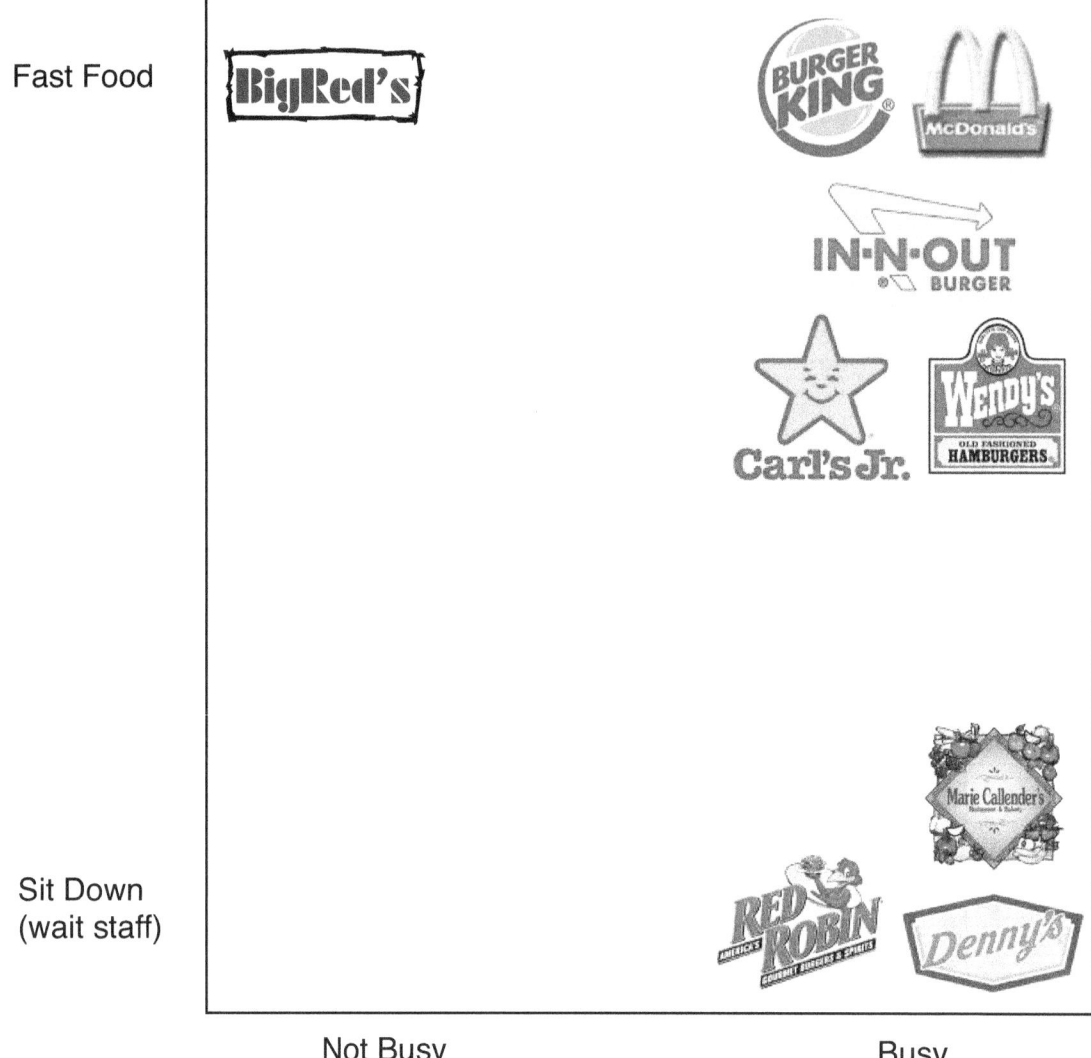

Fast Food

Sit Down
(wait staff)

Not Busy   Busy

Burger restaurants in Fiction, CA.

What this graph illustrates is that BigRed's is a small fish in a big pond. It would be very hard for BigRed's to compete head to head with the likes of McDonald's and Wendy's in the minds of burger customers.

This brings us to the chutzpah question, "How can you get a place in the customer's mind?" The answer is, place yourself in a different brand category in your customer's mind.

The big burger chains own the category, "Fast Food Burger", and they will continue to spend millions to keep that powerful branded position, while constantly fighting amongst themselves for market share. But, BigRed's has chutzpah, they can carve out a new category that the big burger corporations aren't able to occupy.

   We will come back to BigRed's in a little while, but for now, let's talk about your company. Take some time to complete the two question form:

1. Name the business competition in your area:

_____

_____

_____

_____

_____

_____

_____

_____

_____

_____

_____

_____

_____

_____

_____

_____

_____

_____

_____

_____

_____

_____

_____

_____

_____

_____

_____

_____

_____

_____

_____

_____

Place them in the following graph:

You will have to come up with the X and Y categories of your graph based on your company's business type. Some common categories are:

- Small/large
- Low market share/high market share
- Well establish name/unknown name
- Lowest prices/highest prices
- Low customer service/high customer service
- Tourist trade/local trade
- Close to freeway exit/far from freeway exit

You may find, depending on your business climate. that you will need to come up with many graphs for the same group of companies. A company and a group of companies often has the main brand and many secondary brands.

BigRed's Burgers chutzpah assignments

Let's look at how Minnie and Big Red dealt with four chutzpah branding questions.

1. List problems that you solve for your customers.
2. Who are your customers?
3. What is the brand (position) of your business in the community?
4. How does your customer find you?

I asked Minnie and Big Red to fill out these four chutzpah branding questions. They struggled with this. They both wanted to write from their point of view, but the questions need to be answered from the customer's point of view. This is what we ended up with:

#1: List problems that you solve for your customers.

- Friendly environment
- Food is tasty
- Food is made to order and served quickly
- Easy to call in lunch orders for pick up

#2: Who are your customers?

- Workers in the neighborhood
- Moms and dads in the neighborhood
- Moms and dads on the way to soccer or baseball fields
- Single people in the neighborhood

#3: What is the brand (position) of your business in the community?

- Small place with good burgers and milk shakes
- Mom and pop business, feels friendly
- Custom orders makes it easy to get exactly what you want
- Food is good but a little pricy compared to other fast food places in town

#4: How does your customer find you?

- See our sign
- Walk by and see people eating
- Newspaper ads, but we don't think they really worked

When I sat down with Minnie and Big Red, they were frustrated. They explained that they made a much better tasting burger and fries than the big companies. They were frustrated with the fact that the people of Fiction just didn't get how hard they worked putting out a quality product for them to choose!

I bring this up because this frustration is normal in the business world. Your product is superior and you have worked so hard to get where you are. But, that is all about you. To get customers to choose your business you will have to focus on your potential customers' needs. You will have to show them that you are right for them.

I asked Minnie and Big Red to tell me who their average customer was. After a little bit of brainstorming, they came up with this statement.

> Lunch is mainly hard working men looking for filling food and fast service. Dinner is overworked, really busy, moms and dads needing to get food for the family.

Then I asked the biggest question of them all:

How can you help your customers?

With this information I asked Minnie and Big Red, "How can you help your customers?"

"Help 'em? We already make the order exactly the way they want it," Big Red said.

"Yeah, but," I interrupted, "You're talking about the burger, McDonald's does burgers. What can your company do that McDonald's can't do?"

"I think the busy moms and dads would like us to deliver the food," Minnie said.

"Delivery? We have never done that," Big Red grunted.

"It's an idea. Your competitors can't deliver," I said.

Then the ideas started to flow.

Over the next month, BigRed's started three new (very low cost) services to help their customers:

1. Curb side pick-up "Dinner boxes" for the soccer and baseball families.
2. Lunch delivery service for the three business complexes just down the street.
3. Friday and Saturday night home delivery to the four apartment complexes and the six blocks of single family homes all within minutes of BigRed's.

As we will discuss in subsequent chapters, bringing unprecedented customer service tends to be inexpensive and it brings great rewards to the company that does it. By positioning BigRed's as the burger place that caters to its customers, the branding of the company changed. BigRed's left the "fast food" brand they were lost in and developed a whole new category: "Truly Helpful." A brand that stuck in the minds of their growing clientele. In a few short weeks, the fast food burger eating customers changed their thoughts from, "Rush over to Burger King's drive-thru" to "Call or email BigRed's, they'll bring it to us while we…" BigRed's became the extra pair of hands, or extra employee, their customers needed to live their lives the way they wanted to live them.

Chutzpah knowledge is power

Just a little bit of chutzpah information can go a long way. By knowing your customers and figuring out how to give them even more of what they like about your company, you too can re-brand your company as an essential part of your customer's life.

Take the time to answer the following questions. You may even want to start asking your present customers what they like about your company, why they choose your company. Stay open minded by asking yourself, "How can we do it differently?" You are looking for your new, enlightened position in your customers' minds.

#1: List problems that you solve for your customers.
#2: Who are your customers?
#3: What is the brand (position) of your business in the community?
#4: How does your customer find you?
#5: How can you help your customers?

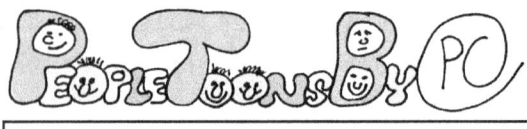

Ninja shouldn't hand out business cards.

2. YOUR MOST IMPORTANT MARKETING TOOL COSTS 5¢

If you had $5,000 dollars you could put up a billboard on a busy thoroughfare by your office or store. Hundreds or even thousands of drivers would pass by it everyday. Over the course of a month you would be able to teach many drivers what you think they should know about your business. For a few moments you would have a captive audience as each driver glanced at your well-designed sign. If traffic backs up your sign gets noticed for minutes or (sadly for the driver) hours.

What if you could place your $5,000 billboard directly in front of your customer's nose? Wouldn't it be wonderful if you could place your billboard in their home, say on their refrigerator, or in that tray where they store their keys? What if your ideal customer kept your billboard in their wallet or purse? Wow - that would be chutzpah marketing!

Well, you can.

Your most important marketing tool is a mini-billboard in the form of a chutzpah designed business card, flier, or brochure. I'm not talking about your standard business card, boring flyer, or fluff filled brochure. I'm talking about chutzpah mini-billboards.

When I suggested mini-billboards to Big Red he looked at me as if I had pudding for brains.

"Mini-billboards?" Big Red laughed. "Why would I want to spend hard earned money on business cards? Who would I give 'em out to? I'm not a lawyer or realtor."

"Mini-billboards can take the form of chutzpah designed, hard working business cards, company brochures, sales fliers, or much need consumer information. Mini-billboards may cost just pennies, but they are designed to keep your business name and offerings percolating throughout your community," I said.

Big Red was not impressed, "But we have never done mini-billboards before, I don't see any reason to start now."

"Fair enough, Big Red," I said. "Let's say you're at the bank and the teller says, 'I've been meaning to get lunch at your place, I love your burgers.' You thank her with a big smile, reach into your back pocket and pull out a mini-billboard and say. 'I miss seeing you darlin' while you write on the back of your mini-billboard 'one free soft drink' and sign your name. While handing your mini-billboard to her you say, 'Let me buy you a soft drink. Even if I'm not there, just give this to the cashier and they'll know you're my friend… they'll treat you great.' Now think about how special the bank teller will feel being treated so kindly by you. I bet you'll see her in a day or two. And she probably will tell her coworkers about how nice you were. Maybe they'll come in for lunch too."

"I could do that, that would be fun." Big Red smiled.

Mini-billboards are powerful tools to get your important information in front of your customers. For just pennies, they keep reminding your customers of your brand. As we go along in this chapter, I will give you lots of mini-billboard ideas that you can start using right away.

Old boring standard business cards

If you ask entrepreneurs why they have business cards they tend to look at you strangely and answer with one of two statements:

- Because I'm in business.
- So I can conveniently give out my basic information: name, address and phone number.

That is not chutzpah talking!

For most entrepreneurs, a business card is just a 2 inch by 3.5 inch piece of card stock with their name, address, and phone number printed on it. Some are more fancy than others with bumpy ink and nicer paper.

They look like:

Ima Professional, M.A.
Licensed Marriage and Family Therapist

1234 Freud St. Suite 69 (123)456-7890
Jung, CA 96002   Lic#: MFT 012345

This is a basic card that makes a few assumptions:

- The reader doesn't need or want more information
- The reader has 20/20 vision
- The reader knows what you do for a living
- The reader knows what services you provide

Some entrepreneurs add a little flash of art to their card:

Ima Professional, M.A.
Licensed Marriage and Family Therapist

1234 Freud St. Suite 69 (123)456-7890
Jung, CA 96002   Lic#: MFT 012345

This adds a nice focal point, but why? What has Ima Professional taught the reader about her business?

Chutzpah business card

A chutzpah business card is a fingertip billboard that lets the holder receive your message in 3 seconds. Ask yourself this question:

> If you had only 3 seconds, what would you want to teach the public about your business?

Don't get concerned about the 3 seconds. That's a lot of time when it comes to holding someone's attention. In the first 3 seconds you have to get the reader to want to spend more time learning about your offerings. If your card has information relevant to the reader, your card goes home with them and it becomes a reference card.

What goes on your chutzpah business card? Your positioning, so that potential customers know what your business can do for them.

Most of this information comes from how you answered the 5 questions in chapter 1:

#1: List problems that you solve for your customers.

#2: Who are your customers?

#3: What is the brand (position) of your business in the community?

#4: How does your customer find you?

#5: How can you help your customers?

Building your chutzpah business card

Most business cards you come across are 2 inches by 3.5 inches and are only printed on one side. Most business cards give the business person's vital information. Our goal is to have mini-billboards that generate lots of business for you.

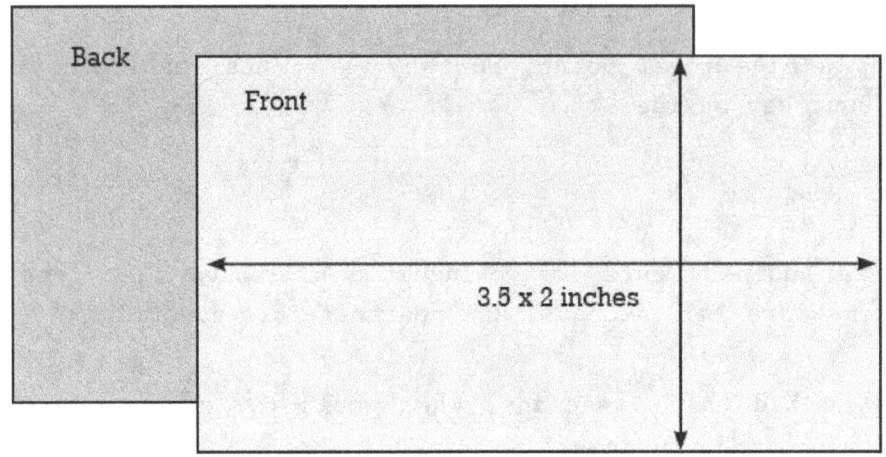

Same size, oriented vertically:

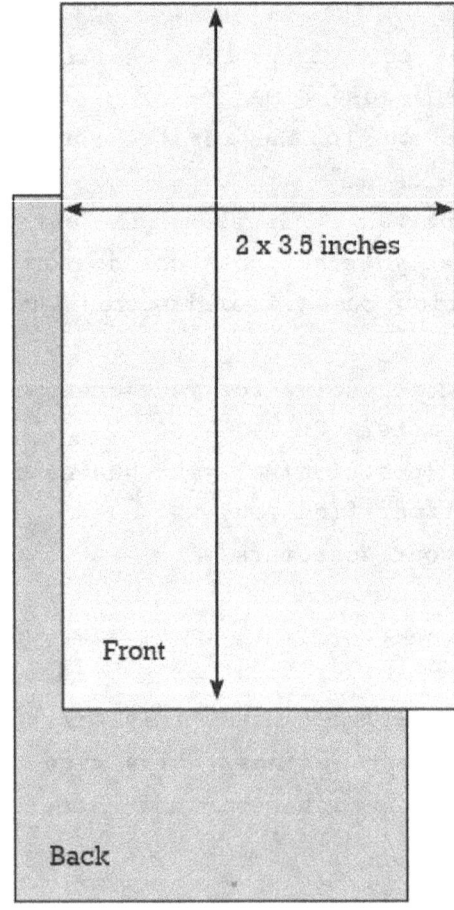

You may find the basic business card size plenty of room for your chutzpah business card. If your business is easy to explain this space may work well.

But…

A business card is not limited to 2 inches by 3.5 inches. Think about this for a moment. If a driver stopped in traffic was stuck in front of your billboard, wouldn't you want it to teach the driver about your services? In fact, with chutzpah thoughts, wouldn't you want your signage to be interesting and informative? Wouldn't you want it to motivate the driver into action; motivate the driver to call you; to refer to your business? Wouldn't you need space to put in all this motivational stuff? In billboards, that means mega bucks. But, in business cards, that means pennies.

The standard card is 2 x 3.5 inches and it has 2 sides. A chutzpah card can be whatever you want. Think of them as mini brochures. A fold over card is 4 x 3.5 inches, two sided. When folded, it is the standard 2 x 3.5 inches with attitude. This card costs a few pennies more, but gives you an easel to create your masterpiece. You have two 2 x 3.5 areas and one 4 x 3.5 area. The card can be printed either tall or wide. Now we're talking the beginning of a chutzpah card. Let's create…

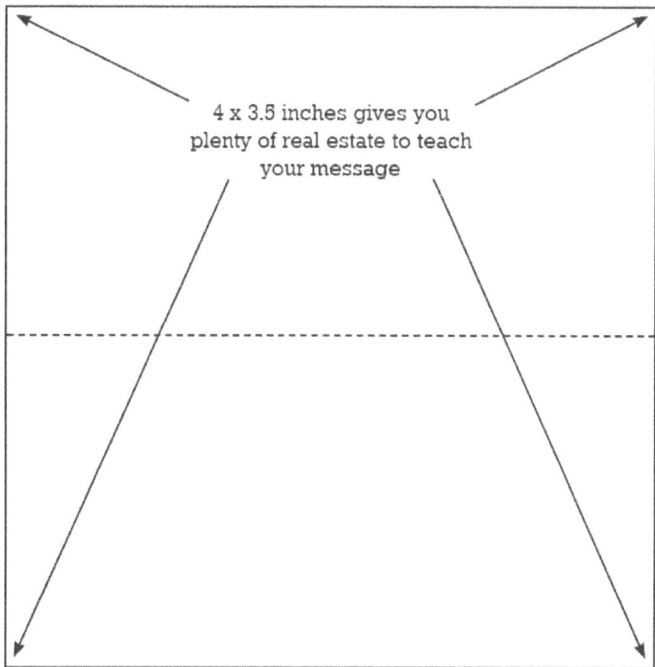

4 x 3.5 inches gives you plenty of real estate to teach your message

When folded it looks like a tent:

Folded the opposite way your canvas looks like:

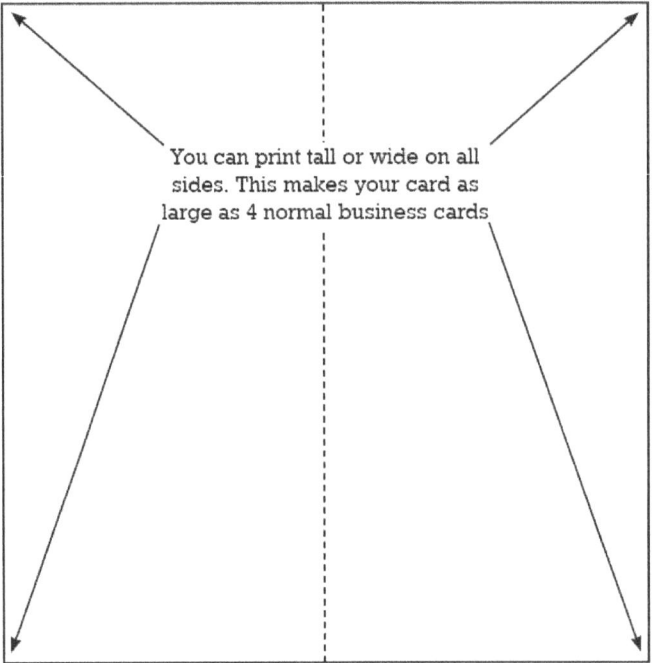

You can print tall or wide on all sides. This makes your card as large as 4 normal business cards

When folded it looks like a book:

Your work area has numerous usable sections:

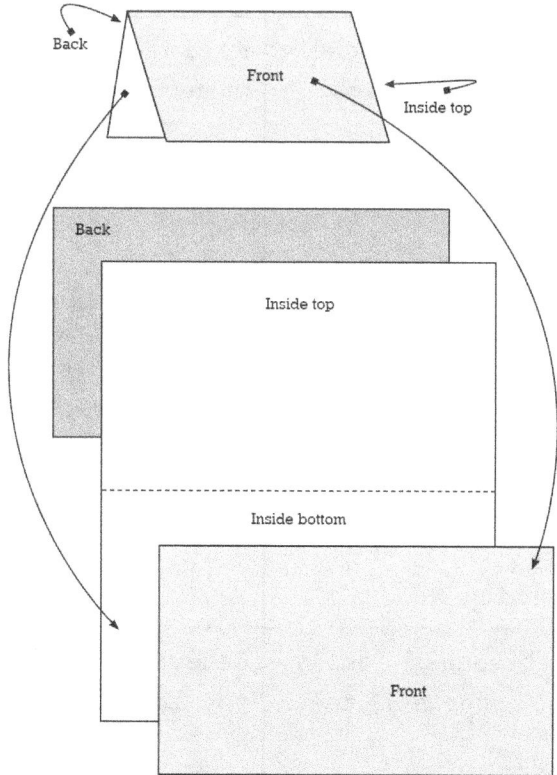

Don't allow yourself to be overwhelmed with all this space. After playing with your copy for just a little bit, you will learn that it is easy to fill this space with chutzpah information that sells your business.

Keep the following in mind while you create:

Use/Stress	Avoid
Clear and accurate words	Misleading statements
Testimonials	Lying
Your qualifications	Puffery

Show how your business is user friendly:
   • Extended hours for your convenience
	Braggadocios statements like:
	   • Friendly staff
	   • Highest quality care

Only offer what you actually do, not what you wish or hope to do.	"Friendly Staff" is meaningless. Who wouldn't say that?
Show that your staff is friendly with action words and/or pictures.	Boring staff pictures of people standing doing nothing.
Show don't tell. Paint pictures with your words. Talk to your customers' needs.	Talking about your wants
Common words	Jargon
Guarantees (Clear easily understood.)	No small print on guarantees. It makes your offer seem like a trick.

Use a logo if it adds to your message:
   • Adds a feeling
   • Teaches something
	A logo for the sake of having a logo:
	   • A shape or swirl is not a logo unless you have a lot of money to teach that it is a logo.

A logo of a family teaches family. Teddy bears, lambs, puppies: teach caring.	Generic logos are generic and make you look generic!

Use/Stress	Avoid
Association logo teaches entrepreneurism.	A picture of your office tells potential customers that they will be paying your mortgage.
Maps can be helpful.	A photo of your cat, dog, or horse tells the reader that you're a little confused about what you sell (Unless you are a Vet).
Use photos as testimonials (happy customers using your product or service.)	Photos of your family. Focus should be on your customer's family.
Use a line drawing to teach a feeling.	If you do not know the purpose of a graphic, leave it out!
Religious symbols may be helpful if you wish to limit your customers to a particular religion.	Religious symbols tend to limit and may leave people feeling excluded.
Why choose you? — Say it! Be positive, uplifting!	Negative statements.
Use large enough print to be easily read. Use clear type styles for optimal readability. Your clients won't be impressed with your artistic flare if they can't read your card!	Don't assume that all your customers have great vision. Avoid hard to read type styles.
Use white space to show importance and to control the reader's eye.	Avoid cumbersome print and hard to read fonts. Make your mini-billboard easy to read and inviting. People will not bother with a crowded mini-billboard.

Chutzpah logo

The purpose of a logo is to convey a feeling and to be a focal point in the reader's mind.

Logos are expensive to use correctly and I can honestly tell you that the average company does not need a logo to grow a thriving business. I have heard lots of sad tales of inexperienced entrepreneurs spending thousands of dollars for graphic artists to develop a "killer" logo for them.

Overall, logos are expensive, but they do work. Having said that, logos are not a necessity. Getting your name out is a necessity. Many of my consulting customers add their logo years after they are established.

For logos to work you have to put them on everything your business produces. The logo:

has been plastered on billions of things over the years. Few people know that IBM stands for International Business Machines. More people know the company as Big Blue: IBM.

A name can be your logo; it works well for Xerox, Kodak, and McGraw Hill.

A graphic is usually the choice for conveying a feeling. A dentist I know uses a simple drawing of a puffy cloud with two soft "W's" for far off birds. His tag line reads "Gentle Care." This is an effective logo for a dentist.

A logo needs to be versatile. It needs to work in lots of different locations, some big—some small. Color is very effective in a logo, but it should also print well in gray scale. Color is expensive to print but adds a lot to the presentation.

To keep down costs, dream up what you want as your logo. Bounce it around for a while. Find an artist within your circle of friends and family. I know a chiropractor who got a great logo from a 14-year old cousin with a knack for drawing. Chutzpah marketers are creative. Be cautious when hiring a graphic artist. They know art, not marketing. A logo is not art—it is a marketing tool.

What makes a logo a good logo?
- Instantly recognizable, makes a clear statement.
- Produces a desired feeling within the reader.
- Clear artwork—even when small.

- Works in color and black and white. The feeling of the art cannot be dependent on the color.
- Your name incorporated, or sits well right next to it.

It's time to start playing with your own mini-billboard mock-ups, yeah! Don't bother cutting up paper into card size shapes. That will just drive you nuts. Use regular, and cheap, 8.5 x 11 copier paper. You'll need lots, so crack open a ream of paper. Half of one sheet is a front or a back cover. A full sheet is the inside of your business card. I advise you not to draw on both sides as it will "bleed" through. As you go along you can tape paper together to make a mock-up.

Now, allow yourself to be creative. Write big! Use colors. Experiment. Get creative. Go too far—then throw that one away. Express yourself. Be honest. Write from the point of view of the potential customer. Clearly show how your company is going to help them.

Getting your card printed

This is the easy part. You take your mock-up to a local printer, office superstore, or an Internet printer. All things being equal, I recommend a local printer because you will get better service and the local printer can be a referrer to your business. However, a local printer will most likely cost more than an Internet printing company.

Ways to save money on printing:

With a Google search for "Print business cards" you will find lots of printers that compete on price. Many boast thousands of free templates to choose from. This is well and good as long as you can manipulate their template to fit your chutzpah card.

You can save money with your local printer when you buy in bulk. Buy business cards, fliers, and menus all at the same time so you can keep the cost reasonable.

Many local print shops take your basic print order and job it out to one of the many huge regional printing companies. You can go directly to the large print company via the Internet.

You should use up 5,000 cards in a few months or you are not chutzpah growing your business. Due to radical changes in digital printing the cost has come down over the last few years. 1,000 cards will cost less then $100, while 5,000 cards will cost around $200.

Build your business card yourself or get it typeset by that computer nerd brother of yours who eats for free at your house all the time. Resist printing your masterpiece on your $100 ink jet printer with the pull-a-part business card paper. It looks cheap, and I'm being very polite when I say that. It also is not cost effective. You are going to hand out tons of your business cards if you have chutzpah. (Relax, I'll show you how shortly.)

If you go the local print route, here is a tip on saving money. When the printer shows you his paper choices, listen politely, then say, "I want that kind of paper there, (point) in a comparable no name brand." He will start with expensive, designer paper. You don't need that expense. You need good quality, moderately priced stock. A chutzpah marketer does not spend a dime if 9¢ will do! You are shopping for value not vanity.

It is worth your time to comparison shop for a printer. Get at least three competitive bids.

Internet printing has come a long way. With little computer experience you can build a great mini-billboard from scratch I do not recommend that you use their art, as it is generic- not chutzpah. But, uploading your art is easy and the cost savings is impressive.

Good web sites to try are:

www.vistaprint.com
www.123print.com
www.printbusinesscards.com
www.printplace.com/
www.uprinting.com/
www.americasprinter.com

Their prices are good and their web sites are easy to use, but for a beginner, there is little hand holding. Also, be forewarned, the web sites are set up to let you easily order "add ons" for an additional price. These add ons can quickly add up to a bloated price. Only buy an add on if it will generate more sales, not because your ego would like it. As I said, a local printer costs more, but will hold your hand, so to speak. Check your Yellow Pages for local printers.

Handing out your chutzpah business cards

In this section I will specifically be talking about business cards. However, any style of mini-billboard can be substituted in the place of the business card. At the end of this section I will give you some examples of other types of mini-billboards, see: **Chutzpah mini-billboards in action.**

I am pretty sure that most business cards go unused, even the boring ones. But, a chutzpah marketer puts the little billboards to work. In this section I am going to give you secrets on how to put your business cards to work. But first, a story…

Back when I had been a therapist in private business for around 15 years, a woman made an appointment. During the initial minutes of the intake interview she pulled out one of my cards from the paperback she had in her purse.

New customer: I've been using your card for my bookmark.
Dr. Phil: Looks pretty beat up…
New customer: I've had it for over 7 years (She started to cry).

It turned out that this woman picked up my card during a PTA meeting at her son's school. When I asked her why it took so long for her to call, she simply replied, "I wasn't ready to talk about it."

Business cards have a life of their own. I have had new customers tell me lots of interesting things:

   · You've been on my dresser for a month.
   · You've been in my wallet…
   · I stuck your card on the bathroom mirror so I would remember to call you.
   · Your card has been nagging me from my change saucer for months.
   · I found you on my sister's refrigerator…

The one that still surprises me…

   · I don't know where I got your card.

A chutzpah business card is a powerful marketing tool. For just pennies you get to place your information in people's hands, homes, and work places.

Shhhh, this is a secret: How to hand out business cards comfortably

The most important secret is that you place your card into every hand you can. (It is really not a secret, but it seems like it is because so few people do it.)

Handing out a card or brochure is like tossing seeds onto the earth. What eventually happens to the seed depends on where it lands. Some seeds will land on rocks. Others will find themselves shaded by stones. Still, others will land under the shade of trees. But, a few will land on fertile moist ground. These few will reap rewards. By keeping the price of your business cards and brochures extremely low, you will be able to toss them into the winds of our society. It only takes a few of them to germinate into new customers. You will not know which cards will germinate, so it is important to put a lot into circulation.

To be able to give out your cards you must keep them handy. A chutzpah card that is four layers into your purse is an unhappy business card. The act of handing your card out should be a seamless part of your conversation. Giving your card is as simple as a smile and a handshake.

"Nice talking to you," as you hand her your card.

"Please feel free to call me…" as you hand him your card.

Please do not make a production out of handing out your card. It should be as socially easy as a friendly handshake.

Once, I handed my card to a doctor at a hospital lunch. She stiffened up and said, "You carded me. I should card you right back!" She went and got her bag and returned rummaging around in it.

"Here's a card for you." Then she proceeded to hand out her cards to everyone else. "I'm carding you, I'm carding you, I'm carding you…" She made me feel uncomfortable, and by the looks on other's faces I was not the only one.

I advise you to practice handing out your card so it becomes more comfortable. Numerous times I have watched entrepreneurs lose credibility in social settings because they were uncomfortable about handing out their card.

A chutzpah marketer always gives two cards. If they say, "You gave me two." Respond with a smile, "That's ok, give one to a friend." I often hear something like, "My friend Susie is always fighting with her husband." Or "Everyone I know could use your help!"

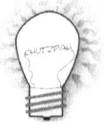 If you are doing business with somebody ask, "Do you have a card?" They usually don't. "Here is one of mine," I say as I give them two.

When you give a tip at a restaurant, assuming you are a fair tipper, leave two cards.

Whenever you are asked for your name, like at a hotel check-in or the vet's office, hand them two cards and say, "All that information is on my card."

When you pay a bill or send something in the mail, always put in two cards.

I have my web site information on my card, www.CopitchInc.com. I have a links page with lots of valuable links to web sites I am comfortable referring people to. As I hand someone my business card I'll often say, "If you go to my web page there is a link to..." I find that people appreciate the leads.

While waiting in line at Costco, I gave out cards to two women who were talking about one of their baby's ear infection. I asked, "Have you been to Healthcentral.com on the Internet? No? They have lots of valuable information about ear infections and children's health. Here's my card. If you go to my web site (pointing to the web address on my card) you can skip right over to get the information you want."

 That same Costco trip I ran into the father of one of the children who does martial arts with my boys. "Hi Dad (I didn't know his name), did you see the pictures of the kids from the last competition? No, oh they're great, if you go to my web site, (pointing at the web address on card) you will find the link to the pictures."

This took only moments, and I got goodwill along with my cards circulating.

 If I need to give someone a number or something, I write it in the margins of my chutzpah business card.

Don't forget to ask friends, who are entrepreneurs in noncompeting businesses, if you can give them a plastic holder filled with your business cards for their waiting room. Offer to put theirs in your place of business if appropriate. Send them replacement cards every few months.

 If you send a thank you card, get-well flowers, or a fruit basket, add your mini-billboards.

Chutzpah mini-billboards in action

"You have to circulate to percolate." The first time I heard this was from a manager who was explaining that if you want to sell cars the public needs to know about you. The more people that know about you the more likely it is that someone you know needs what you are selling. All sales are done through a relationship, the better the relationship, the more trust there is between the buyer and the seller, the easier the sale.

My friend Steve the locksmith and I were pulling into a convenience store to pick up some soft drinks. We had been driving for some time. The whole time Steve had been complaining that business was down. As we got out of the car, Steve took off his bright yellow polo shirt emblazoned with his company logo on the pocket. Wearing only his tee-shirt we went into the store.

When we were getting back into the car, Steve put his yellow shirt back on. "What's up with the shirt?" I asked.

"Oh," Steve complained. "Whenever I wear my shirt into places like that someone always asks me about my work. People are always looking for free advice, it drives me crazy!"

I tell you the story about Steve and his yellow shirt to prove a point. When opportunity knocks he wears work clothes. What Steve didn't realize is that his shirt gave him thousands of opportunities per year to percolate. As he circulated around his community people eagerly talked to Steve about their locksmith problems. All Steve needed were a few mini-billboards and a couple of 9-seconds speeches to give to these prospective customers. For just a few cents he could have netted thousands of dollars. (We will cover 9-second speeches in Chapter 3: **Your Second Most Important Marketing Tool is Free.**)

Instead of dreading "being bothered by prospective customers" Steve needed a chutzpah attitude adjustment. Being a locksmith, Steve had thousands of key blanks in boxes lying around his office, shop, and home. By attaching his business card to a key blank he had himself a low cost and unique mini-billboard.

When someone said to Steve in passing, "Do you fix safes?" or "sliding glass door locks", he would smile and let them know what he could do for them. As he handed them his mini-billboards he would say, "Call my wife at this number and I'll be happy to fix that for you." (By saying "call my wife", many people felt more comfortable inviting someone they just met over to their home or office.)

Name tags make it very easy for people to befriend you in public. I used to have to wear a lanyard with my name tag on it clearly printed with: Dr. Copitch, when I worked in a hospital. If I forgot to take it off and leave it in the car before I went into the grocery store, people would lift their shirts or expose their rumps for my assessment as they said, "What do you think this is?" I would politely respond-looking elsewhere, "I'm not that type of doctor, I'm a psychotherapist." (Sometimes I would have to add, "Yuck! You need to get that checked.")

Name tags make you safe to talk to. Which in turn makes it easier for you to talk about your product or services, and hand out your mini-billboards comfortably. More on name tags in Chapter 7, **Advertising Part D: Your Office, Store, and Vehicles Are Chutzpah**

Marketing Tools.

 Flowers by Dana is a small flower shop down the street from a hospital. As a way to get their name better known, whenever they delivered to the hospital, the delivery person always took lots of extra carnations. Punching two holes in a business card enabled them to slip a carnation stem through the holes with ease, attaching the card to the carnation. The delivery person was instructed to hand a carnation to any woman or child they stumbled across during their delivery and say, with a big smile, "Dana told me to give this to you." This happy gesture positioned Dana's little shop positively in the minds of lots of people. I am told that the nurses never got tired of getting a flower. In fact, many of Dana's cards were kept at the nurses' stations throughout the hospital.

 The Shirt Ladies, as they are affectionately called, used silk screened tee-shirts as mini-billboards. When they met a prospective customer they would hand him a large white tee-shirt with all the silk screening particulars on it. I have seen these shirts in offices around my town. It seems that this mini-billboard spends a lot of time on the desks or bookshelves of decision makers all over town. (One of my sons wore a huge one for years. He thought it was cool. Wow! Free advertising.)

 A lady from my office building stopped me in the hall one morning. I had seen her before but I did not know who she was.

"Oh Dr. Phil, my friend's kid spit in the face of another kid in school. Sally is really worried that her kid is going to get kicked out of school."

"It is really common that schools get concerned about any sort of kid aggression these days," I said as I handed over two of my cards. "You may want to have your friend call me before her meeting with the school. I'll give her a few minutes and some help with knowing what to expect. Tell your friend, because you're worried about her, I'll be happy to talk to her on the phone for free."

I find that a free five minute consult relieves a lot of fear, creates goodwill in my community, and often helps a worried potential customer become a customer. In this situation, I also get goodwill within a company in my office building.

 I am often asked about my sales pitch during these free phone consults. My answer is simply, I have no sales pitch. The purpose of my free phone consult is to dispatch free general infor-

mation. If the caller needs more help, I offer that help. But, if I can solve the caller's needs in five minutes, I do, hoping to also generate goodwill; which may come back to me at a later date.

I was told by a newly minted attorney at a Welcome To The Firm party, that five years earlier she had called my office.

"I was so upset when I called," she said. "You must have thought of me as the most uninformed parent in the world."

"I'm sorry, I don't remember the call," I said.

"It was me screaming about my three year old looking at a **Playboy** magazine. I was frantic that he was somehow damaged."

"You needn't be worried..."

"That's what you said. You calmed me down and told me that my son was just looking at a magazine. He didn't know anything about porno. It was just a magazine. You were so calming. I just wanted you to know that I appreciated your help."

"Thanks, glad I could help." I handed her a few cards.

In the five years since, that single attorney has referred customers to my company almost every month. And, the firm she works for also thinks of me often.

Readers have sent me fun examples of chutzpah mini-billboards. Lot of fun. Enjoy.

Great idea for a fitness trainer or yoga instructor:

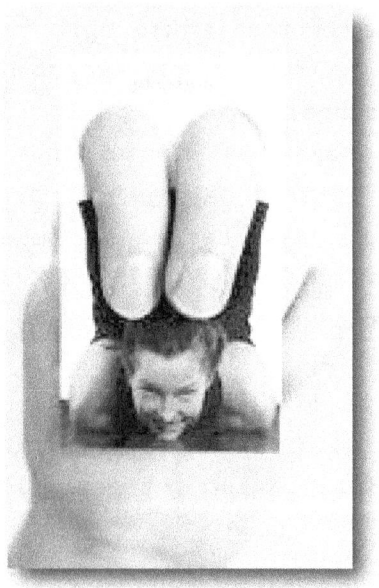

Computer / business chutzpah:

A great Tee-Shirt ad. Delivery service? Mailbox shop?

These last two are dentist cards playing with floss. I like the idea that these cards are so creative that they almost beg to be shown off.

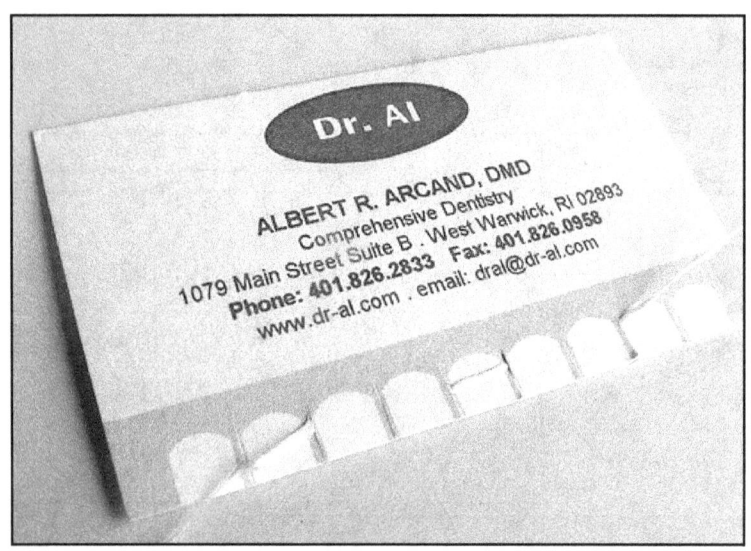

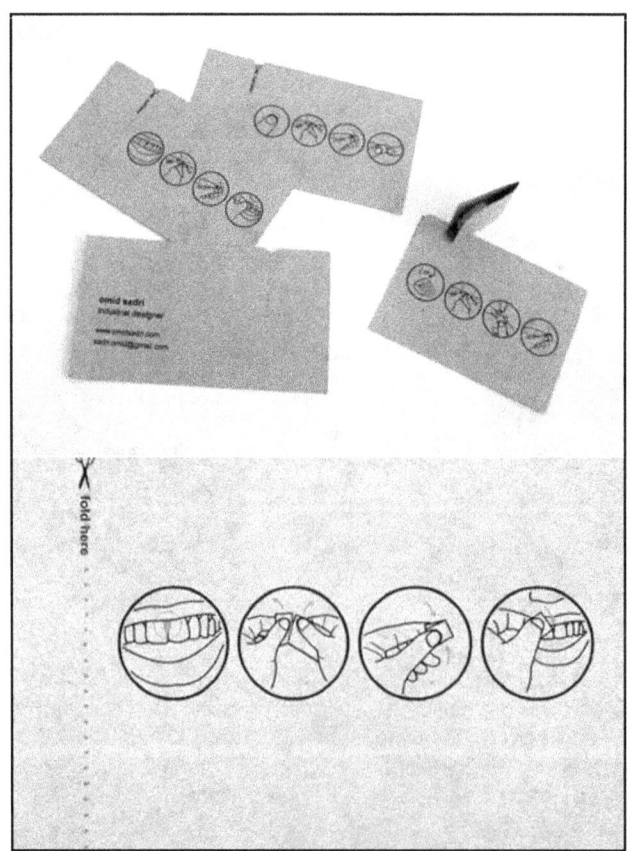

This scratch card is a novel idea. It lets the receiver get involve with your card and "win" something like 10% off or an upgrade of some sort. I found this at www.propulsionprintservices.com/scratch-cards.html

Lots more mini-billboard ideas will be presented in:

Chapter 4: **Advertising Part A: On The Chutzpah Cheap**
Chapter 5: **Advertising Part B: The Yellow Pages and Local Media**
Chapter 6: **Advertising Part C: Chutzpah Gold Mining**

"I was asked to deliver a 9-second speech.
Relatively speaking, that is an eternity!"

3. YOUR SECOND MOST IMPORTANT MARKETING TOOL IS FREE

Yes, free, it will only 'cost' you 9 seconds of your time. We are going to study the difficult task of developing a 9-second speech. A 9-second speech is a mini verbal performance that teaches the listener how to think of your company, refer to your company, or help your company in some way. It is a chutzpah technique for getting people you have had contact with to think of your company at an opportune time, a time when they can choose your product or service, or refer to your product or service. It is a powerful, and often under utilized, marketing tool that is necessary to master if you wish to grow a thriving chutzpah business.

A chutzpah marketer is one hundred percent positive. We do not complain about anything, not the weather, sports, politics, or our kids. We are up-lifting individuals who do not wipe our problems or little grumps on others.

I'm not kidding about one hundred percent. No one in public hears me complain about my family, my job, or that I'm a Minnesota Vikings fan. I save my problems and complaints for my confidants.

I want my referral sources, customers, and potential customers, to know me as uplifting.

The goal of the 9-second speech is for my message to be said so perfectly that it seems unrehearsed. Nine-second speeches are presented comfortably and naturally. Nine-second speeches help you stay on target even if you feel rushed, grumpy, or distracted.

Example of a 9-second speech in a therapist's office

Following a domestic dispute that landed him in hot water with local authorities, Mr. Al Upenset's attorney referred him to my office. Mr. Upenset was a muscular man of sixty. He had been married for over 40 years. For over 30 years Mr. Upenset had been a supply master sergeant in the Marines. After 38 years in the armed services, Mr. Upenset reluctantly retired to a double-wide trailer with his wife and her three small dogs.

Mr. Upenset was angry when he entered my office. He was angrier when I asked him to sit down. He sat, but his chest heaved and his eyes stared at his wringing hands.

The third question of my intake interview infuriated Mr. Upenset. He rose off the couch and angrily stepped over to me where I sat. In one swift movement he ripped his tee shirt off and flexed his body at me. He bent towards me, putting his face 6 inches in front of mine. In a deep, Neanderthal tone he spat his utterance, "I'm going to punch you in the face… what are you going to do about that?"

"I'm going to bleed, Mr. Upenset," I said in a low calm voice. "You will make me bleed, then I will feel a lot of pain."

"What the…" He took a step backward.

"Mr. Upenset, you will make me bleed and feel a lot of pain."

"Yeah, I don't want you to bleed … I'm sorry, I think that I'm just going crazy or something." He went and sat down, took a few big breaths, and tried to put on his ripped shirt. Mr. Upenset was cooperative for the rest of the evaluation.

Many years ago, I learned when someone is in your face and ready to attack, stay calm, and in a low voice tell him or her what will happen next. Let them softly hear what is in their future. When I was a young therapist working with teenage incarcerated murderers this was stressed during in-service training. It has served me well for over 30 years of dealing with angry customers. This reality speech helps the angry customer look outside of their personal anger.

This is also an example of a 9-second speech. If I had to come up with the calm words off the top of my head under these circumstances, the likelihood is that I couldn't. But because I have a 9-second speech, I was able to use it at the correct moment, without thinking it out on the spot.

In emotionally charged situations, a 9-second speech is helpful. It is also a helpful chutzpah-marketing tool. I have many chutzpah-marketing 9-second speeches. I have specific speeches for many particular situations that allow me to sell myself subtly.

I have chutzpah-marketing 9-second speeches that I teach employees, family, and referral sources so they can market me to others comfortably. My 9-second speeches are designed for me to give the best mini performance many times a day as I go through my activities.

Why 9-seconds?

It is my experience that 9-seconds is the longest that any mini-speech should go. Most are less. It is socially acceptable to dominate a conversation for a little bit, while you get your thoughts out. I have found that most people are comfortable with letting me yammer away for up to 9 seconds.

If you had 9-seconds to market yourself to any of the following, what would you say?

Medical doctor	Cab driver	Veterinarian
Dentist	Nurse	Office worker
Minister	Police officer	Florist
Waitress	Entrepreneur	Cook
Funeral home director	Soccer coach	Plumber
High school teacher	Pre-school director	Cashier

Throughout the year you will have hundreds if not thousands of opportunities to talk about your company. If you had only 9-seconds what would you say. In those 9-seconds, **what are the best words to say what needs to be said?**

Building a 9-second speech

You can probably speak 25 words, clearly, in 9-seconds. The problem comes when you have to limit yourself to only 25 words to get your point across. If someone asks you at a party, "What do you do?" What is your reply?

"I'm a plumber."
"I'm an accountant."
"I manage a restaurant."

I recently heard a house painter, when asked this by a surgeon say, "Oh, I'm just a house painter." My heart skipped a beat. The surgeon tossed him a softball, and the house painter forgot to bring a bat! "Oh, I'm just a house painter." Sounded like, "I don't do anything important. Please don't notice me."

In this situation, what would you say? —Even when you were nervous.

You have a potential customer's ear for the next few seconds, what would be the best thing to say? How would you use this opportunity to sell you as a business owner: to sell your business as the one to choose? This is not an easy question. If it were, everyone would be able to do it.

First you have to define what you want to teach.

What do you want to teach about your company?

You are going to be teaching about your company—but not directly. You have to focus on the person you are talking to. You have to *solve a need* for that individual.

If you had answered the surgeon with, "I'm a house painter. I paint houses and sometimes offices." The surgeon probably would have gotten a polite smile on his face and fluttered away like an opportunity lost. Nothing against the surgeon, but you simply would have bored him.

But, if you were to speak to him directly about his needs, he would be captivated. Most people love to talk about themselves and their own interests.

If I were a chutzpah house painter I would speak to the surgeon's potential needs. I would hope that the surgeon owned property and that that property needed painting. If the surgeon didn't own property, I would hope that he knew someone who did own property. To stimulate the conversation towards our mutual interests I would say, "I paint buildings, I specialize in adding value to buildings for resale or investment purposes."

He then might reply, "Value, huh? How much value can you add to a building?" Now you are talking to the surgeon about something that he is interested in and that you can help him with.

If you are *me* focused, the listener hears only that you want something from him. But, if you focus on him, he is very comfortable having the conversation continue.

Teaching others to talk glowingly about your business

The goal of the 9-second speech is to teach the listener about your business. You want to give them information in a manner that is relevant to them so that they can use it, or pass it on to someone else to use.

My friend Sara is a vegetarian. As she often states, "I don't eat anything with a face." When she returned from a trip to Arizona, she told me about this restaurant that is trying to kill people.

"They boast that they have the highest calorie food in the world," she said. "They cook their fries in lard!"

"What's the place called?" I asked.

"The Heart Attack Grill; it's just south of Phoenix in Chandler, Arizona. You'd love it! If you are over 350 pounds you eat for free!"

I would like to point out that a skinny devout vegetarian, who regularly voices concern about my weight, just did a hell of a job selling me on a restaurant that she would never eat at. The Heart Attack Grill did a great job of teaching their 9-second speech. In fact, such a great job that their message traveled over a thousand miles free of charge. This is the power of 9-second speeches. Your message travels!

Develop your 9-second speeches

Your homework assignment is to write 9-second speeches. Think of all the places you run into potential customers: stores, your child's soccer practice, school events, movie theaters, and church. You make hundreds of incidental contacts every week that are great 9-second speech opportunities for you.

Write down your 9-second speech

You need to write down your 9-second speech and practice it. You need to be able to present your 9-second speech naturally, as if it was your first time ever saying it. Your 9-second speech has to feel like an old friend, but be presented as a new vivacious friend.

When writing your 9-second speeches, overwrite. Write too much at first, then cut away the repetition and useless parts. Play around with your word choices. Re-write, and re-write some more. Your 9-second speeches have to feel correct and comfortable to you. I assume that no other entrepreneur could use my 9-second speeches. Nine-second speeches have to be personalized by you, in your style, to the person you are talking to.

Enjoy the process. As the old joke goes, a tourist asks a New York cab driver, "How do you get to Carnegie Hall?" The cabbie replies, "Practice, practice, practice."

Chutzpah marketing 9-second speeches in action

Let's take three different business people and see how they interact with the same person. Please note how individual their 9-second speeches are in about the same situation. The chutzpah entrepreneurs are:

Mr. Marcus Audit, Certified Public Accountant
Big Red, owner of BigRed's Burgers
Ms. Joanne Gutenberg, Owner of ReRead Used Books

Our three chutzpah owners meet Kyle's mom while on the sidelines watching youth soccer.

Mr. Marcus Audit, Certified Public Accountant

"Hi," Marcus says. "Boy I wish I had their energy."
"Oh, me too," Kyle's mom says.
"It is nice being out though, as an accountant I spend a lot of time helping families save on their taxes or estate planning."
"I hate doing my taxes, doesn't it drive you nuts?" Kyle's mom asks.
"Oh no, not at all… I love protecting families."
"I couldn't do it, so much regulation," Kyle's mom says.
"If you have any questions, just call me," Marcus smiles as he hands her two of his chutzpah cards.

Big Red, owner of BigRed's Burgers

Noticing Big Red's name tag, Kyle's mom says, "Are you <u>the</u> Big Red?"

"Yes ma'am, I hope you enjoy my burgers." Big Red Smiles.

"Not much on hamburgers," she says as she pats her tummy. "I'm trying to watch my weight."

"Lots of people find that we're mighty convenient, for families on the go. Ya know we have curb side dinner boxes. Great for bringing to soccer. My Minnie is really fond of the boneless chicken breast. She takes the top bun off, ya know." he says as he hands her two mini-billboards.

"Thanks, my kyle is growing like a weed... always hungry."

Ms. Joanne Gutenberg, owner of ReRead Used Books

Kyle's mom offers to help Joanne as she carries an armful of cut up oranges, a folding chair, and a beach bag.

"Oh thanks, I should have made two trips," Joanne says.

"Thanks for bringing the half time snack," Kyle's mom says.

"No problem, my shop now smells like oranges."

"Shop?"

"Yeah, I own ReRead Used Books," she smiles as she hands Kyle's mom 2 mini-billboards in the shape of books. "We have a great selection in our children's section, everything's at least 50% off."

"My Kyle loves to read."

"Great! Mrs. Kramer, the principal at Fiction Elementary School, runs our children's book club all summer long. There are prizes and lots of laughs. We want to keep the reading skills strong during the summer. You know, club membership is free, and we even have Thursday Morning Rhyming for the littlest readers," Joanne says.

"That sounds wonderful, my name is Gail it's so nice to meet you." Kyle's mom says as she offers her hand in friendship.

Nine-second speeches are free and powerful. Put them together with mini-billboards and you have an unbelievable chutzpah team. In Chapter 10: **Getting Your Staff and Family Into Chutzpah Marketing**, I will discuss how to teach 9-second speeches to your staff and family, helping to make them a marketing army.

Variation: Hollywood elevator speech

A nice variation of the 9-second speech is the Hollywood elevator speech. The idea is that you have just a few moments to get your new movie idea across to a movie executive.

Giving examples that the movie executive already knows, helps paint the picture in her mind.

"It's like Aliens and Kindergarden Cop put together… You have blood thirsty aliens kept at bay by an ex cop turned school teacher."

Or

"It's like The Godfather and Avatar put together… You have an Italian American family that gets shipwrecked on a blue planet with peaceful natives. Within no time hilarity and murders ensue."

Variation: MIT speech

Massachusetts Institution of Technology is a gold mine for venture capitalists interested in funding the next technical innovations. Because of this, graduate students are encouraged to have a 3-5 minute polished speech developed so if their professor introduces them to someone they are ready.

"Marco, This is Mr. Gold, he is interested in funding new ventures, what are you working on?"

When opportunity knocks, it is a good idea to answer the door and have a wonderful speech ready.

"According to the brochure... this experience will help our
David get into medical school."

4. ADVERTISING PART A: ON THE CHUTZPAH CHEAP

In this section we are going to discuss chutzpah brochures. Not the average brochure that you have ignored yourself on many occasions, but a chutzpah mini-billboard brochure that brings in customers. The word 'brochure' may be misleading because it is not a word some businesses I work with typically use. They may call it the take-out menu, information flier, sales handout, or their sales sheet. Whatever you wish to call it, the fact is that it is a piece of paper that sells your business in chutzpah style.

I will use the word brochure, please interchange your industry's term as needed.

The biggest problem with most business brochures is that they are written to make the business owner or manager feel good about the important work they do. This type of brochure is little more than an ego boost for the owner or manager. This makes sense because often a graphic artist or a management consultant sells a brochure to a business owner or manager. These individuals want to keep their customer (you) happy. But, the focus is completely wrong.

The focus of the brochure should be on the potential customer. The brochure is your way to circulate so you can percolate. The brochure is your representative. What would you teach a potential customer about you if you had their attention? A chutzpah brochure is a teaching tool and a call to action.

What is the purpose of a business brochure? It is a sales tool, and hopefully, a chutzpah sales tool. It is not:

- An artistic impression of the warmth of your heart
- A window into your soul that lets potential customers feel safe
- A mission statement
- A vita

I have worked with owners or managers who have spent over $3.00 per brochure (not counting development costs). They loved their beautiful pieces of art. I have noticed them fighting back tears when I suggested that their brochure was a waste of money, and worse than that, not helping to build their business. Very fancy, glossy, and artsy brochures tend to give the wrong message to potential customers. The message is: This business is very expensive and not approachable. A brochure that teaches this is detrimental. Your brochure should teach: Welcome, let us help.

If your brochures costs $3.00 each, you will be reluctant to leave a large stack ($300) of them on a side table at the library. Would you be comfortable dropping $100 worth on a table at the mall, or giving $390 worth to the high school P.E. teacher? A brochure that does not circulate is paper money you forgot to ignite. Would you really be comfortable ordering 5000 overpriced brochures from the printer? Chutzpah marketers don't spend a dime if 9-cents will do. A brochure has to be a hard working tool. It has to pull its weight. It has to make you money, not cost you money.

A chutzpah brochure is a teaching tool and a call to action. You cannot expect your spouse, friends, employees or customers to sell you to a potential customer. However, it is reasonable for any of them to hand your chutzpah mini-billboard brochure to a potential customer and say, "I think these guys are great." Your referrer's sales pitch leaves a little to be desired, but your chutzpah business brochure can fix even a lackluster sales pitch.

Brochure dimensions

The size and shape of your chutzpah business brochure is up to you. I have heard numerous business consultants expound on the need for a 12-page, high gloss, full color brochure so you can represent the quality of your skills, tell your company's story, and build a legend for eternity. For most businesses I think this is a waste of money. Your potential customer is not expecting a high society brochure. Most will assume you are simply pompous or overpriced—or both. If however, your business is very high end, such as a full day spa, herbal bath, and meditation package, then you will need a well-written high society brochure.

To save on printing and postage, I advise that you work within standard paper formats. Start with 8.5 X 11 inch or 8.5 X 14 inch paper. This size is easily purchased in bulk and requires no cutting. It comes in every color and texture. It will cost from about 3¢ to 50¢ for each brochure depending on the quality of the paper. I usually spend less than 10¢ because I prefer index stock. This stock is thick enough to hold up, but still easy to fold, and light enough to mail under first class postage weight regulations.

Most working brochures are 8.5 X 11, either folded in half or tri-folded into thirds. For short orders under 500 most printers fold by hand. Large orders are folded by machine. The fold cost is around 2-5¢ per piece of paper. If your order is folded by machine your printer will inform you that you can have a 5-10 percent loss rate due to the machine devouring them. He will expect you to pay for this loss rate, raising your printing cost by 10 percent. (In actuality the typical loss is only 1-2 percent.) Chutzpah marketers may choose to fold their own or put their kids to work.

If your brochure is going to have photos, you will want high gloss paper. This is a little more expensive, but the only way to go with photos. The photos jump off the page and look crisp on high gloss paper. For graphic art I find that 67–90 lb. Vellum Bristol feels and looks nice. You need to think about the feel of your brochure. Your reader will gather information about you subtly from the paper's feel. I use 67 lb. White or Ivory Vellum Bristol the most. It is inexpensive, holds it shape, and colors stand out well on it.

When talking with the printer, feel free to ask for the high quality, no name paper. The printer typically has this in the back, but he will rarely show it first. (If he does, he is not a chutzpah printer!)

Resist printing your own brochures unless you have invested in a high-end printer. Ink jet printers are very expensive to print on. Laser printers are better and cheaper to run. But, the initial cost of a quality color laser printer is $2,000 or more, and it will cost about 30¢ per side of paper to run. A print house can beat that price and save you up front costs and aggravation.

Typesetting can be done on your computer if you have a real typeset program; or it costs around $50 per hour to use a professional graphic artist. Most find that taking their handwritten copy into a pro is easiest. But, lots of us love fighting with our computers (they are easier than people.) A typesetter just copies your work into a digital format. If your brochure is done cleanly (easy to read) when you hand it to them, it takes little time for the graphic artist to format it. They can show you a list of fonts (fonts will be discussed later) for you to choose from.

In the following pages you will see the most common types of paper brochure folds. One piece of paper can be presented in many different ways to your reader, giving you lots of options in how you present your information.

"SADIE! I chased an ant across your iPad...
I think you bought a book."

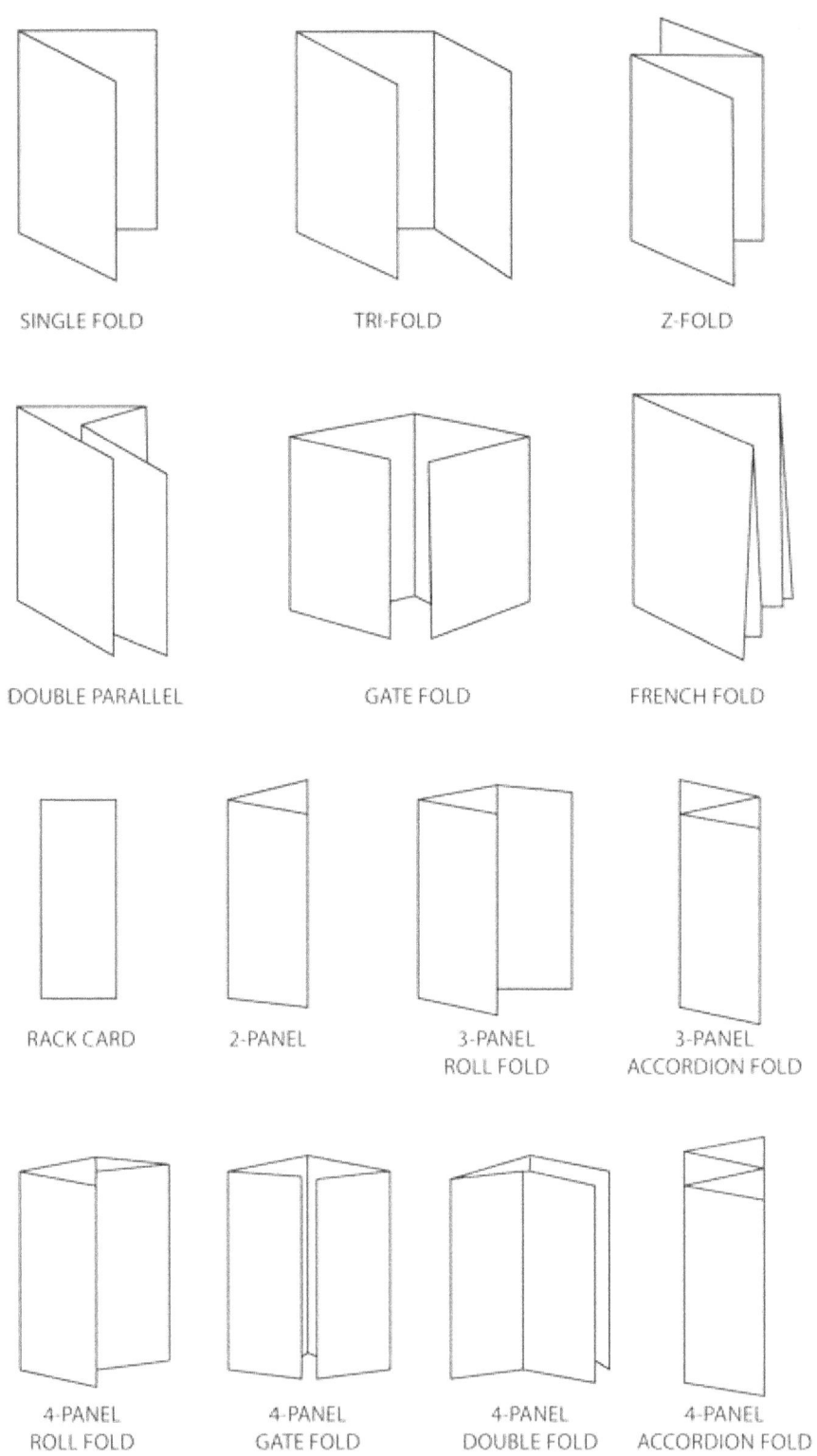

SINGLE FOLD TRI-FOLD Z-FOLD

DOUBLE PARALLEL GATE FOLD FRENCH FOLD

RACK CARD 2-PANEL 3-PANEL ROLL FOLD 3-PANEL ACCORDION FOLD

4-PANEL ROLL FOLD 4-PANEL GATE FOLD 4-PANEL DOUBLE FOLD 4-PANEL ACCORDION FOLD

Common types of brochure folds

Center fold

8.5 X 11 inch paper folded in half makes a wonderful shape. You have an 8.5 X 5.5 front and back, and an 8.5 X 11 inside. The inside can be used as 2-8.5 x 5.5 sections or used whole. The two major drawbacks are that you have only 4 areas to work with, and the brochure will not fit into a standard #10 envelope.

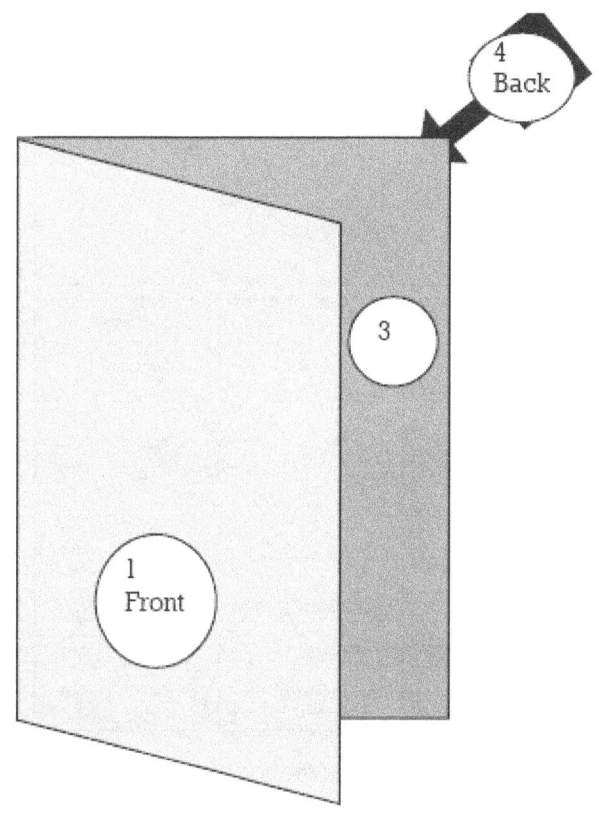

Center fold parts

Another option is that you can put several center folds together to form a roomier brochure. They can be seam glued, stapled, or stitched by your printer.

Tri-fold

A tri-fold gives you six panels to work with. This tends to make for nice columns and separations.

A tri-fold works well to "tell a story" as the reader progresses through your brochure.

The sections are a little complicated because you have to think of the brochure in three dimensions. Avoid the urge to relabel the panels. This is the way these panels are usually referred to in the printing business.

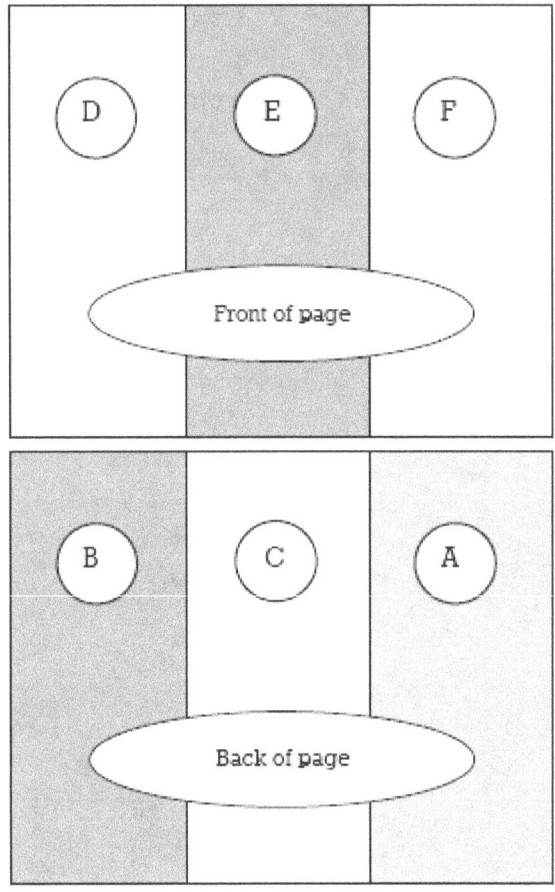

Parts of the tri-fold

When the paper is flat the sections look like the diagram above. There are several ways you can fold this. Think of it as a kind of brochure origami. I will explain a few common ways over the next few pages. Don't allow the alphabet labels (A-F) to confuse you. You may wish to fold paper and play along. What messes people up are the words front and back. Front and back refers to the front and back of the piece of paper, not the brochure. The "front" of the printed brochure is panel A.

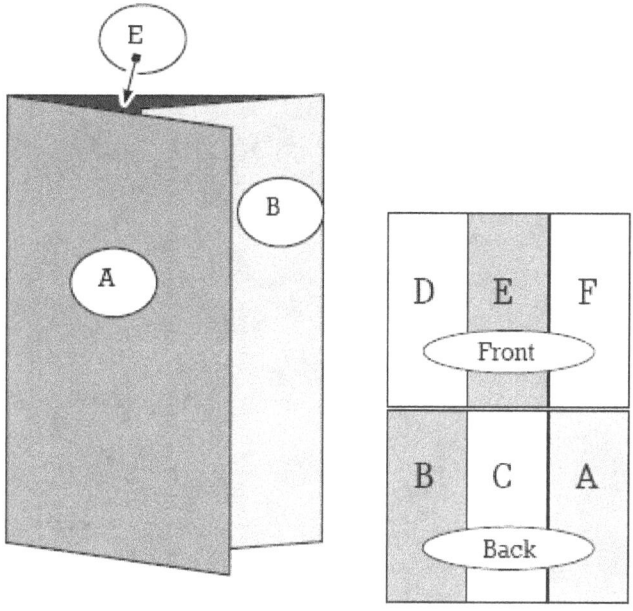

Tri-fold flap style

#A is the first panel of the tri-fold brochure (See above). Usually #B is the inside flap panel, the first panel seen when the brochure is opened. Panels #D and #B can be used together when the brochure is first opened. See below.

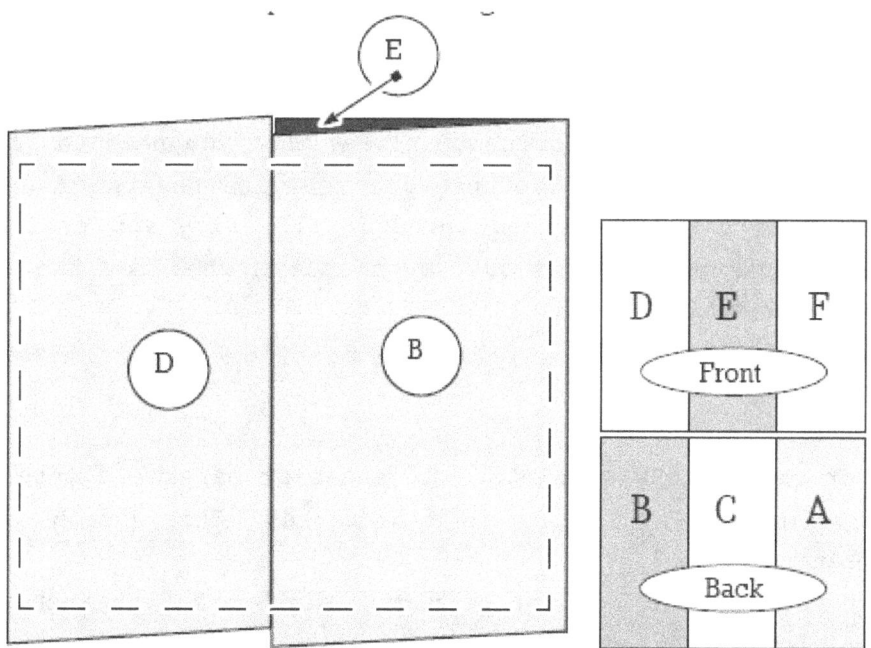

Nice printable area by combining panels #D and #B

You can also fold the paper into a Z-fold or accordion fold which makes

#F the back panel of the brochure. See below.

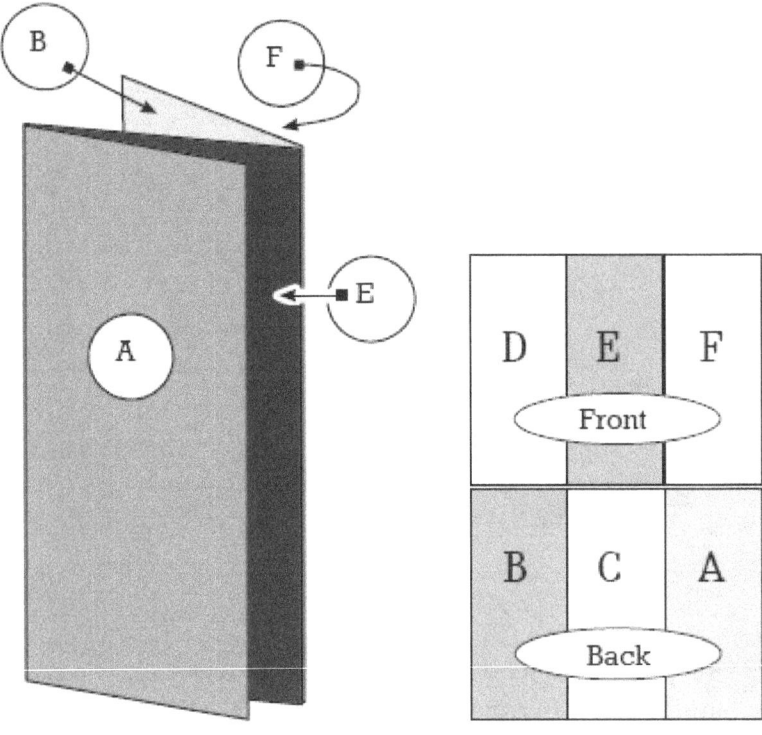

Z-fold style

The front printed page, #D, #E and #F, are the inside of the brochure. You can use them as a full spread or combine #D and #E or #E and #F for a 2/3 1/3 effect. Or you can use each separately for 3-1/3 effects. Lots of choices—giving you a lot of opportunity to say what you need to say.

When you are working your brochure use separate sheets of paper for the front and the back page. The bleed through will drive you crazy. I like to glue stick the mock-ups together to give myself a feel for the wholeness of the brochure.

3-up

A 3-up, or rack card, is an 8.5 X 11 sheet of paper cut into three equal parts. You get three 8.5 X 3.66 inch brochures. This can be great for a chutzpah marketer.

In a 3-up you don't have a lot of room, only 8.5 X 3.66 inches times two. See next page. But, the reader easily sees half your message for just pennies to you. This is by far my favorite shape for most entrepreneur businesses. 3-ups are cheap and powerful. You can blanket your community for a few hundred dollars every few months. At a cost of only 10¢ apiece you feel free to place stacks all over town. You add your 3-up to all outgoing mail with wild abandon. I personally have built my therapy business with my chutzpah business card, my chutzpah 3-up brochure, and my chutzpah nine-second speeches.

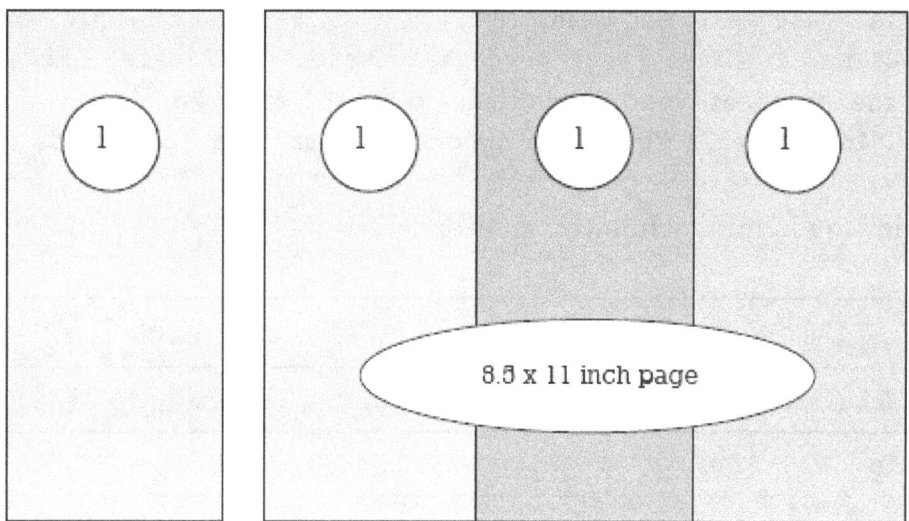

A single 3-up. You get 3 per sheet of paper

A big positive of the 3-up format is that I can easily afford to customize my message. I have a "child" focused 3-up, a "victim" focused 3-up, and a "family" focused 3-up. (I also have a few "business consulting" 3-ups.)

The drawback is that you can't build a relationship with your reader. You simply do not have the time in the space you have. To offset this drawback, use chutzpah graphics or photos. 3-ups are short and sweet, but very effective.

Chutzpah focus

Nothing, and I mean nothing, should go into your business brochure without chutzpah scrutiny. Every section of your brochure is valuable and important.

The purpose of a chutzpah business brochure is to sell. Do not confuse teaching with selling. Many business owners and managers believe that they must teach the benefits of their offerings through their brochure. This is a major mistake. It makes for brochures that are whiny and full of jargon. A chutzpah mini-billboard brochure is made to convince, not to inform! Your goal should be to motivate your potential customer to contact you. Specifically you! The information in your chutzpah business brochure must dazzle! It must draw potential customers to you. A chutzpah business brochure is a magnet for your potential customer. Every word in the copy must mesmerize. It must communicate to the heart of your potential customer. **It must speak to their needs…calling them to action.**

Your chutzpah business brochure should sell you as the right company for your potential customer. You cannot be all things to all people. You need to focus on your market niche, your potential customer. (Please, please, please) Write from the needs of your potential customer. All the same rules apply as we discussed in Chapter 2 **Your most important marketing tool costs 5¢.**

Keep the following in mind while you create:

Use/Stress	Avoid
Clear and accurate words	Misleading statements
Testimonials	Lying
Your qualifications	Puffery

Show how your business is user friendly:
    • Extended hours for your convenience
	Braggadocios statements like:
	    • Friendly staff
	    • Highest quality care

Only offer what you actually do, not what you wish or hope to do.	"Friendly Staff" is meaningless. Who wouldn't say that?
Show that your staff is friendly with action words and/or pictures.	Boring staff pictures of people standing doing nothing.
Show don't tell. Paint pictures with your words. Talk to your customers' needs.	Talking about your wants
Common words	Jargon
Guarantees (Clear easily understood.)	No small print on guarantees. It makes your offer seem like a trick.

Use a logo if it adds to your message:
    • Adds a feeling
    • Teaches something
	A logo for the sake of having a logo:
	    • A shape or swirl is not a logo unless you have a lot of money to teach that it is a logo.

Use/Stress	Avoid
A logo of a family teaches family. Teddy bears, lambs, puppies: teach caring.	Generic logos are generic and make you look generic!
Association logo teaches entrepreneurism.	A picture of your office tells potential customers that they will be paying your mortgage.
Maps can be helpful.	A photo of your cat, dog, or horse tells the reader that you're a little confused about who you treat (Unless you are a Vet).
Use photos as testimonials (happy customers using your product or service.)	Photos of your family. Focus should be on what you can do for your customers' families.
Use a line drawing to teach a feeling.	If you do not know the purpose of a graphic, leave it out!
Religious symbols may be helpful if you wish to limit your clientele to a particular religion.	Religious symbols tend to limit and may leave people feeling excluded.
Why choose you? — Say it! Be positive, uplifting!	Negative statements.
Use large enough print to be easily read. Use clear type styles for ease of readability.	Don't assume that all you customers have great vision. Avoid hard to read type styles.
Use white space to show importance and to control the reader's eye.	Avoid cumbersome print and hard to read fonts. Make your brochure easy to read and inviting. People will not bother with a crowded brochure or mini-billboard.

What's in a name?

It is dumb to start off your brochure with your name. Harsh words, but I believe in tough love.

This brochure is representative of most business brochures I see. It is written from the standpoint of the business owner. It is about the her. It will not get noticed. If a person views it in passing, it barely registers in their conscience. If it is noticed, the reader quickly categorizes it in her mind as…

I know everything I need to know about Sandy somebody… …then she stops reading.

Your brochure has to attract the attention of potential customers. It has to grab them and make them want to pick up your chutzpah business brochure. The initial words also have to get the readers to investigate the rest of the brochure. As the reader investigates they are called to action. They can call for an appointment, they can share the chutzpah business brochure with their spouse, or they can ask a friend what they think about this business! Voila, you are circulating!

Your chutzpah business brochure should consist of 5 major parts:

1. A chutzpah headline grabber.
2. Powerful subheads that interest the potential reader.
3. Dazzling copy that stirs the emotions of the potential customer.
4. Emotion evoking graphics and/or photos.
5. A call to action!

A chutzpah headline grabber

Writing copy (words written to cause a sale) is hard. Especially when the copy is just a few words like a chutzpah headline grabber. You have to look through the eyes of the target audience and solve their problems. Make each word count. Don't use any word that is not absolutely necessary to get your point across. Continuing with our example of Sandra Beach, what does she want to sell? She is a Marriage and Family Therapist so she wants to sell marriage and family therapy:

Sandra Beach's point of view	Potential customer's point of view
I work with children with behavior problems.	• Do your children listen? • Worried about your children? • Is homework a battle? • Solving the homework battle!
I treat teen girls with eating disorders.	• How do you tell her she is too thin? • Are you worried about your daughter's health? • Are you worried about your daughter's weight? • When worrying about your daughter is not enough...
I work with adolescents who are violent.	• Keeping your child out of jail. • Help for violent teens. • Fearful of your own child, we want to help. • Anger management therapy can help your clients (for attorneys who work with teens).

What if love is not enough?

Do I need marriage counseling?

Sandra Beach, M.F.T.

Licensed Marriage and Family Therapist

Which brochure works better to encourage a potential customer to read on?

Smith Magazine celebrates storytelling

We are going to spend a lot of time working to find the correct words to talk about your business. Often I am told that it is "frustrating" or "impossible" to find the correct words. The art of writing powerful copy can be developed, and over the next few pages I will encourage you to start building your headline writing skills.

To show you the power of writing copy, I want to introduce you to a project developed by Smith Magazine called Six Word Memoirs. The rules are simple, share your story in exactly six words.

Learn more and share your story at www.smithmag.net.

A lot can be shared in six words.

On the subject of love:
Married for neither love nor money.

Marriage is glass, cheating is hammer.

Mexican husband. Now swearing Spanish.

Wife makes me a better person.

Marriage is nightmarish, Wake me up!

The laws are different in Nevada.

Dating coach says "Maybe it's you."

I loved you knowing you'd leave.

Out on a limb. Branch broke.

Tried a woman preferred a man.

Never had a Valentines on Valentines.

Dumped through a text… Damn Technology.

Relationship Ended but Proved Love Possible.

He misunderstood the meaning of magnanimous.

I paint my hand holding hers.

I wished I was a man.

I still smell her on me.

A little chubbier, but much happier.

She read between the pickup lines.

Best friend became boyfriend. Lost both.

On the subject of children:
Two toddlers. Too tired to type.

Puppies would have been much easier.

Three years, three kids, I'm tired!
Mysterious disappearance of soiled cloth diapers.
Each new day was my favorite.
Days are long. Years are short.
I am besotted with my boys.
The test was positive; oh s**t.

One of my own:
Chutzpah business marketing percolates to circulate.

Powerful subheads that interest the potential reader

Large blocks of text are intimidating to the average reader. Short text blocks, with clear subheadings, encourage the reader to continue.

When writing the subheadings and text copy, follow the same principles as outlined for the brochure heading. Write to the reader's emotions, avoid jargon, and **promote benefit**.

Again let's follow Sandra Beach's therapy brochure as it progresses:

Sandra Beach's point of view	Potential customer's point of view
I work with children with behavior problems.	**Solving the homework battle!** Many parents find that yelling and screaming battles are soon a thing of the past. In a few short weeks, your family can learn better communication skills that remove the frustration from homework, mealtimes, and bedtimes. Learn the joy of being in the same room again. Family harmony makes your house a home.
I treat teen girls with eating disorders.	**How do you tell her she is too thin?** It is often hard to find the right words. Special care is taken to assist you in finding the correct way to show your daughter that you care for her. I will help you find caring words that she will allow herself to hear. You are not alone. I am here to help.

Sandra Beach's point of view	Potential customer's point of view
I work with adolescents who are violent.	**Help for violent teens** All the love of one person is not enough to protect an angry teen. In addition to individual and group counseling, we work closely with your attorney and the juvenile authorities to help your child. You'll find our team approach brings options to your child's court case that you alone cannot. By allowing us to support your teen, we can protect and help.

Dazzling copy that stirs the emotions of the potential customers

Under each subheading you will need powerful text. Here we are talking about creative writing skills (and you thought high school English was bogus). Your words need to amaze, astound, evoke, and empower the reader. You will need to paint vibrant pictures with your words. Show with emotive verbal pictures; avoid telling in monotone. Show with mind pictures don't just tell with words!

Use verbs, lots and lots of verbs! According to the Encarta World English Dictionary a verb is:

verb (n)
a word used to show that an action is taking place, or to indicate the existence of a state or condition, or the part of speech to which such a word belongs

Your goal is to **show action** and deliver hope. Talk to your prospects needs. For example:

Sleepy [Just words]	Alive with Chutzpah [Alive with emotion]
We care about you.	• For your convenience we offer extended hours. • (Tire company) We run out to greet your car! • (Jewelry shop) After hours and weekend special viewings are available by simply calling Mr. Harding at (408) 555-1234. • (Dress shop) Mother and Daughter fashion shows Sunday 1-3 PM. Free photos and make-up advice.
We are good, smart and really competent.	• Serving Tri-Counties families since 1983. • All of our deliveries are special deliveries. • (Restaurant) See our "brag wall" of happy customers.
I'm respected by peers.	• Past president of… • Founding member of… • Keynote speaker at… • Twice awarded… • Former…

Have the readers read about themselves.

Many display ads tell off, or growl at, the reader:

- Evening appointments by special arrangement only! Talk to the branch manager.
- Payment due at time of service.
- Please read your insurance documentation prior to calling our office if you are unsure about your insurance coverage.
- We try to accommodate as many people as possible, please be understanding if our staff is unable to attend to you immediately.
- Some weekends.

- Closed from Noon to 1:30 Monday to Friday.
- Please have your insurance information available when you call.
- Other colors are available by special order. Please allow a 4-6 weeks for delivery.

Potential customers does not want to know your problems. They are looking for your assistance in solving their needs.

Write your copy about the potential customer. Picture your ideal customer and write your copy to that person. Avoid *we* and use a lots of *you*.

Avoid	Use
We care	· For your convenience… · Your care…
We want you to be happy	· You'll find… · You'll discover… · You'll enjoy…
Our staff My staff The staff	· We are here to support you… · Your care is important to us so we continue striving to…
I, we, and my are not interesting to the reader. Our philosophy… Our mission statement is… My clinical overview is… I have the best staff in town… All focus on the wrong person.	You, you'll, and you will are interesting to the reader. A potential customer is self focused and looking to have their needs met. Your copy needs to be focused on them and letting them feel your helpfulness. You are starting a relationship through your chutzpah brochure.

The last point about your text is its font. Font is the style that the letters take. Your font should be a balance between readability and design shape. The most important aspect has to be readability. But, and this is a big but, your font cannot look like a "retail" store ad. It should not look like a newspaper advertisement.

A chutzpah business brochure for a woman's dress shop should look quite different from a brochure for a tire shop that is aiming to cater to woman.

Limit your brochure to complimentary fonts. A good rule is two or three fonts maximum in a large brochure, and only one font in a small brochure. If your fonts stand out they are probably in the way of your message. If your fonts are supportive of your message, they will blend in.

Black type on white paper is the easiest to read. Colored ink costs more to print, but gets more attention, and can go a long way in establishing a feeling. Be sure to keep ease of readability in mind when choosing a color.

It is easier to read sentences and paragraphs that have both caps and small letters. All caps are difficult for the eye to negotiate. On the Internet, all caps means yelling.

Which sentence do you find easier to read?

WHICH SENTENCE DO YOU FIND EASIER TO READ?

Which sentence do you find easier to read?

WHICH SENTENCE DO YOU FIND EASIER TO READ?

Which sentence do you find easier to read?

Which sentence do you find easier to read?

Emotion evoking graphics and/or photos

Graphics and/or photos are essential to your chutzpah business brochure. With graphics you get to show the story you are telling in the text. A picture is worth a thousand words, so make sure it is the right "thousand words."

Pictures of your staff working with your target reader looking very healthy and happy are by far the best. Avoid before and after pictures of people because they seem unethical and tend to overwhelm and turn off the public. Before and after pictures of your work on a car or building can be very helpful.

I advise you to use pictures of healthy looking active individuals, couples, and groupings. Have the people in the pictures smiling and happy against a light uncluttered background. In group shots, have older people helping younger people "do" something. Each picture must "say" everything is going to turn out wonderfully. Hope and help are just a phone call away.

A call to action!

Probably the most overlooked part of an entrepreneur's brochure is the call to action. I once saw a scene in a movie where the football coach was inspiring his demoralized team at halftime. Over a few minutes he built up the lads to believe in themselves. He proved he was an amazing leader as he pulled them out of despair. Then, he sent his excited players back to the game, unfortunately the locker room door was locked and the team bunched at the door utterly defeated.

As your reader builds confidence in you through your chutzpah business brochure, you have to make sure the door is open for them to come through. You have to give your potential customer that last little push to move them into action - to get them to call your office or drive to your store! Some examples:

Please call (111) 123-1234

**Call now
(111)123-1234**

Free Initial Consultation
(111)123-1234

Next let's play around with the look a little bit. There are a lot of ways to present your information. As long as it fits with your business branding you will stay focused. A company who works with banking officials will have a different font than a company who sells children's toys. Since the purpose of the information is to sell, a chutzpah marketer never forgoes ease of reading for graphic beauty.

First time buyers welcome!
Please call: (367) 555-1234

Smash Dance
One Night only!
Order Your Tickets Now!
(367) 555-1234

Mrs Dowry's

Reading-Is Fun-damental
Tutoring starts now: (698) 555-7895

Rosco's Tattoo

Open Fish to Whenever we shut.

Check in at (745) 555-4110

ZELDARS COMPUTERS

Where Nerds Run the World
First Contact: (852) 555-9513
Tweet us @ZeldarsNerd

Please note: Always put your whole phone number in your brochure. You don't want to miss an opportunity because a potential customer accidentally gets a wrong number calling you from her vacation home or out of area cell phone.

Don't assume that your reader "will just call." Ask them to call.

Inspire, stimulate, encourage, induce, urge, help, cause, and motivate them to call. The point is—if the reader does not call for an appointment, the brochure did not sell!

• Encourage the reader to get in the car and drive on over right now!

• Inspire them to go to their computer (cell phone, ipad) and check out your free PDF offered free from your amazing web site.

• The purpose of a chutzpah business brochure is to sell.

Your job is to write, rewrite, and rewrite some more until your brochure sells you well to your potential customer. Use your business branding to check your ideas against. Stay focused on your target population.

Dr. Phil's Therapy 3-up.

I am very fond of my chutzpah 3-Up. I like it because it is inexpensive and easy to hand out. I get a lot of space to teach what I want to teach, along with white space to direct the reader's eye. Over the years, I have noticed that I tend to give out lots more 3-ups than I do business cards. I'm liable to use business cards more with face-to-face contact, and 3-ups with group and public gatherings. Later, I will explain how I give out these little gems.

In my 3-up, I start with a feeling, my logo, and then teach how I can help. Over the years this simple piece of advertising has encouraged thousands to call in and make appointments. I always ask, "How did you get my name?", often to hear, "My friend/doctor/dentist/waitress/priest/hairdresser gave me…" "I picked up your brochure at…" or "I don't know, but I have had this big yellow card for months." Not bad for a few pennies of advertisement. 3-ups are very hard working, low cost mini-billboards.

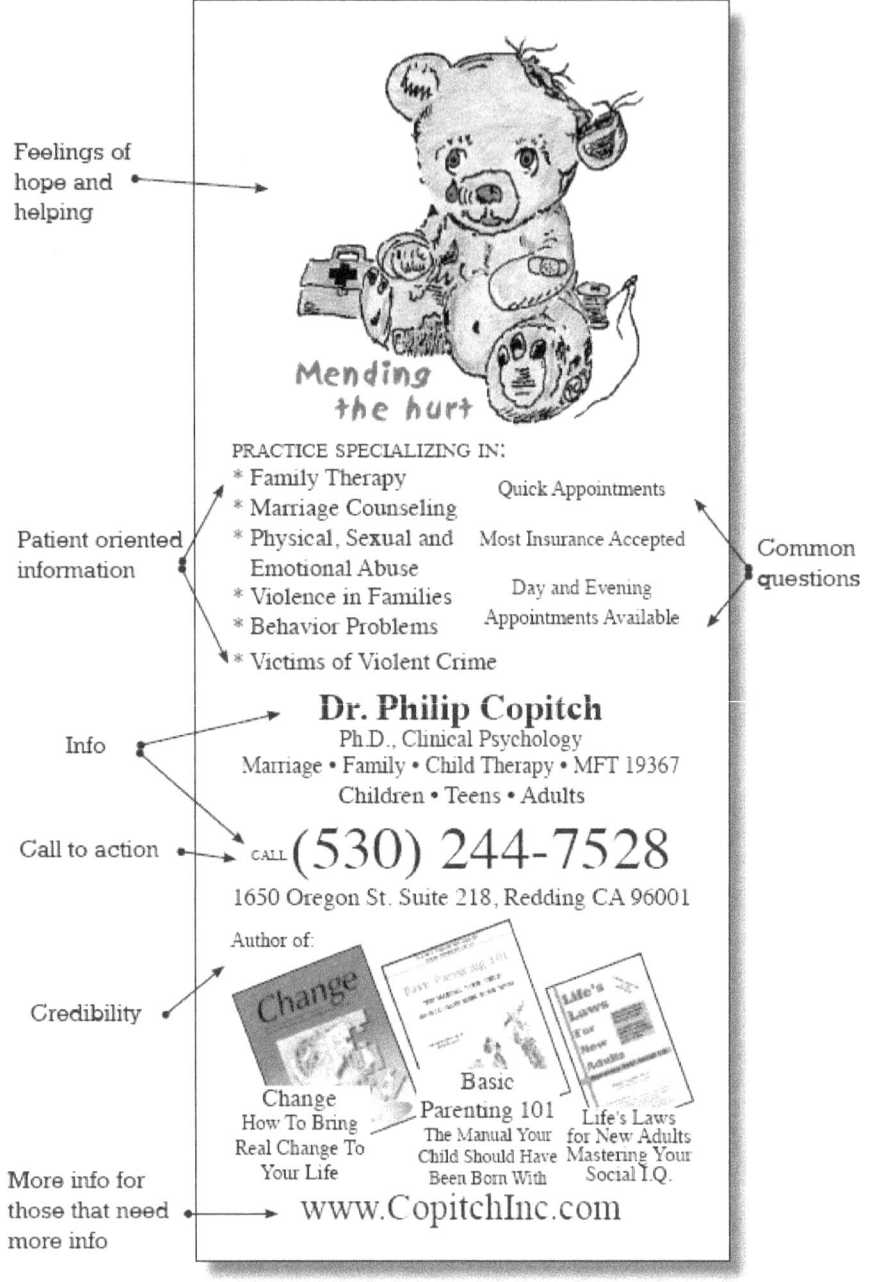

Feelings of hope and helping

Mending the hurt

PRACTICE SPECIALIZING IN:
* Family Therapy
* Marriage Counseling
* Physical, Sexual and Emotional Abuse
* Violence in Families
* Behavior Problems
* Victims of Violent Crime

Patient oriented information

Quick Appointments

Most Insurance Accepted

Day and Evening Appointments Available

Common questions

Info

Dr. Philip Copitch
Ph.D., Clinical Psychology
Marriage • Family • Child Therapy • MFT 19367
Children • Teens • Adults

Call to action

CALL **(530) 244-7528**

1650 Oregon St. Suite 218, Redding, CA 96001

Author of:

Credibility

Change
How To Bring
Real Change To
Your Life

Basic
Parenting 101
The Manual Your
Child Should Have
Been Born With

Life's Laws
for New Adults
Mastering Your
Social I.Q.

More info for those that need more info

www.CopitchInc.com

How to get your brochure out and about

It costs just pennies to make a 3-up, and dimes to make a tri-fold or single fold. Now you have to think of them as seeds. For a seed to grow they have to be sown. There are chutzpah ways to sow that get more seeds to land and blossom.

Donald told me with anger, "I placed a big stack of my brochures at the library and the next day they were all gone. So I put out another stack. Two days later they were gone. I was suspicious, so I checked the garbage can and there they were. Someone had thrown away my brochures."

What Donald didn't understand is that his stack of brochures were not valuable to anyone but himself. I assume his pain actually came from the potential value of his brochures. If you leave stacks of your brochures lying around you have not sown them. You have to make your brochures important.

Let me give you an example.

My 3-up ad is only on the front of the card. The front is what I want potential customers to read. But, Mrs. Smith is not walking around thinking of herself as a "Dr. Phil Potential Customer." She is Mrs. Smith, mom, driver, snack maker, cleaner … you know - she is all the parts of her life. She is the roles she plays. The back of my 3-up is for her, in her many roles. How do I get one of her many roles to pick up my 3-up? I have to give her a want.

If I am talking to a PTA group she is involved with, the want is easier to think of. She may want to take notes on the topic. I want to make this easy for my audience, so I provide a low cost, highly valuable way for them to take notes.

On the back of my 3-up I print a Note and To Do list area. At the begin-

Presenter: Philip Copitch, PhD. Date: _____

NOTES:

To Do:
- ☐ _____
- ☐ _____
- ☐ _____
- ☐

ning of my presentation, I hand out a stack to each side of the group and say, "I have some note cards for each of you. Please pass these around the room." I hand out the cards note side up. Near the end of my talk I softly point out, "If you have any further questions, please call my office… my contact info is on the back of your note cards.

A few people may want my contact info during the presentation. But everyone wants their valuable notes. My ad simply rides home with them on the back of what is important to them, their notes.

Once I was invited to speak to a group of building contractors. I was paid to talk about dealing with drug use in the work place. I had 20 minutes to cover a very large subject and the organization that invited me was happy to foot the bill for a take home package that they would print for me to give to their members. My contact was adamant that since they were footing the bill for the take home package, I could not include my ad, just basic contact information. As it turned out, the take home packet was a well done advertisement for the organization and a microscopic note of thanks to each of that day's speakers.

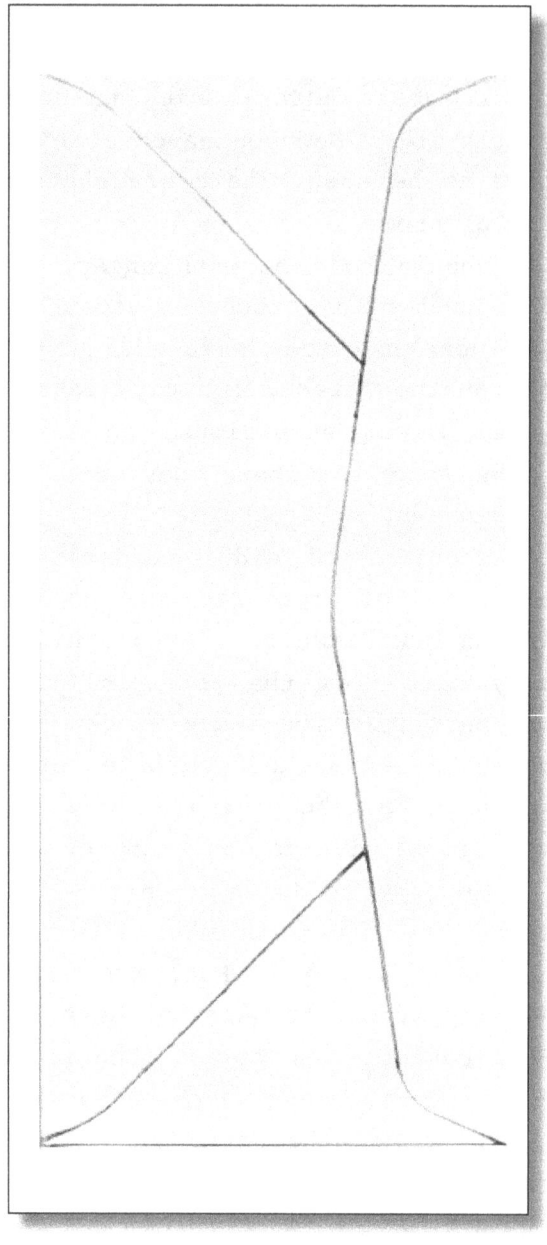

I wanted my advertisement to go home in the hands of every attendee. So I went chutzpah. As I started my talk I said, "You contractors are an interesting bunch. You're constantly on the run, constantly thinking and dealing with a million things at once. In fact, I have noticed that you folks never have note pads, you jot everything on the backs of envelopes. So…," holding my 3 ups, "I have the backs of envelopes for you all to take notes on. Please pass these around." On the back of my 3-up, I printed the back of an envelope. As the 3-ups were passed around the room, the chatter built into laughter.

Later that day, I enjoyed seeing T.B. poking his warm self out of the shirt pockets of many attendees. (They keep their notes private and close to their chests.)

Leaving brochures around

As Donald discovered earlier, if you just leave a stack of your brochures in any old place, they tend to get thrown away. Where you leave your brochure could place you in a bad light. Thumbtacking your ad on the community bulletin board at the grocery or the feed shop, may make you look less than professional.

How should you put your brochure in the public information area at the public library?

It is important to have your brochure fit where you leave it. Because 3-ups and tri-folds are inexpensive, I have different formats for different venues. At the library, I leave my stack of

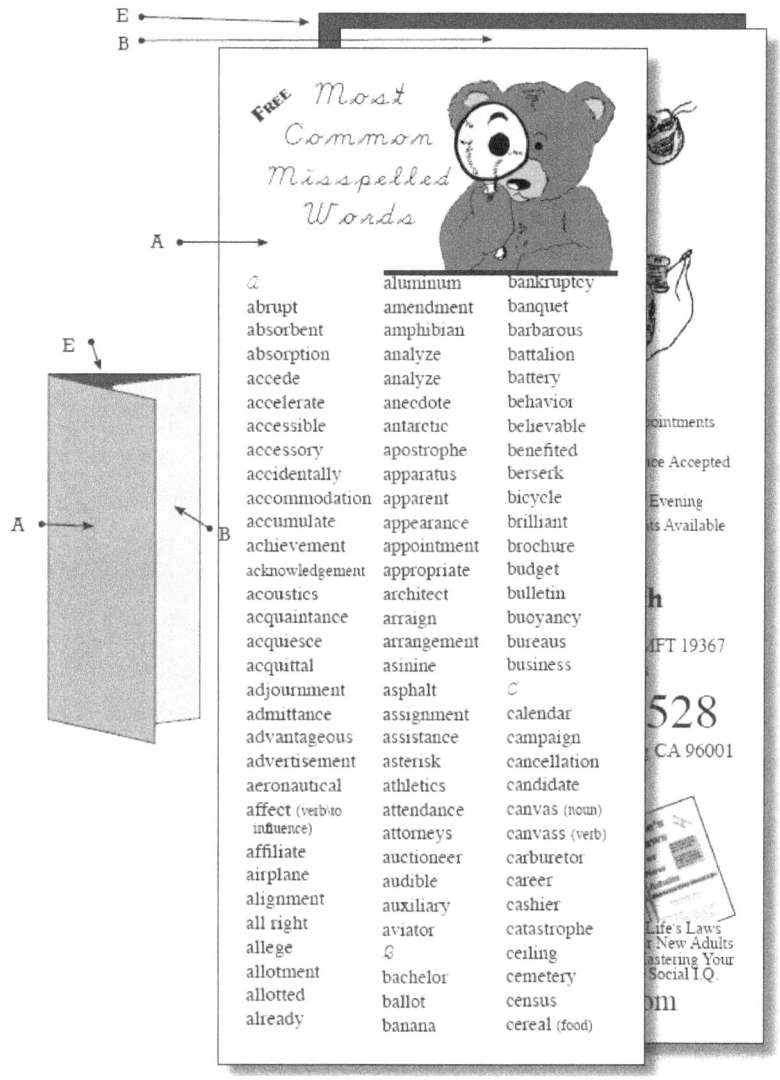

brochures called Most Common Misspelled Words. The list of words won't fit on the back of a 3-up, so I print it on a tri-fold brochure. (A piece of paper printed on both sides. The cost is 5¢ when done in quantity.) My info is on panel B of the brochure, so when the brochure is opened, the ad is right there. I also use this tri-fold chutzpah darling when I talk with school groups, "I'm sending around a list of the most common misspelled words. Take as many as you need." Teachers ask for lots to give out at their schools. This very inexpensive and helpful brochure ends up stuffed at the bottom of lots of backpacks and eventually in parents hands all over the county. I work a lot with children and adolescents with behavior problems. Often parents get concerned about behavior changes in their teens with no idea that their adolescents may well have easy access to drugs. When I talk with this population of parents, I want them to have much more information than I can give them in brochure form. Many parents are so sure that their child could not have a drug or alcohol problem, that they are not even open to taking a free booklet, especially in a public setting like a PTA meeting.

I direct them to my web site where they can download free PDFs on a variety of subjects. I also have a Victim's Have Rights 3-up. Police, social workers, guidance counselors and emergency room nurses tend to hand these out for me.

I hope you have noticed how hard my chutzpah brochures work for me and my potential customers. I keep stacks in my waiting room, and regularly a cop or a nurse will pop in to grab a few hundred. Recently, a police sergeant grabbed a stack of Victim's Have Rights 3-ups and said, "Thanks for these, the state has no money so I can't get their flier." I like the idea that I can help victims of crime with the contact information concerning local and state Victim's of Crime services.

Develop your chutzpah brochure

Now comes the fun part. You get to create your brochures. First, look over your branding goals that you developed in Chapter 1: **Talk too, not at, your customers.** Repeatedly check your creative ideas against your business branding goals. You want to stay on target.

F. A. Q. Most companies find that the brochure is a targeted form of their business card. It is targeted at some branding goal for the company. A common question I am asked during the creative phase:

Most businesses change their advertising on a regular basis … how often do I need to change mine?

If you are Coca Cola or Apple Computer, you are spending millions every month to teach/remind the public about your offerings. If you are like most companies and have a very limited budget, you only need to change your advertisement if your ad stops working, or you stop offering that product or service.

The public will not get bored with your ad, they won't see it enough to get bored with it. You may get tired of it because you see it all the time. I heard Willie Nelson in an interview explaining that there are certain songs he has to sing every show or the audience will leave feeling unloved. He may be bored with a song, but his audience is not.

It is common for me to find an owner or manager that gave up on a good advertising campaign too soon. It takes millions of dollars to get the public to notice your ad and get bored with it. As my mother would say, "You should have such worries." To date, I have not worked with a company where the public got bored of their good advertising campaign that focused on them and their needs.

A chutzpah marketer is focused on the potential customer's needs.

Want my opinion?

After you have gone through the process of developing your chutzpah brochure I would be happy to give it a once over. Send it to me as a PDF. Please don't send me more than 10 pages. Please limit yourself to your brochure in its near final form, or some aspect that is stumping you.

Email: DrPhil@CopitchInc.com

"Next on the agenda... we need to deal with the Yellow Page Monster."

5. ADVERTISING PART B: THE YELLOW PAGES AND LOCAL MEDIA

Embracing the media with a chutzpah hug

The reality of the Yellow Page monster is that if your ad is done right, the Yellow Pages work. For the chutzpah marketer, the Yellow Pages are an essential tool. If done correctly, the Yellow Pages can bring you lots of new customers.

Before we get started, I want you to conduct a thought experiment. Ask yourself these two questions:

1. The last time you used the Yellow Pages, what were you looking for?

2. Did you call someone?

Did you notice that you were motivated before you came upon an ad? When you read a newspaper or magazine you **may** stumble across an ad you find interesting. But, when you look in the Yellow Pages you are **looking** for an ad, you are looking for information in the form of an ad.

Category and action

In preparation for writing this chapter, I surveyed three groups I had easy access to. I asked a total of 76 white-collar working adults, ranging in age from approximately 30 to 60, to write their answers on index cards. I asked three questions.

According to the marketing research group CMR Associates, as reported in "Major Yellow Pages Trends and Opportunities 2006", consumers that use the Yellow Pages spent 25% more on average than the average customer. Also, business users (19 percent of total Yellow Page users) spent 50% more.

Other findings:

88% of Yellow Page users make a purchase. 54% of these users are first time buyers.

1. What was the last thing you looked up in the Yellow Pages? (Category)
2. Did you call a company?
3. Did you know who you were looking for?

I list their answers in order of category preferences:

Category	Call?	Did you know the company?
Pizza	Yes 100% No 0%	Yes 100% No 0%
Restaurant	Yes 100% No 0%	Yes 100% No 0%
Doctor	Yes 100% No 0%	Yes 100% No 0%
Dentist	Yes 100% No 0%	Yes 60% No 40%
Insurance	Yes 100% No 0%	Yes 80% No 20%

Category	Call?	Did you know the company?
Plumber	Yes 100% No 0%	Yes 50% No 50%
Attorney	Yes 90% No 10%	Yes 80% No 20%
Cable repair	Yes 100% No 0%	Yes 100% No 0%
Auto repair	Yes 80% No 20%	Yes 50% No 50%
Appliance repair	Yes 100% No 0%	Yes 66% No 33%
Tires	Yes 50% No 50%	Yes 50% No 50%
Air-condition repair	Yes 100% No 0%	Yes 0% No 100%
Rental car	Yes 100% No 0%	Yes 100% No 0%
Computer repair	Yes 50% No 50%	Yes 20% No 80%
Garage door repair	Yes 100% No 0%	Yes 100% No 0%
Tanning	Yes 100% No 0%	Yes 0% No 100%

My unscientific survey lines up well with industry data. The most striking finding is that Yellow Page users are motivated. They are looking to solve a problem. They are hunting for something.

When a Yellow Page user opens the book they tend to have a defined problem. Their goal is to solve their problem.

Now comes your problem, how do you use the Yellow Pages to your advantage? First let's get the myths out of the way.

Myth #1: The Yellow Pages are very expensive

This really is an illogical statement. What does "very expensive" mean? If I spend $400 per month to get no new customers, then the Yellow Pages are a waste of $400. However, if I spend $400 a month to get 8 new customers, each spending let's say, to keep the math really easy, $100 ($800), then the initial investment of $400 gave me $400 of profit. Plus, I now have 8 satisfied customers that are likely to use more of my services, and hopefully suggest that their friends and family use my services.

Myth #2: Good companies do not need to advertise in the Yellow Pages

Most people who are using the Yellow Pages know something about what they are looking up, but they need more information. They may simply need a phone number, or they may need a jolt of confidence, that final push, to get them to call your company.

I will explain more about this later in this chapter, but good companies do need to advertise in the Yellow Pages.

Myth #3: Unless you can afford the biggest ad, you cannot compete in the Yellow Pages

Happily, this is not necessarily true. In most cases big matters in the Yellow Pages, but that is assuming the big ad is designed correctly. Most companies that advertise in the Yellow Pages do a poor job of designing their ad. After you read this chapter, you will not be one of them. More on size later.

People have been trained to use the Yellow Pages

I am writing this in July 2010. I tell you this because the Yellow Pages as we know them are doomed. Not this year, and probably not in the next five years, but they are doomed.

I come to this conclusion through observation. Let me digress a bit. When my wife and I want to look up a word, we tend to pull out the dictionaries we used in college and delve in. We often get side tracked while looking for our initial word as we stumble across another interesting word, before finally returning to the our original goal. I am 52, and my bride of 24 years, Geri, is 49. We love our dictionaries. They are page worn old friends.

Recently, at the dinner table, Geri and I were discussing the word, cede. "Is that s-e-d-e or c-e-d-e?" she wondered. I had no idea about its spelling. (Just because I write books doesn't mean I can spell.)

Our 20 year old son, Ethan chimed in. "It's c-e-d-e cede: a transient verb. It means to surrender possession of, especially by treaty." He was holding his laptop, reading the definition from ask.com. Geri and I felt old.

The next day, we were out at dinner and I threw out, "Maybe we should go out to a movie since we are already in town."

"I don't know what's playing," Geri said.

"I think I want to see the movie about the brothers who fought the Nazis. But I don't know…" Josh, our sixteen year old, interrupted me.

"Defiant won't be out until next Friday. The Unborn and Seven Pounds are playing at Cinemark 10, I'll check Cinemark 8," he said as he thumb poked his cell phone.

I looked at Geri and smiled. We felt very old.

To our sons, a dictionary is a search engine on the Internet super highway. The concept of getting a dictionary off the shelf is foreign to them. For them, information is always a few finger-taps away. They manipulate information to their advantage all day. To illustrate this fact, did you notice that Josh only relayed the two movies at Cinemark 10 that he was interested in seeing? He limited his information search results to his personal parameters, not his beloved parents' general question.

What does this mean for the Yellow Pages?

The Yellow Page book is evolving into a digital search engine. The book form is going the way of the Dodo bird.

But, not for a few years. Until the book is extinct, it will continue to be a powerful tool. After its demise, we will all be advertising in its digital replacement. Most of what will follow in this chapter will still be true for the digital Yellow Pages.

At this point in time, when a person 30 or older wants to gather information about a local product or service, they are going to use the trusted Yellow Pages.

Motivated buyer

When a person opens the Yellow Pages they have a want. They need something. In Yellow Page nomenclature this person is looking for a category.

Mrs. Lodge gets a call at work from her neighbor. A tree in her front yard has fallen onto her roof. And to make things worse, a large branch has shattered the picture window and made itself at home on her new couch. Mrs. Lodge rushes home through the downpour.

Back at home, Mrs. Lodge is beside herself. Her mind is racing and her heart is pounding. The local fire department had responded to the incident. They cut the tree branches back and covered the broken window with a tarp. As they were leaving, the fire captain told her, "It could have been a lot worse. The roof looks to be in good shape. If you get the carpets dried soon, they will probably be fine. The couch and window frame are probably a total loss."

Mrs. Lodge has a want and is looking for an answer in the Yellow Pages.

She went to the Yellow Pages. "What do I look it up under," she thought to herself. "Emergency!" she decided. Under that category she only found a list of emergency medical options.

Feeling anxious she thought of the fire captain and how stupid she felt for not asking him who she should call. "Fire," she thought and flipped to the F's.

"Financial, Fire," she said.

Looking at the ads she read. "AAA Fire Alarm and Security… Booker's Fire extinguishers… ReStore… We bill your insurance company." She read the top of that ad again. "We bill your insurance company." The next line was "One hour response." This ad talked directly to her needs. This company could deal with her wants.

She called that company. She didn't know who she was calling mind you, because she didn't know the company's name until they answered the phone. Berkowitz Emergency Clean Up, may I help you?" The company's name was in the yellow page ad, but it wasn't the title of the ad. It wasn't even the subtitle of the ad. The title and subtitle of the ad spoke to Mrs. Lodge's concerns. The title and subtitle were probably the most common questions that callers ask Berkowitz Emergency Clean Up.

That is the power of the Yellow Pages. A motivated consumer searching for a company.

Now let's look at building a chutzpah Yellow Page ad so your customers can find you.

"Me too" mentality

I have had a lot of opportunities to look at yellow page advertisements. As soon as a business owner finds out I teach seminars on this subject, they find a Yellow Page book and ask for a free critique. Why not, entrepreneurs aren't stupid!

As I look their ad over I ask, "So, how did you decide what to put in your ad?" Then I steel myself for the usual answer.

"Ah, well, ah, I just copied what others were doing."

Holy not chutzpah batman! This is why most Yellow Page ads bring disappointing returns. They are all the same. If you look through your Yellow Pages, category by category, you will prove me right. I'm a great plumber, I'm a trained plumber, I have a plumbing truck with great stuff in it. I have kids who I feed by being a plumber.

When I travel, I look through the local Yellow Pages to see what businesses are doing. What I tend to find:

- Large bold names of business
- Lots of colors and fonts
- Logos I have never seen before
- Pictures of the owner's family
- Pictures of the owner's building
- Pictures of the owner's trucks
- Pictures of the staff all smushed together in a group shot
- Hard to read fonts on colored backgrounds that make the words even harder to read
- Entrepreneurs stiffly posed in suit and tie
- Tiny print
- Business specific words that the public doesn't understand. (OSHA Approved, ERST Bonded, R-DAR Certified, 100% Digital Service)

This list is an example of the "me too" mentality. Me too, I belong in this category - pick me! This is why most Yellow Page ads do not work that well. If your ad only teaches what your reader expects, you are not standing out in the category. (Also, the nomenclature often loses the reader.)

When I look at a Yellow Page ad, I give the parts the "Well, I hope so…" test. So when the plumber teaches me that he has a plumber's truck I think, "Well, I hope so!" Or how do you get your equipment to my house?

As you look through your local Yellow Pages, do the, "Well, I hope so… " test.

- The attorney went to school. "Well, I hope so…"
- The entrepreneur works with individuals, couples and/or children. "Well, I hope so…"
- The chiropractor helps with back pain. "Well, I hope so…"
- The funeral home listens to your needs. "Well, I hope so…"

- The counselor does EMDR, TFT, sand play, art "Well, I hope so…" Whatever that is.
- The company sells to Christians. "Well, I hope so…" (unless they're outwardly prejudiced.)
- The bail bondsman deals with anger. "Well, I hope so…"
- The rental company rents stuff. "Well, I hope so…"
- The pharmacist educates. "Well, I hope so…"
- The doctor specializes. "Well, I hope so…"

All of these may be important to inform the public, but they will not make you a stand out in the category. A chutzpah advertiser, wants to stand out in any category where they place an ad; the purpose of the ad is to make a sale.

Your Yellow Page rep

The Yellow Page representative is a sales person for the Yellow Pages. Over the years I have had many. And, because I put together ads for other entrepreneurs, I have had a lot of contact with Yellow Page reps.

In my area, the Yellow Page sales person moves into town for a few months, then moves onto the "next book". Most of my reps have been hard working folks trying to eke out a living. They tend to use the soft sell, "I'm here for you". They always push the bigger ad so "you can get your message out". Or, "so you can have a choice placement".

What I want to point out to you is that the sales representative has no power. They can offer what the phone company allows them to offer. They cannot do you any favors. Their goal is to sell the most and biggest ads. That's how they make their income.

It is best for the sales rep if all their accounts get a fair distribution of the potential calls. Then next year, they can return to happy customers who like what they are offering.

But, the reality is, that in the Yellow Pages, you are competing for the eyes of the motivated prospects that view your category. The Yellow Pages places us in direct competition with the other business in our area.

My admonition. Do not let the Yellow Page salesperson make your ad. If you do, it will look like every other ad in the category, and it will fail the "Well, I hope so…" test.

Chutzpah marketers never fail the "Well, I hope so…" test.

I once had a new Yellow Page sales rep who tried to bully me into just redoing my old ad.

"We close in two days. You don't want to be left out for a whole year!" she told me.

I knew that I had meetings set for other company ads over the next two months. So, I politely ended the meeting. I called her supervisor and got a new rep. Do not allow a sales rep to bully you. I have put in ads for companies weeks after the Yellow Pages closed. The phone company really wants your business. They do not want to lose your ad income for a whole year.

For five years I had the same rep. She was based in Oakland, California and spent five days per week, for two months, in my area away from her kids. She said the job paid well, but was very hard on her family. She was an amazing person, full of life.

For four years I had a rep from San Jose who loved to travel. He was outgoing and very funny. He liked that his job paid well enough and afforded him extended time off for pleasure travel.

I tell you about these two folks to make a point. As a chutzpah marketer, an outgoing sales rep for another company is a great referral source for my company. Over the nine years these sales reps worked my area, they accounted for many new referrals. With only a little encouragement from me, the Yellow Page reps repaid me more than my Yellow Page bill cost me. That is called chutzpah marketing. This is the power of the 9-second speech discussed in Chapter 3: **Your second most important marketing tool is free**

Alternative Yellow Pages

About once a month, I get a letter that looks like a Yellow Page bill. It has all my business information professionally arranged. What it really amounts to is a dishonest sales pitch from an alternative Yellow Page company. Their advertisement is made to look like a pre-approved bill. I suspect that many companies simply pay the $500 fee assuming that it was ordered by someone higher up.

The problem with the alternative phone books is that it costs businesses a lot more to cover the same area. I have been told by their representatives that the alternative books are building market share, but I haven't notice it in my area. They tend to be a lot less expensive than the real Yellow Pages, but I doubt that they are cost effective. Legally, they have to give you a free listing without you doing anything. And guess where they buy the listing database from? You guessed it, the phone company. (Do you feel the love?)

At this point in time I recommend against putting your hard earned money into the alternative phone books.

Yellow Page ad size and color

Size

The question concerning ad size is complicated. You have to juggle factors such as:

- Placement position
- The ad sizes of others in your area
- Size of category
- Do you have something to separate you from the category?
- Correct amount of space to tell your story
- Cost ratio of the ad (expense versus income)

Having said this, all things being equal, you want to be the largest ad in the category with a chutzpah message.

But, the message is more important than the size of the ad. When your potential customer peruses the Yellow Page category, she often will not stop searching just because she finds her answer. She will look for options. Even if she is looking for you specifically, she will compare and contrast you against the other offerings.

Think of your category as a buffet table, you most likely want to see all your options.

A woman on the phone told me (in a whisper) "I was referred to Dr. McCoy, but your ad seemed to be right for me. I liked that you care."

This is interesting, this woman didn't know me, but she felt that I was the correct entrepreneur for her. Her feelings were more important in the decision process than her medical doctor's referral.

The size is helpful, mostly because you can get your message across. Please let me prove to you that the smallest ad can have the best pull. If your ad simply said:

100% Free _____ (your product).
(235) 568-2658

The more expensive the product you sell the better this ad will pull!

Your business would be full. This ad would control the category, even against full page advertisements.

Remember, chutzpah content is king, no matter what the size of the ad.

Color

In the old days color was very expensive. Today, color is not as much of as an expense as it is a tool. Use color to tell your story. Do not use color simply to make your ad colorful.

It is very easy to distract with too much color. On the flip side, color used correctly will emote powerful feelings. I once worked for a dentist who loved the color red. Big, bold, bright red letters. "I'm paying to catch the prospect's attention," he explained.

When I affirmed that red was the easiest color to use to capture a person's attention, he beamed with delight.

"But," I continued. "Red is so powerful because it triggers feelings of danger, edible fruit, or interest in mating."

The dentist's face went pale.

I continued, "I don't know if that is what you want your customers to be feeling when they think of you." "What?" he sputtered. "I don't think that the color of eating, pain, or sex is all that good for a family dentist," I said.

In the context of dentistry, customers are already thinking pain. A dentist doesn't want to encourage that type of thought. The further away from blood the

The Red Santa Suit

Until the 1920's Santa was often depicted in lots of different types of dress. He also tended to be portrayed as a kindly thin fellow or even a tall elf.

What we think of as a "Santa Suit" evolved over time as the story of Santa grew. He became plump, lived at the North Pole, and ran a workshop filled with happy elves making toys for good little boys and girls.

In 1931, Coca-Cola hired artist Haddon Sundblom to help sell Coca-Cola during the winter holidays. Before color movies and color television Saunblom's colorful and happy jolly Santa caught the imagination of children of all ages.

Since then the colorful Coca-Cola ads, billboards, and store displays have helped most people to know what Santa "really" looks like.

You can see the rich history of the Coca-Cola ads at www.thecoca-colacompany.com/pres scenter/imageheritage.html#santa

better for a dentist. In the context of Christmas, red is a great color. In fact, we have been trained to think of red as a Christmas color. (See side bar.)

I advise that you use warm rich shades when possible. Brighter colors if your target group is parents of young children, warmer colors for middle age adults, and richer colors for older adults.

For older adults, keep in mind that as we age, our eyes do not separate colors as well as they used to. You will need clear contrasts with no clutter.

A financial planner I worked with wanted to use a warm orange/brown font on a yellow cream background. His target customers were wealthy couples and individuals with a net worth of over five million dollars. As I looked over the mock-ups his graphic designer made for him, I pointed out that the type was way too small, and the color contrast was inappropriate for his clientele. He readily agreed that most of his present customers needed glasses and that the print size needed to be enlarged. But he was adamant about the colors, "My graphic artist said that these are the colors that encourage togetherness. I love them."

I asked him to show the material to some older people.

The next day I got this email:

> Dr. Phil,
>
> I asked my 92 year old mother what she thought of the new sales material. She looked at it intently and said, "Where are the words?"
>
> Any advice on a new graphic artist?
>
> Reginald

For a chutzpah marketer, the purpose of the ad is to sell. Your ad should not be seen as a piece of art.

What about the online offerings from the Yellow Pages?

Last year, (placement 2007-2008) I met with my Yellow Page representative. Near the end of his soft sell sales pitch he said, "and I assume you would like to upgrade your free yellowpages.com listing from simply your name to an ad or a link to your web site?"

"How much for the link?" I asked (I figured if I could get a prospect to my site, I'd have a good chance for that prospect to see if I was the right entrepreneur for them.)

"Only $24.95," he said.

"A year?"

"Ah, no a month, it is part of your monthly phone bill," he clarified.

"$300 to link my name to my web site?"

"Have you been to yellowpages.com? It is the leading Internet Yellow Pages."

"But, setting a link takes only seconds, isn't $300 excessive?" I asked.

"It used to cost more," he said.

I didn't pay for the Internet Yellow Page ad. Their numbers were too small to warrant the cost. It would have cost me $200 per month for me to place my ad on their web site. With their low numbers and high cost I do not need them. Let me explain my reasoning.

- The people who call my office to make the appointments, for themselves and / or their families, are over thirty. They are comfortable with the Yellow Page book.
- The largest search engine by far is Google. Google is reasonable to advertise with.
- I know that in 2005-2007 I had only three new contacts via the Internet. I track this data precisely. All three contacts came from individuals that got my name from someone, then they Googled me to check me out. Interestingly, all three contacts were men who were computer programmers.

This year (placement 2008-2009) my Yellow Page representative gave me a different offer. Linking my yellowpages.com free listing to my web site was only $4 per month. I signed up. Not only because of the price, but more so I can see if the link translates into customers. (See below)

It has been four months since the new Yellow Pages came out, I have had only one Internet contact. He is an information technology (IT) specialist who got my name from my book. (He received the book from his sister for Christmas.)

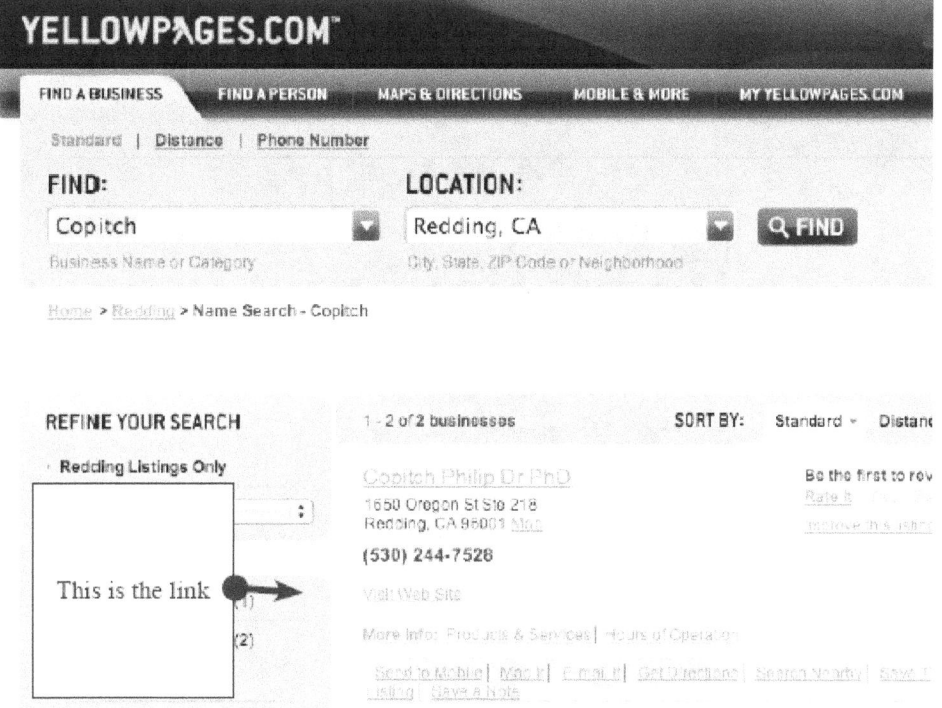

I played with this site a bit, and found it lacking when I compared it to Google. Yellowpages.com is cumbersome and busy. The flashing ads down the side are distracting. It seemed more like an ad for the yellowpages.com than for me. When I searched for "Entrepreneur Redding CA" I got a long alphabetized list of entrepreneurs in the county. I had to limit my search to get just Redding. A savvy search engine should not have you re-request to get the search information you want. The "C's" started on page 2. I suspect that I could pay to move my listing to the top, and still compete with more flashing ads.

My rep says that the phone company is planning to spend millions to increase its market share. So, for now I will keep an eye on it.

What belongs in your display ad

A display ad is the type of ad you find in Yellow Page directories, magazines, newspapers, billboards, or on the side of a bus. It is simply a display of your offerings. The difference between the various types of display ads is the audience you're targeting.

If you were developing a display ad for The New Yorker versus Guns & Ammo your ad would need to be targeted to each specific audience.

Your display ad is developed based on your reader. Because we know that the Yellow Page reader is motivated by category, the ad is easier to develop.

All chutzpah ads have four major components.

1. Chutzpah headline
2. Chutzpah supporting information
3. Chutzpah supporting secondary benefits
        ------Name and address
4. Chutzpah call to action

The basic ad looks like this:

Without logo/art-

Chutzpah headline up to
10 words

Chutzpah supporting information : supporting the headline.
Chutzpah supporting secondary benefits
showing benefits benefits benefits ben-
efits benefits benefits benefits benefits
benefits benefits benefits benefits benefits
... and more benefits!

Name rank and address.
Chutzpah call to action:

235-555-9874

With logo-

Chutzpah
headline up to
10 words

Chutzpah supporting
information : supporting the headline.
Chutzpah supporting secondary benefits
showing benefits benefits benefits benefits
benefits benefits benefits benefits benefits
benefits benefits benefits benefits ... and more
benefits!
Name rank and address.
Chutzpah call to action:

235-555-9874

Let's look at the parts.

Chutzpah headline

This is the most important part of your advertisement. If you do not catch the reader's attention, you are sunk. Look at this ad and notice the power of a good headline verses a ho-hum headline.

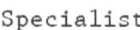
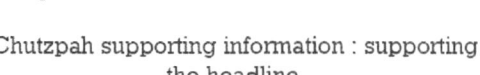
Both ads say about the same, which one catches your eye? Which ad will most likely capture the eye of a frantic parent searching through the Yellow Pages for help? Even with the power of the ducks and kitty, the question is substantially more powerful than the entrepreneur's name and clinical interest.

The goal when developing the headline is to find the best combination of ten words or so that addresses the concerns of the reader.

If the reader comes to the Yellow Pages looking for help with her out of control three and six year olds, she may well be asking, "I'm going crazy, is there help for me and my kids?"

The goal of the headline is to anticipate the reader's needs. If you get it correct, they will continue to read your advertisement. You only get to focus your heading on one target.

To make your headline, start with your branding that you developed in Chapter 1: **Talk too, not at, your customers**. What is your ideal customer looking for when she goes to the Yellow Pages? You may find five or six good answers to this question, but only one is your core customer, the one that fills most of your appointments, or tables, the one that is your meat and potatoes.

With your core customer in mind, answer the question she is asking. Write it and rewrite it so every word is perfect. Now you have your chutzpah Yellow Page headline.

A common assertion I get at this point in a seminar is, "But I have five ideal customers." If so, you need five ads. Pick the most common ideal customer for your Yellow Page ad. The other four ideal customers will be targeted in other publications, 3-ups, or brochures.

Your ad headline will not limit your company. Once you are seen as good at one area of your general category, people will expect you to be good at everything. If you find a plumber that did a good job on your emergency water leak wouldn't you assume that the same plumber is also good on kitchen clogs and toilet repairs? Remember, speak to the potential customer in their words. The words that they are most likely using when they are looking for your type of company. Remember to avoid nomenclature and to focus on solving their problem.

Chutzpah supporting information

The second part of your ad needs to be supporting data for your headline. Depending on your type of business, this could be short declarative sentences, or full complicated and specific paragraphs. It will depend on your customers' need for information.

If your headline lends itself to bullets, great—use bullets. Just make sure the bullets support the headline. Make sure the bullets show clear benefits of using your services.

If your headline needs fact filled information to support it, you will need to write concise fact filled paragraphs that show clear benefits for using your services.

I have been told that no one will read a long paragraph in a Yellow Page ad. I disagree. It depends on the question the headline is answering.

If your business specializes in working with highly intelligent individuals, such as engineers, mathematicians, and physicists, you will need at least a paragraph to convince your potential customer that they need your services.

An emotional headline will need a declarative paragraph emoting feelings that allow you to be the correct company to call.

Examples for a pet cemetery:

When pets are called home to heaven we are left to grieve…

or

It does not seem fair, when bad things happen to our loving pets.

Chutzpah supporting secondary benefits

As we discussed in Chapter 4: **Advertising Part A: On the Chutzpah Cheap** in the sections **Chutzpah focus** and **Dazzling copy that stirs the emotions of the potential customers,** copy counts!

Your supporting secondary benefits need to point out, very clearly, why you are the best choice for the prospect. It is important that your picture or graphic is seen as part of this secondary support. You can't just say it, you must show it. We are talking about creative writing skills (and you thought high school English was bogus). Your words need to amaze,

Eye tracking research shows that 65% of eye contact with an ad is spent looking at the illustration or the photograph, while only 35% is focused on the text.

This research suggests that the reader is much more interested in illustrations or photographs.

Perception Research Services (http://www.prsresearch.com)

astound, evoke, and empower the reader. You will need to paint vibrant pictures with your words. Show with emotive verbal pictures; avoid telling with monotone work salad. (Show not tell!)

Use verbs, lots and lots of verbs! The potential customers do not want to know your problems. They are looking for your assistance.

A potential customer is self focused and looking to have their needs met. Your copy needs to be focused on them and letting them feel your helpfulness. You are starting a relationship through your chutzpah ad.

What if your product or service is hard to picture as having secondary benefits? If you find yourself stuck, it means you have not been listening to your customers. They verbalize the secondary gains for you.

Call to action

The call to action is a polite nudge. As the prospect reads your advertisement, he gets to the action, usually a phone number. Inside his head he hears, "call 530-555-1234." This gentle nudge is powerful because it seems to come from within. It feels like internal dialog. Yawn. Go ahead, it's ok, yawn. As you read this, do you notice that your body is reacting as if you need to yawn. Just reading the word yawn triggers a behavior.

A call to action statement will increase your customer contacts.

· Call now: 530-555-1234

- More info at <u>address@website.com</u>
- Free information, call now: 530-555-1234
- We are here, call now:
- Join Us For Happy Hour 5-7 Every Thursday
- For a FREE consultation call 530-555-1234
- Meet your date at The Rusty Crow!
- Free parenting information at <u>www.copitchinc.com</u>

 A friend of mine, who lives in the San Francisco Bay area, told me that when she checked her child's medical symptoms at the Kaiser Permanente's web site, she was offered a link that read, *Set your non emergency appoint now.* This took her to a page that showed her the doctor's open appointments for the next day. What a great call to action! (She was even telling people about how her insurance company was helping her.)

Local print media advertisements

Local print media is a much broader field than most entrepreneurs believe.

Most entrepreneurs think of the:

- Local newspaper(s)
- Shopper / Throwaways

But there are a lot more:

- Local free children/parenting magazine
- Local free entertainment weekly
- Local senior magazine
- High school newspaper
- Junior high and elementary school newsletters
- Sports boosters signage and handouts/fliers
- Church and charity newsletters
- Community bulletin board sponsorship ads
- Community map sponsorship
- Coupon mailers
- Bus signage
- Taxi signage
- YMCA newsletter/ bulletin board

Now you are probably thinking that I am suggesting that you shell out your hard earned money on taxi signage. Well, sure, if it is the correct placement for your ad. A well done ad for alcohol treatment or gambling addiction will get a lot of attention on a taxi.

Drunk? Take a cab!
When you sober up,
Call New Start Counseling Center
(456)555-7898

For the chutzpah marketer, the ad needs to appear in front of the eyes of your potential customers or potential referrers. So, when you think about where to place your ad, you have to ask, "Where are my customers looking?"

A colleague of mine is highly involved in her nonprofit community dance studio. She sponsors the monthly newsletter and garners a lot of attention. Her donation of $500 per year is easily offset by the 15 or more referrals her ad generates, year after year. "When I first offered to cover the cost of the newsletter I had no idea how many people read it," she told me. "Parents and grandparents read it every month. I am often thanked by people in the grocery store."

"Over the years, lots of families come and go from the dance program," she continued. "Every now and again I will hear from a family that hasn't been in dance for years. They think of me when they have a family problem."

What goes into your ad?

To develop chutzpah advertisements, you need to focus on the *gateway* to your business. From the perspective of your potential customers, what need do they have that will get them to call your office, buy your product, or patronize your business?

If you desire to expand your business, you need to expand how many people know what you are offering. Print advertising lends itself to this well.

There are three major rules that chutzpah marketers must understand about print advertising:

1. Print advertising is a small part of marketing your business. You can get prospects to look at your offerings, but you better have what you advertise, or they will just walk on by.
2. Print advertising is expensive. A monthly ad budget of $1000 is small.
3. Print advertising takes time.

A small ad in a small local paper can cost $250. In a large metropolitan paper, the same ad can be $1800. If it only took $1800 to get lots of prospects beating your door down, that would be, well… cheap. But, it doesn't work that way. A prospect needs to see your ad a minimum of seven times to notice it. But, it isn't as easy as it sounds. Just because you run your ad seven times doesn't mean the prospect saw it seven times. So, depending on the type of ad you develop, you need to run it many times over many months for it to start generating business for you. In the next few pages, I will show you how to improve your chances of getting noticed, but I can't stop your prospect from being too busy on any particular Tuesday to read the paper.

Three types of print ads

There are three types of print ads:

1. The name recognition ad
2. The direct response ad
3. The combination ad

The name recognition ad

The purpose of the name recognition ad is to get your name and what you offer implanted in the prospect's mind. The goal being, that if the prospect needs what you offer she thinks of you. It sounds a little Pavlovian, but it works.

A little test. When you think of the items in the following list, what company do you think of?

Canned soup reminds you of _____?
Rental cars remind you of _____?
New books remind you of _____?

The companies you thought of paid a lot of money to get their name implanted (branded).

Rhubarb reminds you of _____?
Zucchini reminds you of _____?

These last two items do not have money backing them. (However, rhubarb does have Prairie Home Companion support.)

It takes a lot of ad repetitions to get a prospect to think of your name. But, if upon getting to the Yellow Pages, your name is known to them just a smidgen more, they will give more weight to your Yellow Page ad.

Like the Yellow Page ad, the name recognition ad has the same parts.

All chutzpah ads have four major components.

1. Chutzpah headline
2. Chutzpah supporting information
3. Chutzpah supporting secondary benefits
        ------Name and address
4. Chutzpah call to action

Week after week you will switch out the headline, but the rest of the ad should stay the same. The headline gets the attention, and over time the public learns what you do. I advise you to keep the same ad location, week after week.

Name recognition advertising takes time. So, before you begin, you need a realistic budget, and the stick-to-itiveness to see the process through. Often, three or four weeks in, entrepreneurs start to notice only a few new customers and a huge outgoing expense. Before you start this type of ad campaign you have to know that it will take at least four months before you can judge the campaign's effectiveness. The cost is loaded up front. As your name becomes known in your community, you will be able to decrease your ads, but keep the name recognition. The benefits over time, say one year, are how you truly judge this type of ad campaign.

My friend the dentist developed a newspaper ad that people looked for. His receptionist would ask customers if they wanted to be in the ad, and if they said yes, she would snap a picture of their smiling face. Often customers would ask to be in the ad and whole families would dress up to pose for the camera.

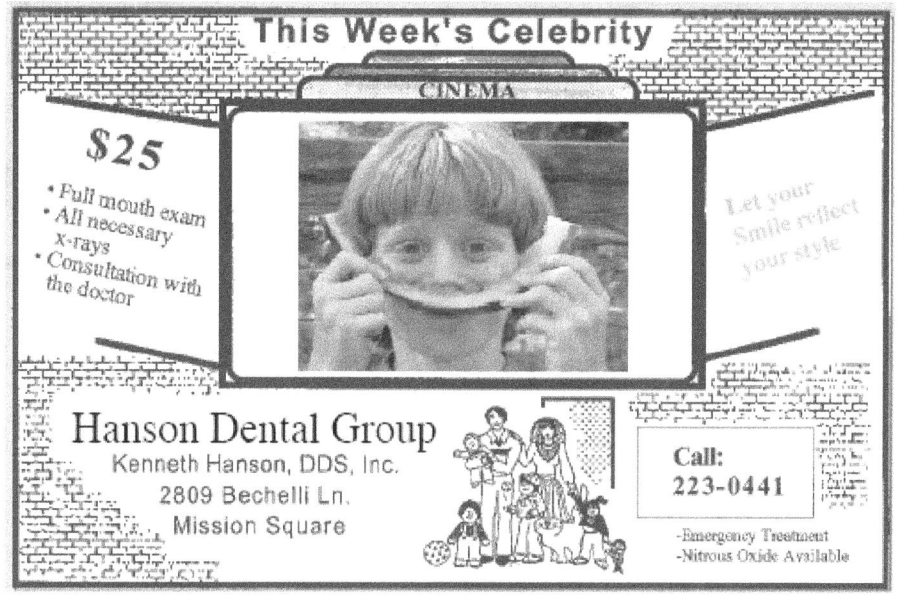

Dr. Hanson ran this type of ad every Tuesday and Thursday for years. Often he would skip a Tuesday or a Thursday. His customers were sure he ran it everyday. Anyone that was pictured in the ad got lots of attention and often reported how many people told them that they "saw them in the paper." Parents often cut out the ad and showed it around or put it on their refrigerator. That's a lot of extra free advertisement.

The direct response ad

The direct response ad is a call to action ad. On the surface, this sounds great, but it is a little more complicated. The direct response ad gets attention in short spurts. I have seen it bring in lots of business, but it's not a steady flow. Let me explain.

In the direct response ad, you have to offer an incentive to get the prospect to show up. Unlike the Yellow Pages, where the reader is already motivated and looking, you will have to motivate the reader into action. This is usually done by giving something away. Examples of chutzpah low cost giveaways with a great return:

- Free initial consultation
- Free copy of Dr. Tom Orrow's book *How to Break the Cycle of Procrastination*, a $25 value.
- Free child care available during all our adult exercise classes.
- Free motorcycle lessons - Even if you are not ready to buy just yet.
- Six free archery lessons with every bow we sell.
- Free oil changes for a year. A $129 value!

- We come to your windshield, just call and we will do the rest.
- Dental ex-rays only $25
- Free pool chemicals with every refinish.

Although these giveaways lead to responses, they often attract customers who "expect" a lot for free. Also, these promotions cost money, lowering your profit margin. If your offer is perceived as valuable, but it is actually low cost, you are using your chutzpah skills. For example, Dr. Orrow's book cost only $4.55 to print. But, a book has a perceived value that is related to the retail price not the wholesale price.

If you use an offer of a lower fee, you run the chance of being seen as the discount company. This will run off customers who are looking for an upscale service provider. A pizza place in my area puts out coupons for $3 OFF. I have heard people say, "Let's not go there for lunch, I don't have a coupon. Inadvertently and at great expense, this company has taught the public that it is a discount pizza choice.

Direct response ads work quickly, but they can come with unforeseen complications.

A direct response chutzpah ad has four major components with special emphasis on the call to action.

1. Chutzpah headline
2. Chutzpah supporting information
3. Chutzpah supporting secondary benefits
      ------Name and address
4. Chutzpah call to action

It is best to put a time limitation on your direct response ad. "Good through…" or "Valid till 01-02-01" will encourage potential customers to act now. For print ads, 30 days seems to work well, for email ads, 7-10 days works well.

I once met a man on a plane who told me about his main advertisement problem and solution. His pizza parlor was well established in his college town until a chain pizza joint move in down the street.

The chain bought a bigger ad in the college weekly than he could afford and started pulling business away. Their ad offered six $2 coupons for money off their pizza (One per visit). So, the small pizza owner changed his ad to read, Bring in any Pizza ad with a money off coupon and we'll give you $3 off the best pizza in town.

He knocked out their bigger ad and multiple coupons for only $3 per paying customer. I love the chutzpah.

Print now and save! Good through xx/xx/xx.

Make sure you don't print this in small print. You want your reader to read this and to be motivated by it. So, draw attention to it.

The combination ad

The combination ad is 80 percent name recognition ad and 20 percent direct response ad. You follow all the rules of the name recognition ad plus build in a no cost or very low cost incentive for your potential customer. Like the direct response ad you don't want to give away the store just to get foot traffic. "Let me buy you a cup of coffee…" is a nice invite to a family friendly restaurant.

Invite shoppers in for a "Bottomless bowl of soup when you order any soup and sandwich in December. We want to keep you warm while you're hustling and bustling about for the holidays."

 An attorney friend of mine offered a free Q&A session from 7-8 PM Tuesdays at a local cafe. People would come to the cafe and he informed them that he would happily answer any general questions for about an hour, and more private questions after the public Q&A. He often spent two and a half hours at the cafe and generated new customers every week. His sister, who owned the cafe, loved the extra business on the slowest night of the week. A small ad in the Monday paper motivated people to show up.

 Similar to this, on CNN I saw an attorney who owned a hotdog cart in some big city. Noon most days, as an employee sold foot longs, he dispensed free legal advice and handed out his cards.

 I like to play a game I call Stump The Shrink. When I am invited to talk to a group, I ask how they intend to publicize the event. Often they say something like, "Well I guess we can put something in the church newsletter?" I ask if it would be ok if I provide the copy. They are usually very happy to oblige. I provide the newsletter editor with the same ad in three different sizes: 1/4 page, 1/2 page and full page (On a CD and also a printed copy). The newsletter editor has options with very little work on her part. The groups want a big gathering and I tend to get a lot of free publicity.

Combination type ad for Stump the Shrink

The nice thing about playing Stump The Shrink is that I don't have to have all the answers. When I get to the meeting, index cards and pencils are handed out (provided by the organizer). I ask people to write down any questions they have secretly wanted to ask a shrink. The cards are collected, and I scan through them. I try to pick questions that are of general interest to the group I am talking to. If I know the answer, I answer, if I don't know the answer, I open the question to the audience. This leads to funny and often heartwarming moments. This isn't for every entrepreneur, but I love playing Stump The Shrink, and the members of the audience leave knowing that they got some helpful information. When you emotionally touch individuals in the audience, you are generating future work for yourself.

I have seen variation on Stump the Shrink such as:

Ask an:
- Author
- Wedding planner
- Police officer
- Horticulturist
- Dentist/hygienist
- Heart disease specialist
- Home security specialist

If your business is interesting to others, advertising that you will answer audience questions will get you lots of attention. More on this in Chapter 11: **Chutzpah Presentation, Speeches, and Trade Shows.**

Here is a nice example of a handout given out to all the Friday attendees to the Home Show. If they had lead with the speakers' names this ad would not have worked as well.

Latest News
Low - Flow
Toilets
Save $540/yr

10 AM - 11 AM Saturday, May 11
Wayne Home Show
Fairgrounds · FREE

Plumbing contractors
Rob and Mary Swank
answer questions on saving
money on bathroom remodels

Dealing with local newspapers and magazines

The first thing to remember about local newspapers and magazines is that they need you. The revenue from the ads pays for the newspaper.

As I write this in 2010, local newspapers are hurting for ad revenue. As their costs go up, their readership has decreased. This is important to you, the ad buyer. The fewer eyes on the paper, the less return on investment for your ad dollar.

The scariest part of dealing with newspapers and local magazines is the fact that they have entrepreneur sales people. Their job is to get you to buy ad space. And, as we discussed before concerning the Yellow Page reps, they work for the newspaper, not you.

Newspaper sales reps are like busy bees. They have to get out and find ad sales then get back and get the ad into the paper. These sales people are very aware of time, because they know that they cannot sell an ad for an issue that has been printed.

Newspaper representatives present as very friendly, and they love whatever it is you want to do. But, they are pushy. They want your ad now and they want it printed now. Then, they want another ad, and they want that ad printed now!

Every workday the ad manager meets with the ad sales people and attempts to motivate them. The ad manager's job is to motivate the sales force into rabid closers. The tactics used are usually coercive at best. A friend of mine was very upset after a meeting when the new sales manager coldly said, "One of you will be unemployed at the end of the month. Low sales numbers will get you fired." This type of pressure is not conducive to harmony in the sales department. Another common tactic is to offer a big gift to the lead sales person; TV's, expensive dinners, or trips are common. The goal of the sales manager is to get ad sales. The rule of thumb in ad sales; "Sell or walk!"

It is important that you do not get caught up into the publication's business problems. You do not need to feel rushed. You want information from them concerning ad costs and ad placement. You run your ad campaign. Expect to hear that the sales rep has a special deal that expires in two days. "I love your ad, I can give you 20 percent off if you sign for a 90 day run. This manager's special ends at 5 PM Friday!"

Chutzpah marketers know that this is just hype. At 5:01 Friday there will be another unbelievable, don't miss it, deal. The correct ad in the right place is the focus: the deals are secondary. In reality, the sale is 'over' when you get what you want. You are in charge, not the sales rep.

Ad and ad size placement

Your chief goal is to get your ad next to something that your potential customer or referrer is interested in. Over the years, businesses I have worked with have had profitable results in the following areas:
- The TV page
- The movie section
- The senior page
- The local sports page
- Local events section
- The comics section (Most commonly read section of the newspaper)

So, for example, if you are interested in expanding your posh foods offerings, the Sunday or Tuesday food section is a logical choice. Interested in expanding your alteration business, the Sunday wedding or bridal section may work well (Women tend to check out this section well before their wedding announcement will be printed). Where most entrepreneurs go wrong with ad placement is putting their ad where they look. (Good if you are growing an entrepreneur marketing group.)

Ad size counts, but not that much. The power of your title line is much more important. If you need size to tell your supporting information, then you need size. The size of your ad alone will not sell your product.

The sales rep will always push for ad size. "You want the reader to see your ad, don't you?" Do not buy into the up sell. Take a deep breath and calmly ask the ad rep, "I notice lots of ads this size in your paper, are you telling me that you sell ads to people that you know will not get seen?"

Again I reiterate, you run your show.

Common up sell fibs sales reps use

Fib #1

Sales rep:	I can't place your ad on that page unless you have at least a 1/4 page ad.
Chutzpah you:	Oh, I'm sorry, I didn't know … Thanks for coming in, sorry I wasted your time. (Then stand up indicating the meeting is over. The sales rep will "find" a way to help you. You are her paycheck, and she wants to have a pay check.)

Fib #2

Sales rep:	By placing an ad everyday, you will be seen everyday.
Chutzpah you:	That makes sense, but I need maximum coverage for a more reasonable placement fee.

Fib #3

Sales rep:	If you sign today, you get a great deal as part of our February is for lovers promotion.
Chutzpah you:	If I have to answer now the answer is no. Let me think about your offer and I will call you with my answer by Friday. ('If I have to answer now the answer is no,' is my favorite line from my parenting book. It works well with children, adolescents, and pushy sales reps!)
Sales rep:	We are putting out this special supplement, *Children in the North State* it is perfect for your type of business.

Newspapers love to put out special supplements. Such as: Health Care In The Tri-County Area, Senior Issues In Worsening Economic Times, and Summer Activities In Your County. Be careful. This is hype. A special supplement is just a newspaper section that the newspaper sales rep can use to target a section of the community with. The sales manager rubs his hands together and snarls at his sales reps, "This health special supplement has 419 ad slots. Get out and sell them to any business that deals with health." There is nothing special about these supplements. They are just normal newspaper articles packaged to make ad sales easier. The ad price tends to be 20-40 percent higher.

Any ad person worth their salt reading this will say, "But what about the fact that people will hold the supplement longer, referring back to it for months?"

This sounds good, but people hold the whole newspaper for months until they say, "I have to clean up this fire hazard!"

I have not seen any evidence that supplemental ads work better than normal ads, except from newspaper sales reps.

Yellow Page and ads: my chutzpah perspective

Most entrepreneurs find that print ads are a waste of money. I partially agree. The reason is that most entrepreneurs spend money on poorly conceived ads.

Over the years I have worked with many companies who learned to love their print advertising. But the ad has to be done correctly and done over a long enough period (at least several [4+] months).

If you are working with a limited budget, a small Yellow Page ad is a must. Print ads are for your future. I wasn't joking in earlier chapters when I called some things, "the most important chutzpah tool" or "the second most valuable tool". Chutzpah business cards, brochures, and 9-second speeches are substantially more valuable when building a thriving company (plus cheap).

But, this is the big but, if you want to go from a small company to a large company, you will need extensive advertising. Print, radio, and television are all viable options.

Want my opinion?

After you have gone through the process of developing your advertisement, I would be happy to give your copy a free once over. Send them to me by Email PDF attachment. Please don't send me 10's of pages. Please limit yourself to 2 or 3 of your best.

Email: DrPhil@CopitchInc.com

On advertising:

Don't bunt. Aim out of the ball park. Aim for the company of immortals.

David Ogilvy

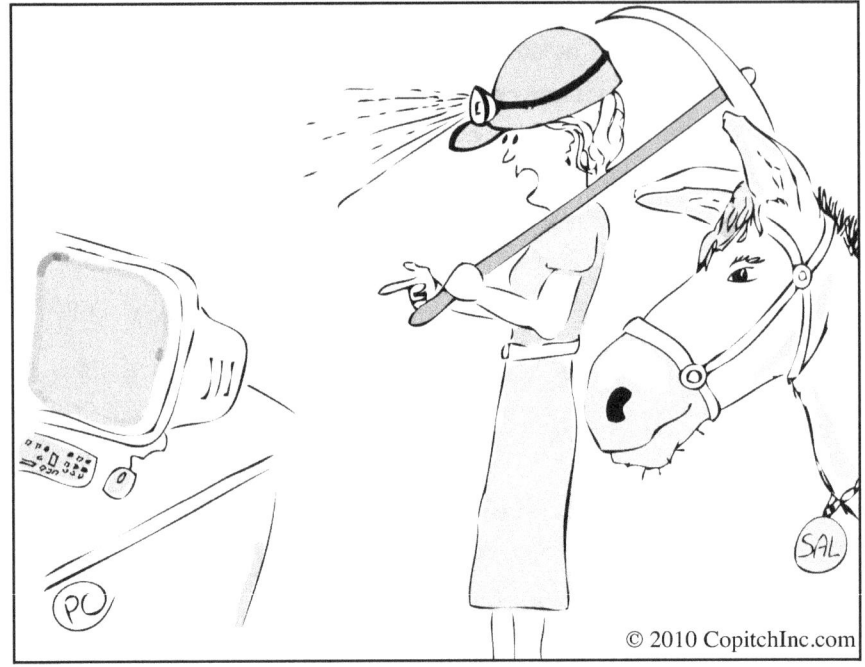

© 2010 CopitchInc.com

"Give up the gold or I'll show you chutzpah!"

6. ADVERTISING PART C: CHUTZPAH GOLD MINING

In this chapter we are going to look at the chutzpah technique of using your customer information wisely. I begin with the assumption that your present and past customers respect your work, trust your opinion, and like you as a person. If this is true, you have a gold mine that is waiting to be harvested.

A customer is a valuable commodity. You spent a lot of money to open your business and to generate your first customer. (Not counting the cost of your training.) The vast majority of entrepreneurs I work with do not keep contact with their customers after the first sale is over. I think it is because most entrepreneurs assume that once a customer, always a customer. Unfortunately, this is not a fact. The truth is, loyal patronage has to be cultivated.

Your database

A database is a collection of data arranged for ease, speed of search, and retrieval. All the contact information you have on every customer you have ever seen is your customer database. All the contact information you have on every company you have ever worked with is your Business to Business (B2B) database. All the contact information you have on every person who ever downloaded anything from your web site is your Internet database.

If you read this and think to yourself. "Holy cow, I have only eight people in my database," don't worry. I'm going to help you fix that.

Most entrepreneurs think little to none about their database. Nevertheless, your database is filled with ready contacts that know you. The fact that they know you (or of you) helps if you would like them to buy more from you.

In the real dog-eat-dog world of business if you have not had contact with a customer for six months, you most likely do not have that customer. I am not saying anything negative about customers or entrepreneurs, but the fact is customers are people, and as people they do what they want. Let me give you an example.

In the cola wars, I like Diet Coke. All things being equal, I vote with my money and I buy Diet Coke. While standing in the soft drink cavern of Costco, my bride of over twenty years asked me, "Do you want Diet Coke or Diet Pepsi?" To tell you the truth I thought it was a dumb question. She knows I'm a Diet Coke drinker. She continued, "I have a coupon for Diet Pepsi, two dollars off per case." I looked at the large signs above the pallet's of soda cases, Pepsi products were fifty cents less per case. We bought Diet Pepsi. At $2.50 less per case I was motivated to suffer with Diet Pepsi.

Now, I want you to think about my soft drink decision. The cola giants spend millions to get me to buy their product. Millions! But for $2.50 I switched. At the beginning I said, "All things being equal I vote with my money and I buy Diet Coke." The coupon, and the lower starting price, made my usual cola choice unbalanced.

My friend the dentist is a great dentist. I say this selfishly, because over our very long friendship, my family and I are stuck going to him. As long as he is an (even) OK dentist, if I want to maintain our friendship, I have to go to his office. If I get a coupon from another dentist I drop it in the trash. The mailing from every dentist in the area is a waste on me. I don't need a dentist, I have a great one.

I tell these two stories because your customers will keep coming to you, or talking about you, all things being equal. But, it may not take much to make them stop thinking about you. Please do not overestimate customer loyalty.

Use of you database to keep in regular contact with your customers. This is chutzpah important if you wish to grow an ongoing and thriving business.

Computer database is a must

The computerization of a modern business is not within the scope of this book. Over the next few pages I will simply touch upon the basics of using a computer database in your business.

A computer database is an organized collection of information. Most entrepreneurs I work with have this information in individual customer index cards or in customer files. A growing percentage have this information in a computer database. The advantage of a computerized database over a paper database is ease of use. With a computer database you can easily sort the information, say by city or zip code.

Kathryn Luddite had been in part-time business for less than five years. She had a file on every customer she had ever seen; a total of 84 files. When I suggested that she organize the files into a computer database she was reluctant. On top of that, when I suggested that of the 84 files, probably half were outdated, she got upset with me.

"How do you know that my files are outdated?" she snapped.

"Nothing personal," I said. "But about 20 percent of the population moves every year. So, there is a good chance that many of your customer addresses are outdated."

A well managed database has a life span of about six months. After six months, many of the addresses will be incorrect. If you are using an outdated database to mail 100 letters to past customers offering some new and exciting item you are now offering, probably only 80 percent will get your mailing. If the mailing costs you $1.00 each, that is a waste of $20.00. Add another "0" to the equation and the numbers get scary. ($200.00 in waste)

There are a lot of database programs on the market. The most popular are part of a program suite such as:

Program	Estimated Cost	Operating System
Microsoft Office	$250-$600	Windows & MAC
Apple iWork	$79 (Free with a MAC)	MAC

These suites are packaged with other features: word processing, spreadsheet, and presentation software. Within each suite, you will find a powerful database tool. If you are new to computers I highly recommend Apple's iWork. Apple computers are much more people friendly and have the fastest learning curve.

For a small business, I recommend the freestanding database program, Bento 2, by FileMaker. This is an easy to use dedicated personal database. (Cost about $50)

For mid-size and larger companies, I recommend the powerhouse of database programs, FileMaker Pro. (Cost $300) This program has a serious learning curve. However, it can do almost everything you can think of in the database world. Unless you are a computer geek, I recommend you take a community college course versus self learning this program. For a few dollars at your community college you get a great learning environment and some academic hand holding. If you are looking to hire an office manager you may wish to add FileMaker Pro knowledge to your list of job requirements.

The program suites (Microsoft Office & Apple iWork) are each great starting tools. But, you will have to learn the program. Be kind to yourself. Don't plan on learning the database component and building your database in an evening. Realistically, twenty hours over two weeks will have you up and running. Having someone show you how to use it can save you half the time. If you are going to learn the program by yourself, I recommend you purchase a book to support your education. In the old days, computer programs came with massive documentation, not any more. The program will come with an Internet based help program which tends to be very comprehensive. The problem with the help program is you need to know the right questions to ask. In a book, you will find tutorial chapters that teach a set of skills. This will be much less frustrating than trying hit-or-miss on your own.

I advise the (computer program name) The Missing Manual printed by Pogue Press, or the (computer program name) Bible printed by Wiley. Avoid the (computer program name) For Dummies (For Dummies (Computer/Tech)) books. They seem to me to be rushed to print. Often, they are the first on the market, but not well organized or documented.

The computer books are expensive, usually in the 30 to 40 dollar range, and there are lots of choices. These tomes are mouse killing, massive, 400-500 page, paperback books. Don't let that intimidate you. You're going to read it chapter by chapter, a page at a time. Often you will be given a tutorial to try; for example the first database I developed was for a fictitious coffee company. All the basics I learned building the tutorial coffee company have been the building blocks for every database I have developed since.

One last thing on getting a computer book. Make sure you get the exact book for your exact program. My local Barnes and Noble bookstore tends to carry outdated computer books for a year after the program updates. If you own FileMaker Pro 10, the FileMaker Pro 9 book will be of moderate use, and probably confusingly frustrating. In computer program lingo, FileMaker Pro 10 and FileMaker Pro 9 are children of the same family, but they are not the same child.

What to put in your database

If you are a professional such as a CPA or a plumber you will have access to more customer information than say a mom and pop shop and rob (convenience store). The latter company will have to use data gathering information that will be discussed later in this chapter, to build its database.

If possible, start with the basic information: name, rank (title), address, and phone number, then you build onto your database from there. However, since a database is sortable you want to have each chunk of data in its own data field. My name is Philip Copitch. In my database I am First Name = Philip, Last Name = Copitch. To database newbies this tends to seem like an extra step: having 2 data fields for just 1 person. It will prove to be very useful in the use of the database information.

Each piece of data needs its own data field. In the old days I only had data fields for *home phone number* and *office phone number*. Nowadays I also need data fields for *cell phone numbers*, and *email addresses*.

The more data fields the more powerful a database becomes. Please let me explain.

What if I wanted to sponsor a senior self defense class at the local YMCA? With my database I can sort for females, born before 1960, who live in zip codes 96001, 96002, and 96003. This will give me the address of every woman I know, who is age appropriate for the class, who lives within one hour of the YMCA where the class is to be conducted. The database information can be printed on labels to be placed on fliers. Or, I could merge the data into a personalized letter.

Dear Mary, (First name = Mary. Used as a database merge field)

Thought you would like to know of the exciting event we are sponsoring at the…

It is this sort-ability that makes a database program very chutzpah. In a few minutes you can organize data into distinct specifications for your task.

The biggest problem with databases is that you can only sort for information that is in them. If your database has only names and addresses, you will not be able to sort out your seniors to invite to the event.

Most professional businesses build their database from their file data. With this in mind, it is usually best to have the computer database entry form in the same order that the data is on your intake form, contest entry, or email sales promotion registry. This will allow the data entry to take on a comfortable, common feeling. The goal is to get the correct information into the correct data field.

Below you will see the first part of my Patient Intake Form.

Confidential Patient Information

Philip Copitch, Ph.D., Inc.
1650 Oregon Street, Suite 218
Redding CA 96001

Patient Intake Form

Please Print

Patient Information: ONE form per person...please, please, please. One form per person.

Patient's Name: _____ D.O.B.: _____ Age: _____

Patient's Gender: ☐ Male ☐ Female   Patient's Social Security #: _____

Patient's Address: _____ Home Phone: _____

_____ Work Phone: _____

Email Address: _____ Cell Phone: _____

If minor, parents' / guardians' names:

☐ Mother ☐ Step-Mother ☐ _____   ☐ Father ☐ Step-Father ☐ _____

Name: _____   Name: _____

Address: _____   Address: _____

_____   _____

Home Phone: _____   Home Phone: _____

Work Phone: _____   Work Phone: _____

Cell Phone: _____   Cell Phone: _____

Social Security #: _____   Social Security #: _____

If the patient is a child, I may have three full sets of data: child, mom/stepmom/guardian, and dad/stepdad/guardian. If my identified patient is an adult, I tend to have one set of data to record.

Information is valuable. In addition to customers, I also add business contacts to my database. If I am handed a business card, I jot down where I met the person and other stuff I learned about them, such as: "has two kids, likes the 49ers." I also estimate the age. If he looks around fifty, his birth year is estimated as 1968. Business to business contacts give implied consent to stay in contact through the business information provided on the business card or brochure they gave you.

Printed on the Intake Form above, you may have noticed a space for Social Security Numbers. This private information is not placed into my marketing database. I do not like phone solicitation, so I do not use it or recommend it. Thus, I do not store phone numbers for marketing purposes in my marketing database. (In many states phone solicitation is regulated. Yeah!)

I advise an opt-in policy. I ask for permission to send mailings or email to customers. I ask right from the beginning, "Is it ok for me to put you on our email list? We send a newsletter out about every six weeks with information concerning health and science." As part of every contact, we offer a clear and easy opt-out option. (See: Email later in this chapter.) My goal is not to bother anyone with my newsletter, as well as not to waste money on sending someone something they are not interested in.

What to do with your gold mine

Once you have your database set up you have lots of options to keep your customers aware of how you can help them. (Short on customers? New in business? See: **Ways To Generate Custom Mailing Lists** later in this chapter.)

"How you can help them" is what your gold mining is all about. Most marketers try to talk existing or new customers into buying their products or services. A chutzpah marketer solves problems for people, and helps people get their needs met. We do no talk anyone into buying anything, we offer a quality product or service, and let people understand the benefit of it for themselves, personally.

Your chutzpah business mailings and emailings should sell you as the

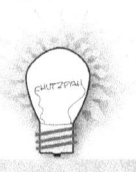

An attorney I worked with decided to develop his database prospecting (finding gold in a database). He gathered all the business cards he had collected over the three years he was in private practice, and was overwhelmed with the total-1,500. After getting no volunteers to type all the data into the computer, he decided to go hi-tech. He purchased a nifty card scanner called the Card-Scan Executive 8.0 made by DYMO Mac/PC). He did the job himself on two consecutive Sundays while watching football. Cost: $260 for the scanner, and a little more for the pizza, beer and chips.

A cool addition to the story is that he keeps a copy of his database on his iPhone.

right company for your potential customer. You cannot be all things to all people. You need to focus on your market niche, your desired potential customer. (Please, please, please) Write from the needs of your potential customer. (Discussed in detain in Chapter 1: **Talk To, Not At, Your Customers**)

The 4 best ways to grow a long term clientele

The 4 best ways to stay in contact with customers in order of chutzpah value:

1. Postcards
2. Newsletters and eNewsletters
3. Email
4. Direct mail solicitation

Postcards

Postcards are a powerful way to stay in contact with long term customers. The ratio of cost is reasonable for the benefit. The cost is around a dollar per postcard, which includes postage, labeling, printing, and labor. The benefits are the ease of getting the postcard out, and it will get looked at. This second benefit is very important. Most mailings are not read. The recipient receives the letter, has to open it, unfold it, and then read it. That is a lot of opportunity to lose your reader's interest.

With the postcard, you have a great chance of getting the postcard headline read. Thus, the headline is very important. You only have seconds to capture the reader's interest.

Since the reader already knows you, you have a second-second to get the reader's cooperation. This second-second is very helpful.

My wife and I received this postcard from a nonprofit that we are members of. We like this museum and support its efforts. Let's take a look at the card they sent us. See below.

I am impressed with the work Turtle Bay does and highly recommend that if you are ever in northern California you take a day to explore the park. It is an amazing combination of education and natural beauty. But, this card has a few limitations.

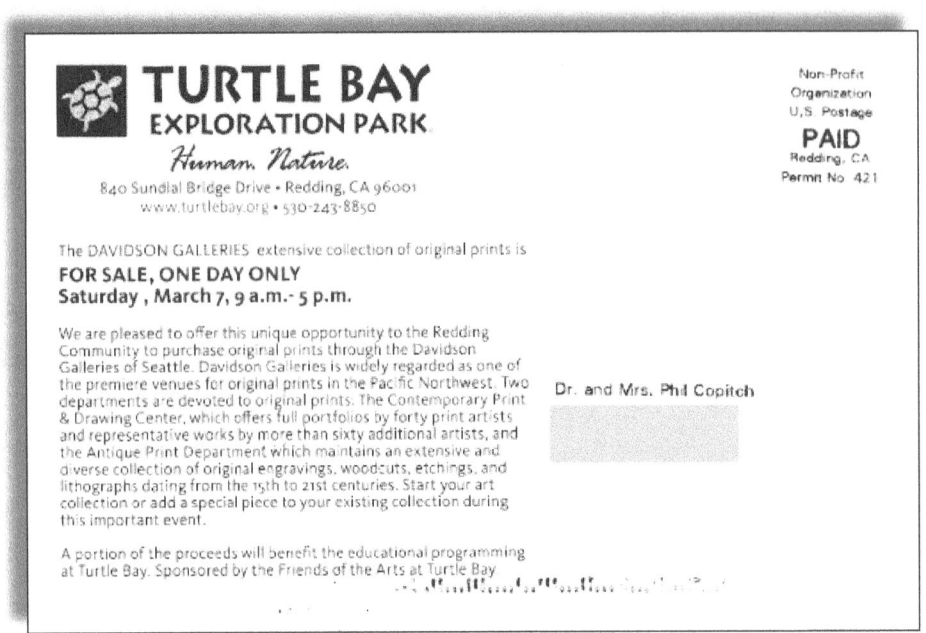

Turtle Bay postcard address side

Turtle Bay postcard side 2

I point out these limitations because they are so common in many of the mailers and advertisements you are constantly exposed to. The card is sender centric. It focuses on them. They are having a one day print sale. So? Am I looking for a print on sale? In fact, what is a print anyway? The answer may be in the copy on the address side. Thus, another problem. Where are my damn reading glasses? Am I interested enough in finding out more about this post-card to put them on?

I'm not joking about the reading glasses. I'm fifty + years old and I haven't seen 9 point print in five years. Please take a moment to think about this, one of the reasons this charity sent this card to my wife and me is because we are of the age and income bracket that can afford to buy collectable art. We are good prospects. We have bought art from other charity fund-raisers over the years. (Our names are on a mail list of people who buy art from charity fund-raisers; see buying a mail list later in this chapter.)

When you develop your advertisements, business card etc., please keep the recipient's needs in mind.

What would you print as the eye catching headline on the address side of this card? How are you going to get the reader's attention and hold it?

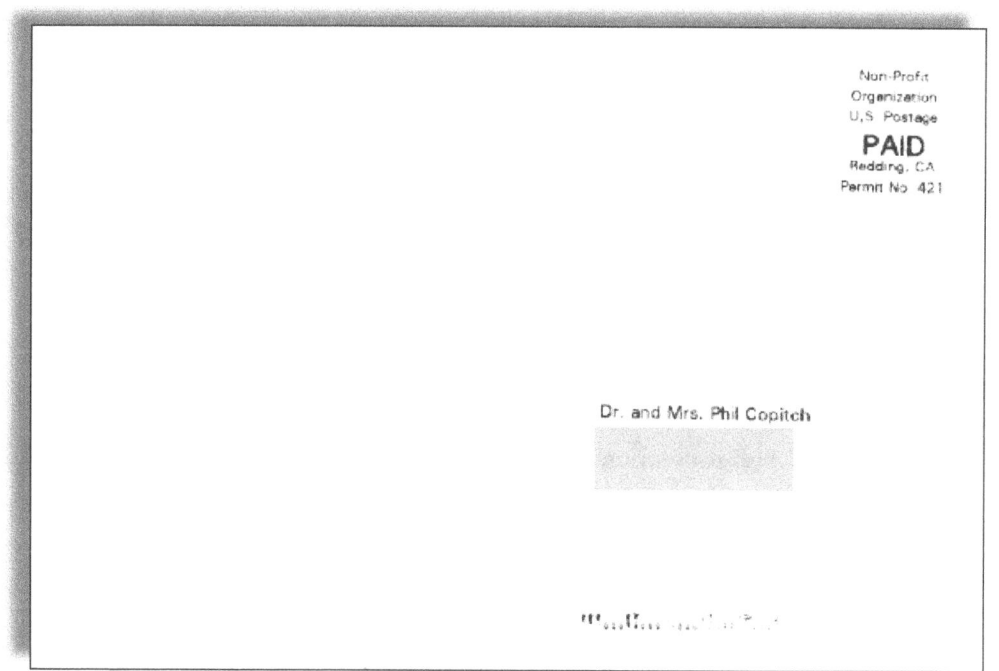

What would you suggest?

Grabbing attention

Your card has made the trip though the mail service's machines, air-planes, and trucks. It is now in the hands of your prospect. You have a few seconds, how are you grabbing the prospect's eyeballs?

Just as we did when building our chutzpah Yellow Page and print ads, let's use chutzpah copy. (See: Chapter 5. **Advertising Part B: The Yellow Pages and Local Media**)

All chutzpah ads have four major components. When it comes to post cards you want to ad a 5th component!

1. Chutzpah headline
2. Chutzpah supporting information
3. Chutzpah supporting secondary benefits
      ------Name and address
4. Chutzpah call to action

Plus a 5th, if possible— save/stick/pass-ability.

Save-ability, stick-ability, and pass-ability is the act of making the postcard so valuable to the receiver that they keep it and even want to show it to others. Ways to motivate a prospect to keep or show your postcard are:
- Coupons
- Contests
- Important information such as time or dates that they are interested in
- Valuable information that they wish to save, such as: directions or a cool factoid (a brief, somewhat interesting fact)
- A funny picture, joke or puzzle that they will want to share
- And my favorite... cartoons

I am an unemployed cartoonist at heart. I even joke that I write books just so my cartoons have a home. Many years ago, the local school districts went through severe budget cuts. Of course, I drew a cartoon. It was like Christmas, summer vacation, and my first kiss, all rolled into one when I noticed my cartoon (below) on a staff information bulletin board at the County Schools' office. The only thing that would have made it better would have been if it had my company information tacked on the board along side of it.

> I once met a man on a plane who told me about his main advertisement problem and solution. His pizza parlor was well established in his college town until a chain pizza joint move in down the street. The chain bought a bigger ad in the college weekly than he could afford and started pulling business away. Their ad offered six $2 coupons for money off their pizza (One per visit). So, the small pizza owner changed his ad to read, Bring in any Pizza ad with a money off coupon and we'll give you $3 off the best pizza in town.
> He knocked out their bigger ad and multiple coupons for only $3 per paying customer. I love the chutzpah.

"I hear we only have 20 kids in our class this year."

"Welcome Bobby... your desk is the mop bucket."

A postcard can do just that. It takes your chutzpah marketing information and places it right next to save/stick/pass-ability. Our goal is to have the reader act on our offer right now, or hold and share the information with others in the near future. (I'm super happy if they do both.)

Dr. Hanson was moving, and being the chutzpah marketer he is, he didn't want to lose any of his patients during the move. So, he sent them all a giant postcard (we will look at postcard sizes and cost later in this section).

The postcard measured 11" X 6" so it had to go First Class letter rate. But, for the cost of a stamp, he put the information right in the hands of his clientele. The logo family and recognizable name got the reader's attention ("My dentist is moving?"). The map added stick-ability. I'm sure the postcard ended up on refrigerators all over the county for the rest of the family and visitors to see. See below.

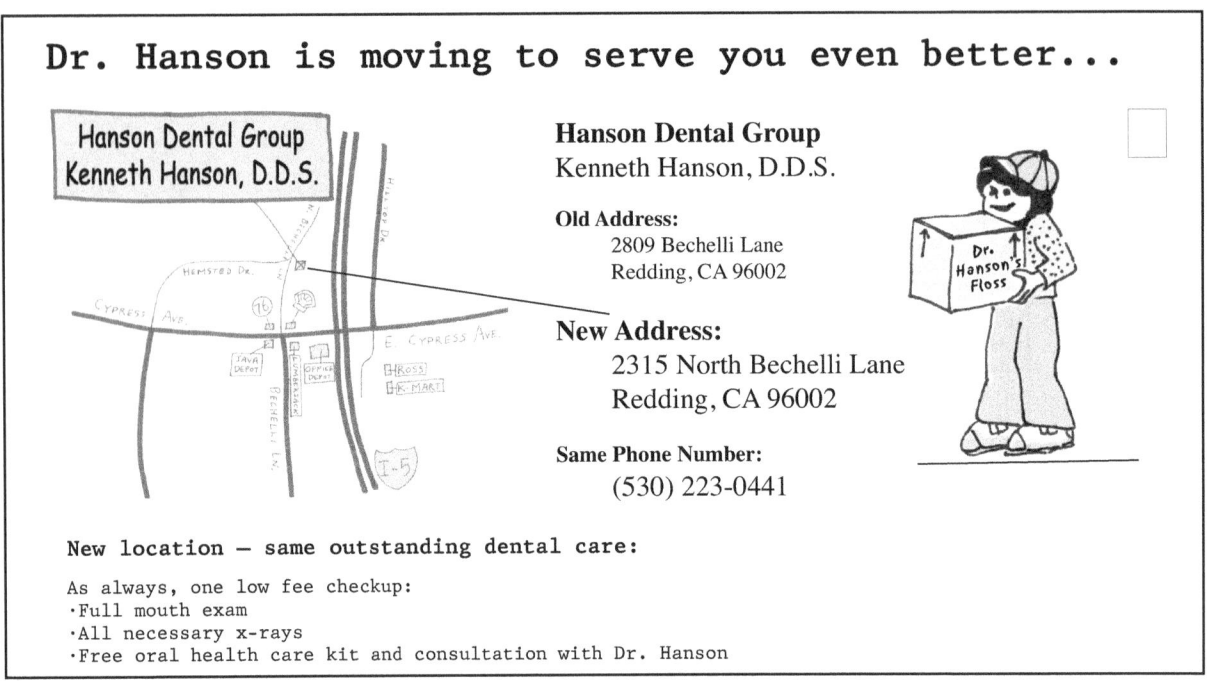

Dr. Hanson's moving card. Address side (reduced)

Dr. Hanson's moving card. Side 2 (reduced)

When looking at Dr. Hanson's card, please note the great use of art and white space. His headlines are solid, and the subheadings talk to the customers about the benefits of the change. The logo family helping the business move adds the feeling of family to family dentist.

When striving to stand out in a community with lots of lawyers, Mr. Berg chose to show off his professional credentials. There are lots of attorneys, but only a few are *Certified Specialists In Criminal Law By The California State Bar Association*. This impressive distinction separates the experienced trial attorneys from the pack. Along with a little playfulness and chutzpah, Mr. Berg is well known in northern California. See below.

Mr. berg understands his target market. The tongue-in-cheek nature of side 2 speaks to the devil-may-care attitude of many of his potential customers. This playfulness is in stark contrast to his logo, the dueling pistols. The logo represents the law business's motto and refusal to give up attitude. Mr. Berg's legal tenacity is as in-your-face full intensity as is his motto: *In a legal battle, choose your weapon carefully.*

Mr. Berg's postcard side 2

Mr. Berg's postcard address side

Mr. Berg's card allows me to illustrate how targeted a postcard can be, and how reasonably priced it should be. This card is printed in black and white. It lines up perfectly as a 4-up on an 8.5" x 11" piece of card stock. That is pennies a card. A reduced copy of the 4 card master is below. With a design like this you can economically print postcards in house with a decent laser printer.

When a man throws an empty cigarette package from an automobile, he is liable to a fine of $50. When a man throws a billboard across a view, he is richly rewarded.

Pat Brown
Quoted in David Ogilvy, Ogilvy on Advertising, 1985

Mr. Berg's 4-up postcard master side 2 (Reduced)

According to USPS regulations (available at www.usps.com), the address on a postcard needs to be parallel to the longest edge. That way your postcard can be machine canceled. The rest of the print is up to you. With three major exceptions:

1. The return address needs to be on the same side as the mailing address.
2. No numbers that could be confused with a zip code should be in the area of the mailing address.
3. The stamp or permit number must be on the same side as the address.

Additionally, the area under the mailing address may get a postal barcode printed on it. This bar code can make your information look sloppy or even unreadable. An example of this USPS bar code can be seen in the **Turtle Bay postcard address side** printed earlier in this chapter.

The following example will help you keep track of the areas where the post office will be mechanically looking at, and possibly, printing on.

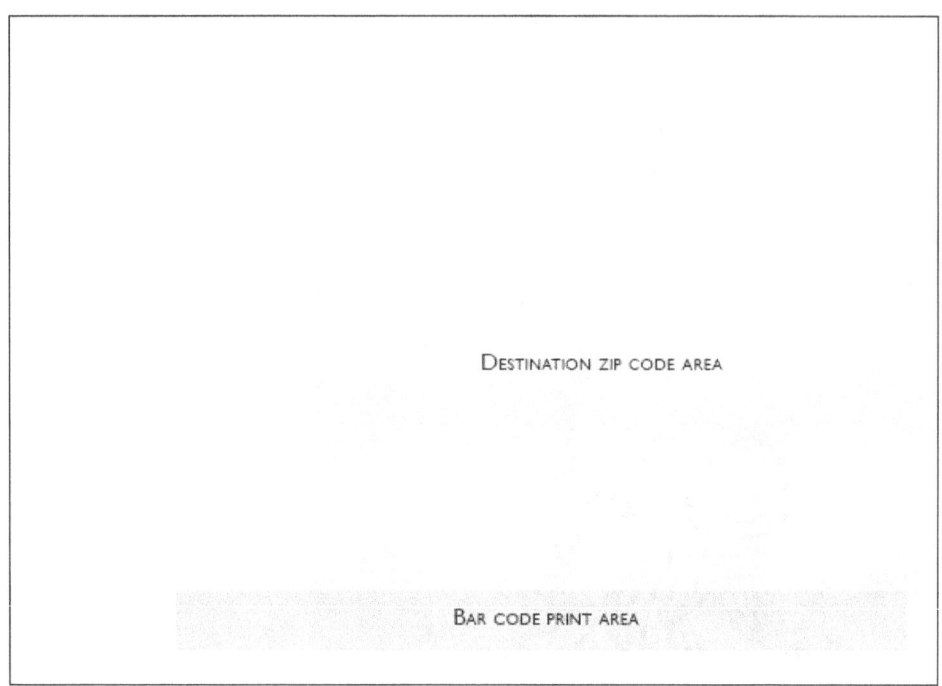

DESTINATION ZIP CODE AREA

BAR CODE PRINT AREA

Post office cautionary areas

The reality is that you are giving up valuable real estate to the post office on the address side of the card. However, I suggest you do not over-stuff the print in the first place. White space around your copy invites the reader to do what you want them to do—read.

A postcard is a very chutzpah tool to push one request: Buy my book, visit my web site, or think of me. However, it won't allow you to do all three in a single postcard. Overcrowding will not encourage the recipient to read your offer.

About two weeks before any of my books were available, I mailed (and emailed, and told) everyone in my database that the book would be available on such and such a date. See below. This is the front cover of the book in full color. The address side offers general information about the book. I use the same side 2 for targeted postcard mailings if I am going to be at a book signing or event. Instead of "Available March 20," it reads, "Meet the Author." See Below.

Postcard of book release side 2

Meet the Author
Dr. Philip Copitch

Basic Parenting 101
The Manual Your Child Should
Have Been Born With

*A must read for all parents,
stepparents, teachers, and counselors.*

Meet Dr. Phil on June 6, 2000

Book Signing 7- 8 PM
Q&A 6:30 PM
Children welcome

REDDING BOOK STORE
California & Placer
Downtown Redding

1650 Oregon St. 218
Redding, Ca 96001

BULK RATE
U.S. Postage
PAID
PERMIT NO. 1
IGO, CA

Book signing postcard invitation address side

Next, are two cartoon postcards. The first is an integrated cartoon and the second is the stand alone cartoon.

The integrated cartoon, at first glance, is a little crowded. Much of the white space is used by the cartoon. However, people like cartoons and will take the time to figure them out. Thus, drawing their attention to the message.

> The first rule of any technology used in a business is that automation applied to an efficient operation will magnify the efficiency. The second is that automation applied to an inefficient operation will magnify the inefficiency.
>
> Bill Gates

Integrated cartoon/text postcard address side

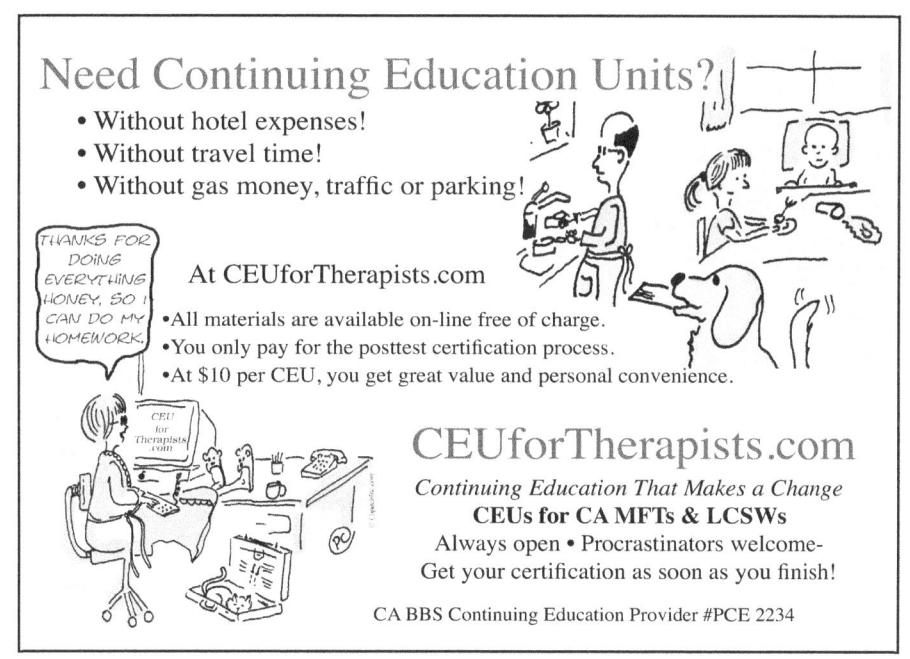

Integrated cartoon/text postcard Page 2

The following example shows side 2 of a cartoon postcard. We use this postcard in November and December. The attention grabbing cartoon is the focal point of one side of the postcard. The address side is similar to postcard page 2 above without the cartoon subsection. In this particular card we play off the holiday season without being too commercial.

"All I want for Christmas is a few quiet
hours at home to get my CEUs"

www.CEUforTherapists.com

Always open • Procrastinators welcome

Cartoon postcard side 2

Size and cost

It may not cross your mind often, but the United States Postal Service (USPS) moves a lot of mail. There are a few ways to get the USPS to take your postcard and give it to your customer or prospect.

The size limits on your postcard can be found in the table below. If you go over it, even by a smidgin, you will be charged the same rate as a first class letter (today that is 16¢ more/postcard).

The most common way to mail a postcard is First Class. For the price of first class postcard postage (28¢ in 2010), your postcard is on its way. The USPS even gives you a self sticking stamp. (The USPS no longer makes stamps with the lovely tasting glue.) So, if you want to mail 638 postcards the postage alone will be $178.64. That is real money but not too bad. But, what if you want to mail, 8956 postcards? That is a postage bill of $2,507.68. By using Bulk Mail you can lower the price per postcard about 5¢. In addition to the savings, you also get very specific rules you must follow so that the bulk postcards can go through the USPS Bulk Mail Centers. These "highly mechanized mail processing centers"[2] allow the USPS to keep the cost down. The machines route the mail by bar code. Your bar coded mail list must be pre-certified by the USPS before you can use it. There is also a $180 annual fee to use bulk mail services.

Mailpiece Dimensions

SHAPE		LENGTH	HEIGHT
Postcard	minimum	5 inch min.	3-1/2 inch min.
	maximum	6 inch max.	4-1/4 inch max.
Letter (up to 3.5 ounces)	minimum	5 inch min.	3-1/2 inch min.
	maximum	11-1/2 inch max.	6-1/8 inch max.
Large Envelope	minimum*	11-1/2 inch min.	6-1/8 inch min.
	maximum	15 inches	12 inches
Package	Weight cannot exceed 70 pounds. Length + girth (distance around the thickest part of the package) cannot exceed 108 inches. (Parcel Post cannot exceed 130 inches.)		

* Large envelopes exceed one or more letter-size maximum dimensions.

Most of you will not be mailing out the quantity to take advantage of the USPS Bulk Mail savings and if you are, you still may not wish to. The USPS regulations[3] are stringent and if you do not follow them exactly, the USPS will refuse your delivery (trays of mail). Most find the savings they would get are eaten up by staff power costs and time, plus aggravation.

The news is not all negative. There is a whole industry dedicated to putting out your bulk mailing for you. Once you get to the bulk rate size, a specialty company can do the mailing for you. Your cost is about the same, but they take care of the headaches. See bulk mailers in the Yellow Pages.

All things being equal, I like the first class postcard postage stamp. So, when I have a mailing of fewer than 2,500 I put stamps on them. When the recipient gets the postcard it does not look like "junk mail." Some recipi-

2 USPS

3 See: http://pe.usps.com/businessmail101/welcome.htm

ents have a personal rule to toss any mail with a bulk rate stamp.

If I had my choice, I would hand print each address to make the postcard more personal.

Label and stamp party

Chutzpah marketers rope anyone they can into "fluffing and folding" mailers. If I tote a box into the house, my kids and the dog vanish. "Fluffing and folding" is boring work. So make the process easier on yourself. A few hints:

- Whenever possible, have the address printed onto the mailer with mail merge. This will save you from having to pay for labels that need to be placed on each piece of mail. Earlier, we discussed database programs. All of them have some form of mail merge capability.
- Make sure you have enough room to place the stamp (and the label) on it with ease. When you are stamping and labeling 1000 postcards, having a little extra space around your target area makes the job much easier.
- When you are developing your postcard keep the placement of the stamp in mind. It just stabs me in my chutzpah heart when I see a beautiful headline look off center because of the stamp. Your goal is to send a chutzpah postcard that works magic for you. The little details count.

Build your own postcard

Now let's have some fun. You will need a stack of blank 8.5" x 11" paper. By folding it in half along the long side you get 8.5" x 5.5". Turn the paper and fold along the long side again to get 5.5" x 4.25". Make the creases crisp then open the page. Not exactly origami, but you do have four postcard size quadrants of 5.5" x 4.25". (If you are printing in house, this gives you four postcards per sheet, with no waste and only two cuts.)

To start developing your postcard you will need your business branding to check your ideas against. Then play… But remember all chutzpah postcards have five major components.

1. Chutzpah headline
2. Chutzpah supporting information
3. Chutzpah supporting secondary benefits
------Name and address
4. Chutzpah call to action
5. Save/stick/pass-ability.

Newsletters and enewsletters

The purpose of a newsletter is to keep your name in front of the customer. Remember, the customer is thinking of themselves, not you. So, by popping up in front of the customer every now and then you state *remember me*! A second reason for your chutzpah newsletter is to entertain and teach. You want your newsletter to be infocational: informative and educational. Your newsletter should contain snippets of "cool" information presented in a fun, uplifting way. This may sound difficult to do, but I'll show you lots of options.

Electronic newsletters are the "in" thing if you listen to Internet gurus. I'm not so sold on them. The best thing about an enewsletter is that it is very inexpensive to distribute. The hope is that your enewsletter is picked up and distributed to tens of thousands of interested readers. The reality is that your distribution goal is another's SPAM. This brings us to an important fact: Chutzpah marketers do not SPAM.

I prefer to build a content packed newsletter. I want to distribute it to my target group the way they would like to get it sent to them. If they want it mailed, I mail it. If they prefer it in their email box, I happily oblige and send it to them as a PDF attachment to an email. I'm even happy to do both. No matter the format, I gently encourage them to distribute the newsletter to friends and family. On my web site I offer free PDF downloads to the world. When I am playing "Stump the shrink" with a parenting group, I can casually mention, "A few months ago there was an article about the latest research concerning this in my free newsletter. You can get it for free at my web site." (You and I know this is really a 9-second speech.)

Dr. Peri O'Steum, a chiropractor I worked with, bought the mail list of a chiropractor who was retiring. This left Dr. O'Steum with 6800 families that had purchased chiropractic services from the other chiropractor sometime in the last 20 years. Dr. O'Steum was reluctant to send each name on the list a letter inviting them to use his services. The postage alone would run $2,992.00. So we devised a postcard campaign to be rolled out over three months. Each month, 2,300 postcards were mailed. The postcard was a coupon for a free exam (side 2) and an offer for a free enewsletter from Dr. O'Steum's web site. Over the course of the year, Dr. O'Steum garnered 117 new families for a total of 209 new customers. Dr. O's business averages $560 per year per customer. That totaled out to over $117,000 from new customers alone. Not bad for a postcards/coupon/ newsletter campaign.

It is best to send at least three mailings over the course of a few months. So I suggested that he continue mailing to the non-responsive families over the course of the year. In the end, he chose not to because he was too busy and didn't want to bring in an associate.

For the rest of this section I will be discussing hard copy chutzpah newsletters, but rest assured these newsletters can live forever as PDFs circulating the Internet.

Newsletter design, chutzpah style.

It is best if your newsletters have a "feel" to them. After reading a few of your newsletters, your reader should know your newsletter on sight by its "feel." The easiest way to do this is to have every edition of your newsletter built on a template with a predictable organization.

Word processing programs such as Microsoft Word and Apple Pages have newsletter templates built right into them. These have become quite sophisticated and easy to use. You simply paste your information into the template. The biggest problem is that the program comes with a small number of templates and your newsletter can easily get the same "feel" as the church down the street or the elementary school across town. However, these newsletter templates are a great beginning. For the computer savvy

What is a PDF?

(Portable Document Format) The de facto standard for document publishing from Adobe. On the Web, there are countless brochures, data sheets, white papers and technical manuals in the PDF format.

PDFs solved a chronic font problem, in which the target computer may not have all the fonts specified in a document. For a graphic artist, font selection is an important part of page design, but, quite often, only basic fonts are chosen to ensure they will be available in every user's computer.

In contrast, PDF files do not rely on the fonts installed in the computer that displays or prints them.

Document designers are free to choose whichever fonts they have at their disposal, and those fonts are embedded within the PDF document. Because the fonts are not distributed for general use, they comply with the font license and do not violate copyrights or patents. Most importantly for page designers, they can use all the fonts they have at their disposal and be guaranteed that the page will display and print correctly on any computer with PDF rendering software.

Answers.com

More information is available from Adobe Systems Incorporated

www.adobe.com

the program InDesign (PC/Mac, starting at $700.00) is the industry print/ publish standard. See: www.adobe.com.

Below are examples of two templates from Microsoft Word. It is for a standard 8.5" x 11" newsletter in full color. (The creator of these templates must get free color cartridges.)

Microsoft Word template example #1

Microsoft Word template example #2

What you do is replace the filler words with your copy. Then replace the filler photos with your photos, and voila, you have a newsletter.

Your newsletter can be from 2 to 6 pages, which is up to three pieces of copy paper printed on each side, then folded in half. Staying within 3 pieces of paper keeps you under the 1 ounce, first class, postage requirement. By using the bottom of the last page as the mailing label area, you save an envelope. You will need mailing seals (2¢ each at office supply stores.) These are perforated, 1" white or clear labels, that keep the mailer closed during shipment, but makes opening easy without damage to your mailer. Mail seals are even printable, with free computer templates available at www.avery.com/avery/en_us/Templates-%26-Software/Templates/_/Ns=Rank.

As with postcards, it is very helpful and money saving to mail merge the address directly onto the mail piece.

Below shows my newsletter (custom made) template produced with Adobe software.

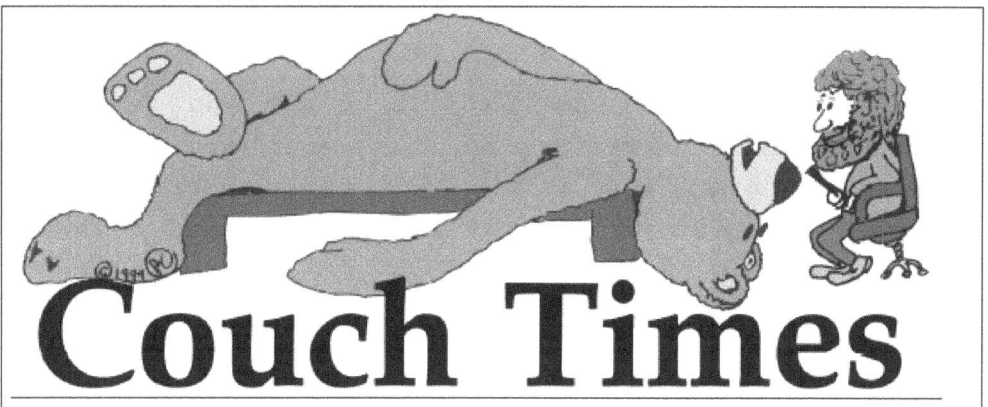

Dr. Phil's newsletter template (reduced) The big hairy thing is Dr. Phil (chair).

Color

Color can add a lot to the look of your newsletter. The problem is that color is expensive and your newsletter is a freebee.

My advice, develop the newsletter in color, but print it in black and white (gray scale) on a quality laser printer. Why bother with the color if I'm advising you to print in black and white? The reason is the PDF. Color in a PDF is free. When your newsletter is viewed on a computer screen, iPhone, iPod, or iPad screen, it shines in all its glorious color— for free.

Color pictures print nicely as gray scale on a laser printer because the color shades are reproduced as shades of gray.

It is nice to have the option to print in color. You may want to print the first page in color making the whole newsletter brighter. Or, use color for your holiday newsletters.

If you print in color have it done professionally or splurge on a color laser printer (PC/Mac $500.00 and up plus expensive color toner costs). Avoid ink jet color, it looks less professional and comes at a really high toner price.

Content counts

The whole reason for your newsletter is to get your name and services front and center in your customer's mind. The second reason is the hope they will share your newsletter with a friend or family member. If 80% of your copy is interesting stuff, you get to fill the other 20% with informative stuff about your business.

This is where interesting topics count. Not interesting necessarily to you, but interesting to your target audience. What does the reader want to read about?

People like to read short articles about:
- tricks of the trade
- cool facts
- secrets
- money
- sex
- health
- helpful hints
- safety
- themselves

If you read the cover of Reader's Digest the next time you are in line at the supermarket, you will see the quintessential national newsletter. Reader's Digest's April 2009 cover boldly stated:
- How To Hide Anything
- Your anxiety
- Extra pounds
- A spare key
- A water stain
- Passwords and more...
- Plus, Eat Better, Pay Less and The Shocking Truth About Cancer Tests.

That's just the cover. Personally, I love the little stories and jokes but never find the time to read the magazine that sits in my own reception area. (I did enjoy one a few months ago at my dentist's office.)

11 chunks of chutzpah newsletter advice

1. Long prose is death! Short is sweet, interesting, and fun.
2. Cover lots of subjects. Keep it interesting. Keep the subjects related to human behavior as it relates to your customer. Stay extremely up beat and positive.

3. Give information in numbers— 8 ways to walk pounds off you heinie. (11 chunks of chutzpah newsletter advice)

4. Allow humor. Heinie is funnier than buttocks. It is even spelled funny. But, be careful. Be funny not raunchy. "G" rated humor is the safest for most businesses.

5. Avoid specific advice. Give general advice. Playfully ask a question, then answer it.

6. Quote others liberally. Being well read is impressive, being a know-it-all is uninviting.

7. Proof read, prof reed, prooof reaad! Your newsletter represents you. Then proofread again.

8. If possible, write so an average 8th grader can understand. Use small clear declarative sentences.

9. Follow the 80/20 rule of information to sales pitch. If the reader feels that you are asking them to read a sales brochure disguised as a fun newsletter they will think less of you.

10. Publish at least 4 times per year and no more than monthly. A newsletter is a long term project to keep word of mouth going concerning your business. Plan the publication dates a year at a time. If there is a slow period at the office and you think people are not talking about your business enough, publish a special issue.

11. Never play leapfrog with a unicorn (not relevant to your newsletter but it is good advice) Have fun so your reader enjoys reading your newsletter. Sprinkle jokes, cartoons, sayings, and puzzles throughout your publication.

Email

Email is tricky. People seem to love it or hate it. People love to get pertinent email, and they hate to get spam. This is a huge problem for you if you are looking to communicate with your customers by email. Unlike regular mail, email for a lot of people seems very personal. So, if your email is unwanted your services may quickly become unwanted.

The best way to deal with this is with opt-in only email. What this means is that you only send email to people who give you prior permission to send them email.

However, this opt-in rule is still not enough. Every time you have contact with the individual you also need to offer them a clear way to opt-out of receiving email from you. People change their minds. This needs to be respected.

The Opt-in and Opt-out procedure should be simple for both the email receiver and you. If your email database is managed by your Internet Service Provider (ISP) make sure you familiarize yourself with their procedures. It could be some time before you get a complaint about the system if there is a problem. Most customers will simply feel unloved and choose a different company to work with verses tell you about the problem. Most people do not like conflict.

A manual system of opt-out is easy to set up. It is part of your email signature and looks like this:

If you wish to have your name removed from the CopitchInc.com email alerts simply send: "Please remove my email address" to:

DrPhil@CopitchInc.com

If you have had this alert forwarded to you and would like to have your email address added, simply send: "Please add my email address to the CopitchInc.com email alerts." to:

DrPhil@CopitchInc.com

Please add the above address to your address book or white list so your spam filter will let us through, Thank You.

This way you, or your designate, gets an email telling you to remove them from your email list. Nice, clean and simple. Please note, as your email is sent from friend to friend, you will also get new opt-in requests. An enewsletter often takes on a life of its own once you let it fly.

"So why bother with removing them?" you may ask. The first and by far best reason is "Chutzpah marketers don't SPAM!" And once you know you are emailing someone who wishes no contact, your email is spam. The second reason is Internet justice. Like in the old west, there are self appointed Internet sheriffs who will teach you a lesson.

I have a friend who is, by day, a mild mannered entrepreneur. But at night, he is the Internet version of Zorro. He is obsessed with email purity, so when he gets an unsolicited email he responds with a polite, "Please remove me from your database" email. And he saves the unsolicited email in a file he calls simply "Z". If he gets a second unsolicited email from the same person or group he responds with a stern, "REMOVE me from your email database, if you do not, you are giving me permission to send you unsolicited email."

 If he gets a third unsolicited email, he sends the naughty emailer the contents of his "Z" file which is massive. This will play havoc with the naughty emailer's service provider. No matter what you think of this tactic, it is not uncommon. There are reports of some major companies having their web sites knocked off the Internet when an angry individual asked a thousand (or 10,000) of his closest friends in a user group to simultaneously email their computer operating system, every hour, to the errant company's web site. This level of usage will disrupt even the largest ISP, and most likely get the attention of the FBI.

What to put into your email

This is simple to say but hard to do. You want to send information your customer wants to read more about. Content is king!

The goal of your email is to get information in front of the eyes of your opt-in customer. They want to hear from you, that's why they opted in. Now give them what they want. Quickly.

Consistent format is helpful so your customer can find what they want every time: clean, easy to follow information. Your email is an invitation to learn "more." It would be nice if it was seen by the customer as "an old friend" in the email window. Give them the headline and then a sentence or two with a follow up "More..." link (hypertext link) to get lots more information. This link should go to a specific place in your web site (called an anchor). Internet patrons have no patience. If you drop them at the beginning of your web site and expect them to search for what you interested them in, they will click off your page and be gone. Your hyperlink should take them right to the item you interested them in.

This destination web site page should have full navigational abilities giving them full access to your web site offerings. More on your web site can be found in the white paper, **Chutzpah Web Site Marketing for Professionals.** (www.store.copitchinc.com/ChutzpahWebSiteMarketing.html)

Direct mail solicitation with chutzpah

The subject of direct mail is a weighty topic that can cover volumes. We have already covered the chutzpah value of postcards, for most purposes the best form of direct mail, and the usefulness of a chutzpah newsletter. But, there are other methods that a chutzpah marketer should have in her arsenal to be pulled out at the right time.

In this section I am going to cover the low cost, high value, direct techniques that can be used to nurture a growing business. My focus will be on low cost and high value, the chutzpah way.

Chutzpah direct mail is a targeted sales method. Unlike L.L. Bean and Costco that can afford to place a catalog in everyone's mailbox, your funds are limited. Don't let this discourage you, because it is an advantage. Inside the mailbox of the correct individual you can compete easily with the million dollar players in the direct mail business.

The vast majority of direct mail is a total waste of money. I was once told by a magazine editor, "Ninety percent of my direct mail is a waste of money, I just don't know which ninety percent." This is strange math in the real world, but not in direct mail. Most direct mail campaigns have an expected read rate of ten percent and a sale rate of 1-3 percent. So, if you knew which 1-3 percent would buy your product or services, you wouldn't need to bother mailing to the other 97-99 percent.

By using your own list you have upped your odds dramatically. People that have bought from you in the past are more likely to buy from you in the future. This makes sense, but there is more. People similar to those who have bought from you in the past are more likely to buy from you.

As we have discussed before, it is important to follow your business branding and direct your message to your potential customer's pressing needs. When developing your mailer, use the same process as you did with your postcard ad campaign.

There are many types of low cost direct mail ideas. A chutzpah marketer keeps an eye out for the opportunity:

Inserts

Inserts are advertisements that are placed into another company's package or mailing; like when you add your 3-up brochure to every statement you mail to existing customers. Well, almost every other business does the same thing, and if you ask nicely, with the correct motivation, they may let your 3-up ride along.

Ride-along inserts

Three entrepreneurs who met a few years back in the hallway of their building work together to support each other. They help each other keep costs down by buying their general office supplies in bulk from Costco. The three office managers each take turns doing the weekly shopping, and distributing the items. They also place the other two entrepreneurs' fliers in their outgoing statements. This way each entrepreneur gets to place his name in front of the other entrepreneurs' customers for the chutzpah cost of the insert.

A social worker who is highly involved in her church's women's group asked the church school director if she could pay to have a small ad placed in every monthly bill mailed to the parents. The school director politely said, "No."

The social worker talked to me about the uncomfortable conversation, and I suggested she ask again, but from a different angle. Instead of "ad" I suggested "sponsorship".

At the end of each statement, "Thank you to Mary Richmond, M.S.W. for her donation to offset the cost of this mailing. Mary is a social worker who works with teen girls, junior high through college age. Mary's office is located at 1917 Columbia Street. Her phone is (608) 555-5879."

Mary pays half the postage, and the church school director is now looking for someone to sponsor the other half. (Please note: Mary has no printing costs.)

When Mary talked to the school director in advertising terms with the word "ad", the director was turned off right at the beginning. But when Mary talked about helping with the ever growing cost of the school statement mailing, the school director was eager for help.

Stand alone inserts

When you open a magazine or newspaper and stuff falls out, that stuff is called stand alone or free standing inserts. This type of insert takes a ride with periodicals, thus no postage. To get your flyer into the periodical can cost a pretty penny. A few low cost ways have crossed my desk over the years.

 A psychologist who lives in a large apartment building, noticed that residents would recycle their barely used magazines by leaving them on a table in the mailbox area. He placed his 3-up into each magazine to see what would happen. About a week later, he got a call. When he asked, "How did you get my name?" the caller said, "I saw your ad in Architectural Digest."

Over the next couple of weeks this enterprising psychologist started taking extra copies of magazines and leaving them, along with his inserted flier, on the "free" table at the public library.

 An athletic trainer who was a frequent visitor to the used bookstore in her neighborhood, asked the owner of the store if he could put his insert into the books in the health and fitness section. The owner was ok with the idea, but joked, "For every sale you make, you owe me lunch." To date, the trainer has brought him three meatball subs. The bookstore owner liked the deal so much, he now has a deal with the Jiffy-Lube on the corner. The Jiffy-Lube manager gets to put a coupon in the automotive books and magazines, and the bookstore owner gets a free oil change every three months.

 Inserts don't only get to travel by book. A charity I was involved with was having a Wine & Art Auction. One of the sponsors was an upscale specialty food and wine shop. In addition to the sponsorship, I asked the owner if he could have his baggers stuff a flier into every bag that left his store. He agreed as long as the insert had no advertising from any other store on it. When I suggested that the insert could be all about the Wine and Art Charity Auction and how gracious his company was to sponsor it, he volunteered to pay for the printing of the insert. A few days later, he called and asked permission to print information about the Wine and Art Charity Auction on coasters that he had to buy anyway for another business. As it turned out, he also owned an upscale bar that specialized in micro-brewery beers and ales.

Mailbox inserts and card decks

Companies like Val-Pac (www.valpak.com) and Welcome Wagon (www.welcomewagon.com) mail packs of inserts concerning goods and services to homes throughout the country. It is common for entrepreneurs to get national card decks, a pack of post cards mailed in a plastic shrink wrapped mailer. Card decks often tout specialty books or product deals.

Often local card deck advertising are coupon driven ad campaigns. I tend not to recommend coupon driven ad campaigns for entrepreneurs, because in most situations, entrepreneurs who give coupons accidentally teach the public to wait for another coupon before buying from them. Larger companies with lots of different types of items to sell can afford money off or percent off coupons as loss leaders.

1.If your company is doing a charitable activity where you need the community to get involved (and maybe learn your name), then a mass card deck mailing may help.

When a local service club wanted to gather glasses to refurbish and send overseas, Dr. Eage offered his Optometry clinic's lobby as the main drop off point. The following year, still pleased with the goodwill from the prior year, Dr. Eage, paid the cost for an insert in the Community Saver Pack. The local service club helped get a lot of glasses to needy people, and Dr. Eage got a lot of goodwill and added foot traffic.

Not all communities have mailbox/card deck companies. To find a local company look in your Yellow Pages under Direct Mail.

Coconut?

You may wish to think outside the envelope. The postal service will mail almost any non dangerous item for a price. I mailed a coconut from Hawaii to friends instead of a postcard. I just put a stamp on the coconut shell, wrote a note and the address with a marker, and the USPS delivered it in a timely fashion. No box needed. My friends still have the coconut to this day.

In my small city, you can get a letter delivered across town for $4.00 by a private messenger service. They mainly deal with attorneys, but they are happy to pick up and deliver to any address in 3 zip codes. Check your local Yellow Pages under Delivery, private or Messenger Service.

Ways to generate custom mailing lists

It may sound simplistic, but the best way to build onto your mail list is to ask people for their address. Business people will happily give you their business card, while others will give you the information if they feel they are getting something from you.

When I give a talk, I encourage listeners to place their names and addresses on a list that I pass around. The offer is usually a free white paper. (I have learned to beg for penmanship.)

As will be discussed in detail in Chapter 11: **Chutzpah Presentations, Speeches, and Trade Shows,** if you do a health fair, job fair, or charity event, have a raffle. Make sure the raffle ticket has ample space for name and address (no phone number). By making it clear that "You do not need to be present to win," you will greatly increase the participation. On the bottom of the ticket write: "The winner will be informed by certified mail." This costs only a few bucks but sounds very official and special.

One year, my dog Jazz was expecting. So, just for fun we had a Guess The Birth Date raffle. On the "Official Entry Form" there were spaces for name and address along with spaces to guess the date of birth, start time of birth, and number of pups. First prize was a large coffee table book of "Puppies." ($10 bargain table at Barnes and Noble) I left a large stack of Official Entry Forms in the waiting room and told people, "Give them out to friends, let everyone play." Over the next few weeks, hundreds of entrees got turned in. Jazz did all the work, but a lot of people enjoyed playing the game. The winner was a school teacher who I had never met from a school across town. Her class sent Jazz 30 very nicely written congratulation cards and the book became very popular in the classes' lending library.

You can even get addresses over the phone. If someone calls looking for information, offer to mail them your business brochure or newsletter.

List brokers do's and don'ts

Your physical location is very important to a potential customer. If a customer has to fight traffic or parking to get to your business, they may simply look elsewhere. This information may be ego deflating, but many people pick a business based on location. With this information in hand, it may be advantageous to inform people within a few mile radius of your office that you are there to serve their needs. This is when a list broker may come in handy.

List brokers sell public information in a tidy fashion. If you know specifically what type of person you are looking for, a list broker can get you a list of names that meet your parameters.

Your job is to think of the parameters. The list broker's goal is to sell you names—the more the better. They get paid by the name anywhere from 6¢ to over a $1.00. The list broker has the list, and runs a computer sort to fine tune their whole list to your target group.

Examples of lists:
- Every home in a particular zip code.
- Every homeowner in a particular zip code.
- Every new homeowner in a particular zip code.
- Every homeowner with a car less than one year old in a particular zip code.
- Single parent households with children under 5. Children over 5 but under 12. Teens only.
- Homes in your area that get Parent Magazine or Guns and Ammo.
- New renters in your area.
- Homes of a particular income bracket.
- Businesses in your area that…

As you can see, if a computer can gather the information from public records, a list broker can sell you that information. It is kind of spooky how much is in the public domain.

Mail list brokers

Mail list owners tend to be large banking and credit corporations with access to huge amounts of consumer and business data. Mail list brokers lease the lists from the mail list owner and rents it to you. Yep, that's right, you, the end user can only rent a list. Usually the list is rented for a single use or for unlimited use during a specific period of time, for example one month.

The mail list brokers offer two types of lists:
- Compiled list
- Response list

A compiled list is computer generated from public and business records such as telephone directories, birth records, divorce records, credit reports, and annual reports.

A response list is computer generated from information gathering areas like, magazine subscriptions, warranty return cards, business contact databases, government reports, and government records.

Response lists tend to be more targeted and are more expensive to rent.

Freshness counts

When you rent a list you have to be aware about freshness. A list that is one year old is very old. It may be 30-40 percent inaccurate. People move, companies go out of business, or move. You do not want to pay to mail your target list to the wrong mailbox.

A fresh list is considered 92 percent accurate. It tends to be about a month old. List owners and brokers regularly clean up their lists. There is competition in the list rental game, and the list broker wants to keep you coming back to rent from them. It is appropriate to ask how old a list is, and when was the last time it was pruned. The list broker cannot guarantee that people on the list will buy your product, but they should back that the list is accurate (92% or better).

 Beware of "expired lists." I have been offered expired lists on a few occasions. The cost per name was nice, but a expired list is very old, and when you think about the cost of the mailer and postage, an expired list is probably a black hole that will simply devour your money.

Lists: A numbers game

Most list brokers want to sell quantity. It is common in the industry that a list broker sells the names for, say 15¢ each, with a minimum list price of $500.00. This $500.00 minimum was the standard for at least the last 10 years. However, just recently, a list broker I worked with a few years ago sent me an email offering "Inflation Busting Special" of a $350.00 minimum.

Seeds

 List brokers add a few seed names into every list they sell. The seed addresses are legitimate addresses monitored by the list owner. If you use the list again, without paying for it, you will get a call, bill or nasty lawyer letter. Or perhaps all three.

Where to get

List brokerage is big business. You can find local list brokers in your Yellow Pages.

Some of the big players on-line are:
- Experian's Small Business Services (www.experian.com/small-business/services.jsp)
- List Brokers, Inc. (www.listbrokers.com/)
- Lists Are Us (www.listsareus.com)
- Century List Services (www.centurylist.com)
- 1000Lists, Inc (www.1000lists.com)

The following companies offer concept (start) through mailing services (finish) for a price:
- Salesgenie.com (www.salesgenie.com) More B2B
- Keenote Marketing and Media (www.keenote.com)

National Organization:
- Direct Marketing Association (www.the-dma.org) This site has a wealth of information.

Email brokers

MX Logic reported in 2005 that 3 of every 4 email messages were spam. It bothers most people to get spam. This has also taught most people to mistrust email marketing. With this information, and the fact that most states and the federal government are regularly drafting anti-spam legislation, it is potentially dangerous to buy and use email addresses for marketing purposes.

I advise you not to email anyone who did not opt-in to your company specifically.

"No Dr. Freud, this meeting is concerning your cross-marketing... <u>marketing</u>!"

7. ADVERTISING PART D: YOUR OFFICE, STORE, AND VEHICLES ARE CHUTZPAH MARKETING TOOLS

Your office or store should be a symphony of cross-marketing. Just as a musical symphony blends the brass with the woodwinds and magically incorporates the percussion instruments, so should your office or store gently and constantly inform whomever enters it… "This is what I offer."

First, an example of how hard it is to "teach" others what services you offer.

For five years I have been working with a married couple who own a large chain of mini-marts. Every couple of weeks we get together to iron out problems between the two of them concerning management issues. I am their business consultant and sounding board. For their convenience, we have met hundreds of times at my therapy office. Hundreds of times they have sat in my waiting room.

My waiting room is child friendly, it is large and colorful. There is a homework area, and a child play area adorned with a large doll house and a larger toy chest castle. There are hundreds of children's books, stuffed animals, and a Lego work table. The walls are adorned with large pictures of kitties and puppies.

The "adult" area has comfortable chairs and tables with magazines. The chairs in the adult area face the homework area and the play area.

I tell you all this because recently, the couple I mentioned above, came into my office for their corporate appointment. As they sat down they both burst into tears. "Our daughter has been expelled—expelled from school for fighting," the mom said. "I don't know who to talk to!"

To tell you the truth, I was a little confused.

"I work with children, what's the problem?" I asked.

He said, "You work with children? I thought you only solved business problems."

Before this incident, I thought I had 100% cross-marketing going for me. What I learned was that it is hard to get some people to see 80% of your waiting room.

Chutzpah cross-marketing

Internal cross-marketing is any and all marketing that you do inside your business. From the signs on your office or store door, to the letterhead you use for business letters. Internal cross-marketing is huge, it encompasses what your staff say and do, to the smell of your rooms. Even your bathroom.

The best thing about internal cross-marketing is that you have a lot of control over it. As a chutzpah marketer, you can get a lot done for pennies.

In this section, I am going to go over many internal cross-marketing techniques. The more you incorporate into your company, the larger your company will grow. Most of the things I will share with you will honestly only cost you pennies, but they will bring you thousands of dollars of business—over and over again.

Business signage

The signage for your business is very important to a chutzpah marketer. Obviously, your external signage helps your customers find your office or store, but that is just the tip of the signage iceberg. Your external signage sets the tone of your business for your customer.

Signage is not inexpensive, but it is amazingly valuable. An external sign can be a 24 hour beacon inviting potential customers into your company.

Signage has a preventive job also. Under no circumstance do you want your office or store to make a customer feel dumb, not even for a second. When signage works, people don't pay much attention to it. But when it doesn't work, they feel dumb. Once that occurs your customer associates feeling dumb with your company. This is not good.

External signage

Most companies rent or lease office or store space. If that is the case for you, you probably have limited control over your site sign (the big sign out front). Nonetheless, let's start our discussion at the big sign, then we will move inside.

Let's step outside and look at your sign. Is it inviting? Is it legible? Is it new, clean, and crisp, or is it flaking and sun worn? Your sign represents you.

I was hired to do a business evaluation on a well established law firm. I took my camera and went to the firm's office. The complex was very nice. It had easy access from a main road, plenty of parking, and nice green spaces. The buildings were clean and well maintained.

When I got out of my car, I looked around, took a few snap shots, and just stood there. (The pictures were for my evaluation presentation.) My goal was to go to Suite 101. The problem was, I had no idea where Suite 101 was. As I walked towards the building, I noticed a dentist's office and a hi-tech firm of some kind. But no attorney. I moseyed to my left and found four doors, one labeled "Private." I knew I was at the correct building, the large sign near the street confirmed that, Mallard Business Park.

The building wasn't that big, but somehow I had gotten lost.

I took a few more photos and went around the corner. I met a woman smoking who smiled at me. I asked where Suite 101 was, and she directed me. "You want to go just around that corner over there," she pointed. "And you'll see the path to 101."

When I got to Suite 101, the receptionist peeked over the hundreds of files on her counter and welcomed me. "Any trouble finding us?" she asked with a smile.

"Well, kind of," I said. "I found the building with no problem, but your office was kind of hard to locate."

"Yeah, I hear that all the time, do you have an appointment?"

A few directional signs fixed the problem. The cost was less than $100.

Your main external sign or signs are a low cost and powerful tool. Every car that drives by is a potential customer or referrer.

Because the sign works 24 hours per day, make sure it is well lighted. By using energy efficient lighting, it is also reasonably priced to let your sign sell your services all night long.

People shop in their own neighborhoods. They desire a dentist, a medical doctor, a pharmacist, a grocery store, and takeout food within twenty minutes of home or work. Ten minutes is even better. If you are located in a larger city, your customers will want you close to a transportation hub.

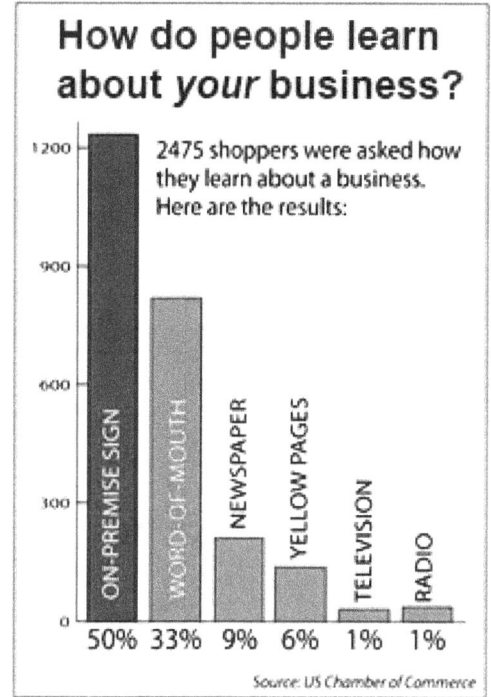

US Chamber of Commerce

Treat your major external signage like it is your chutzpah business card, simply a giant version of it.

In the sign business, the big sign out front is called a site sign. They come in lots of forms: monument, pylon, window graphic; just to name a few. I personally find that the wooden sand blasted signs look professional and connote calmness. I am not fond of florescent signs for professionals. However, as we have discussed before, if it fits your company style, then it is correct for you.

Now the good news. Signage has gotten less expensive over the last few years. As a result of the use of computer generated letters, and the reality of the Internet, signage is not limited to businesses in your own area.

I recently had two door signs made in 36 hours that are spectacular for $19.95 each. Ten years ago the same door sign would have taken a month and cost $50 each. Also, I would have been limited in colors and graphics.

Examples of signage:

Monument sign with movable message section (Pricey)

Wood framed plywood sign, painted. (Reasonably priced)

Banner sign (Reasonably priced but may be hard to put up.)

Fluorescent sign (Mid-range cost plus bulb maintenance and electricity.)

The bathroom sign above is a sign at Beijing Capital International Airport showing lines of people waiting to use the restroom, the Chinese below translates to, "If we reduce the population, everyone will feel relief."

Sand blasted sign. Nice carved wood look but much lower in cost. (Mid to high range)

For the average company the purpose of the site sign is to mark the company's territory. The purpose of the chutzpah site sign is to motivate new customers to use your services.

You may need a local sign installer to do larger and fancier signs. Start by consulting the Yellow Pages for companies in your area. Often there are city and county regulations concerning signs. Local shops tend to be very aware of these rules and regulations, but I advise you to check your city's web site for the most up to date information. Many cities tax site signs annually. Make sure you know all the expenses before you commit to a sign.

Banners

Banners are large signs designed to get noticed from a distance.

Truck stop sign gets lots of attention and laughs.

As I walked into Safeway, I noticed a sign on the automatic door. "Our pharmacist gives flu shots." Because I like signs, and didn't know that pharmacists gave shots, it caught my attention. There were two problems with this sign:

- It was on a moving door as I was walking in. This makes the sign difficult to notice, and it leads to the problem of people bumping into each other at the door as someone pauses to read the sign. Researchers have found that people do not like being touched in stores and will buy less if they feel crowded or touched. Research has also shown that any sign at the door is not noticed by regular customers. They know where they are going and thusly are not looking for directional information. To get a sign noticed, it needs to be inside the door at least 6 feet. Then, as people traverse the door area, and start to scan the store, the sign is in their line of sight.
- The sign demeans the service. Safeway should be shouting from the roof of its store, "We love you one and all and want to help you prevent a nasty flu."

The following 5 foot by 2.5 foot banner could be hung from the store: (towards all the passing cars)

> **Keeping you healthy...**
> # Flu Shots
> **available in your Safeway Pharmacy**

This banner shouts that Safeway pharmacy loves you.

Inside the store the message needs to be reinforced with 3 by 6 foot posters on sign pedestals placed six feet inside the store.

> **Keeping you healthy**
> # Flu Shots
> **available in Pharmacy**
>
> Oranges available in produce.
> Vitamins available on isle 3B.
> Get well cards,
>   for your friends who did
>   not get their flu shot, aisle 17C.

If you ever do anything in the community such as health fairs, church bazaars, or sports boosters, your banner should announce your business.

Banners tend to be printed on nylon, poly or vinyl, depending on the length of desired use. They are colorful, durable and come in almost any size. The price is reasonable.

Banners boost traffic. Plain and simple. So in situations where you need to boost traffic, you need banners.

One non-profit I worked with had its office in a remodeled school building across from a busy transit Park And Ride lot. The program offered after school homework support for grade school kids, and if needed, family therapy. The grant they had provided no money for advertising. One large banner sign "Low Cost Homework Help For Kids," filled their program in four days. Their mission was to help working poor families, and they found these families at the Park And Ride.

I am often asked by medical doctors, chiropractors, or health care business owners a kind of round about question.

"Every year my hospital puts on this huge weekend health fair in the parking lot. I feel obligated to have a booth, but, um, ah… how do I get out of it?"

"Why would you want to get out of it?" I ask.

"Well it takes a weekend, and I don't tend to get new patients."

The problem tends to be that the doctor is not getting noticed in the sea of booths. So I advise that they spend $500 to solve this problem. The money is for a big TV and an even bigger banner. The banner reads, "Free TV Giveaway!" People love free TVs. Even if they already have six, they would like seven.

The weekend of the event, the office staff hand out entry forms and collect the important name, address, phone number and email address data from each entrant. Each form says that the winner will be called Monday evening. You do not need to be present to win. Everyone who comes by the booth is handed the company's brochure.

As the people hand in the entry form, the staff asks, "Do you have any questions for Dr. Smith? He will be here from 3 to 4 today, or you can write him a confidential note, and he will call you back." People who want to write a note are given a clipboard with notepaper, pen, and an envelope. The envelope is stamped "confidential." The notepaper reads, "Confidential question for Dr. Smith" and has a place for the person's name and phone number. When the clipboards and notes are returned, the staff person says, "Thanks, all confidential paperwork is given to supervising nurse Thompson. I'll give it to her right now."

Over the next few days, Dr. Smith calls all the people who submitted questions. He either answers the question or suggests the need for follow up care, whichever is appropriate. If it is follow up care, he asks the new patient to hold so that Sally can set an appointment for him.

The sign drew people in and got Dr. Smith noticed in the sea of other doctors and services. For relatively little money, many potential customers were garnered.

These web sites will answer a lot of basic questions about signage:

- www.signarama.com/
- www.buildasign.com/

For engraved signs, such as marble, brass or stainless steel, check out: www.plaquemaker.com

Internal signage—Part one

Your internal directional signage should anticipate your customers' questions.

- Whose office is this?
- Where are the restrooms?
- What forms do I fill out when I first enter the waiting room?
- Do you accept charge cards?
- Which door is the exit?

Remember, the goal is to prevent your customer from feeling dumb. We want them to feel like honored guests. Your signs should enhance your office's motif. They get noticed when your guest is looking for information, but they are not the center of your office design.

The basic rule for the internal sign is that it should be in the customer's line of sight when the customer asks themselves the question.

The office door sign should be visibly inviting. In some offices you will be limited by the building's signage rules. The building management is not concerned with marketing as much as signage consistency. One building I rented from early in my career, had as part of the lease contract that they made all the signs in the building, passing the cost onto me as a surcharge in my second month's bill. You can't do much about that if you want to rent from them, but your internal signage is all your choice.

The following is an example of companies that do not have control over the site sign. I would think the following sign conflict is not good for either company.

If you have say over your signage, develop an appropriate sign for the building with chutzpah.

Welcome to the office of
Mary Farnsworth, M.A.
Serving families since 2001

Example of a welcoming office door sign

For years, my wife and I had a parental pet peeve. Our boys would race to be first into the supermarket and then abruptly stop just inside the doorway and become road blocks. The reason was they didn't know what to do next. Were we going to the produce section or to the deli?

The same thing will happen in your office or store, patrons will walk in for the first time and feel uncertain about what to do next. They're left feeling dumb.

If you have a receptionist, and she is identified with a sign, then the new customer knows to go towards her.

Navigation signs

Internal directional signs are a must. It is nice if your signs are consistent. To that end, all of my directional office signs start with my helpful logo, T.B. I advise you to add your logo to all your signs. It takes thousand of contacts with a logo for a customer to connect the logo with the company. So, don't miss an opportunity. Recently I was given a gift of a Panda calendar, "I saw this calendar and thought of you," she said. I didn't have the heart to tell her that pandas are not technically bears. The calendar is cute, and I am using it this year in my therapy living-room.

Basic sign template - Blank

These signs are always printed in color on white card stock. The white card stock is pasted onto yellow card stock leaving a 1/2 inch yellow boarder. This chutzpah workhorse of a sign costs 25¢ to $1 depending on the size.

Exit sign

This charming little sign is chutzpah, low cost, and extremely important. Common navigation signs needed in most business:

- Reception area
- Restrooms
- This way out
- Recycling Can
- Please do not disturb
- Private
- Exit

You tend to know that you need signage if a guest in your business asks a question about your physical plant.

Internal signage—Part two

The second form of internal signage is informational. At the beginning of this chapter, I spoke of how hard it is teach customers of the many ways you can help them.

Almost every entrepreneur has an experience where they have a customer put them in a pigeonhole. A friend of mine who is an eye doctor was frustrated when a long time customer showed him a $360 pair of protective sports eyewear.

"I told him, 'Why didn't you come to me, we have those for $280 and your insurance will cover half of that.' The man just looked at me and said, 'you have sports glasses too?'"

The eye doctor continued, "What really pisses me off is that this guy has been a patient of mine for over ten years, and we play pickup basketball together twice a week at the Y!"

What my friend didn't understand was that his patient, who respects and appreciates his medical skills, sees him as an eye doctor, not a seller of sports eye glasses.

This is the type of lost business that internal informational signage can rescue.

Small and large posters, tent signs, and item displays, are extremely useful. Most entrepreneurs do not think that they have offers worthy of a sign. Wrong. A non profit counseling service makes real money with a lobby sign that simply reads, "Anti Rape Whistles Only $10. Available at the front desk." I would advise more exposure and an additional line. The line would be, "3 for $28, protect a friend." (Chutzpah marketers up sell.)

Place signs throughout your office to get added exposure. Place one in the waiting room, another in the restroom, and one more in each meeting room.

The following simple and inexpensive sign is chutzpahlishous. It is a simple tear sign with pizzazz. It is printed in black ink on pink card stock. It would work well inside also.

Chutzpahlishous ballet sign

Tent signs are easy to construct. They are made of card stock so they stand up. I have noticed that a lot of scrap booking skills are being added to tent signs. These very colorful points of interest get attention.

Remember, the point of the sign is to inform.

Tent signs that elaborate customer choices and options are very powerful. Unfortunately most tent signs used in business are orders issued to customers:

Examples of tent signs

Signs that give choices tend to work best.

Clear plastic tent frames are available at office supply stores and eBay in many sizes to allow you to put out tent signs printed from your own computer and printer.

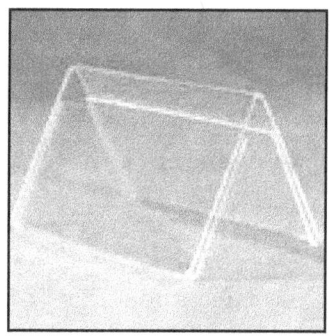

As you look around your office, don't forget to make available, in numerous locations, your business card and company brochure. As a customer picks up a business card or company brochure I often hear, "My friend at work is having a problem with her child, I think I'll give her this."

My 9-second speech is, "Thank you very much for your trust in me, take as many as you would like."

 One company that specialized in helping teens with academic issues had their office in a mall store front right next to a private (after school) learning center and two doors down from a music store that offered instrument sales and rentals along with lessons. The mall traffic was vibrant with active families.

Outside of their door they had a nicely appointed rack of tri-fold brochures with inviting titles such as: Homework Shouldn't Be A Battle, Bullies, What Parents Need To Know, and Schools Are Obligated To Service Your Child's Needs.

Odd place for an advertisement?

Men's and women's restrooms are often quite different. Many women restrooms have pictures on the walls and a small flower arrangement on the vanity. Most men's restrooms are more subdued. This does not have to be. The restroom can be a wonderful marketing area.

 Recently I was at a conference in a nice hotel. Above the urinals were small bulletin boards affixed to the wall. On each bulletin board were fliers entitled, "Todays Events." The flier listed the events the hotel offered as well as the hours of the hotel's restaurants.

Similarly, in the restrooms of a private collage I saw community health information sheets above each urinal and paper towel dispensers. The fliers were put out by the colleges health center. The sheet I read was entitles, "V.D. Fact Sheet." Now that is chutzpah targeted marketing.

A sports bar has televisions in the bathroom wash area. Scrolling below the game were the specials of the day and the hours for happy hour.

With this in mind, I wonder why my large department store doesn't place ads such as, "Baby Wipes, isle 3b" above the baby changing station in the restrooms.

A captive audience may not mind being advertised to if it is useful information.

Areas such as elevators and waiting lines are also good for cross marketing.

Uniforms and name tags.

Name tags can be very helpful if you have front office staff. The receptionist can have a name tag that either pins onto his shirt and/or a desk plaque. This way, any customer can easily recall the person's name without having to feel awkward by having to figure out how to ask his name, or by avoiding the use of his name altogether.

I recommend name tags and some type of uniform, matching shirts for example, if you and your staff are out in public or giving a seminar. A local realty group volunteered to join many other volunteers at a park cleanup day. The group's crisp red shirts and caps got them a lot of attention throughout the day. I think that many people thought it was the realty group's activity, not the park's activity.

Name tag guy

Scott Ginsberg has worn a name tag every day since November 2, 2000. This little name tag schtick has gotten him a lot of attention. He has been interviewed on national television, written up in newspapers and magazines, and even is mention in **Ripley's Believe It Or Not** under the heading Off The Wall.

What started out as a fun experiment has grown into a thriving business for Scott, the Name Tag Guy. He speaks to audiences around the world on how to bring customers to their companies. Scott is a true chutzpah entrepreneur who is very comfortable being the center off attention. He also has a flair for getting noticed, even his books are inviting. This one is a 2 for 1 flip book. Nice chutzpah presentation. (Great Save/stick/pass-ability.)

You don't have to go as far as Scott did to invite customers in, but he has an excellent point that inviting a customer to feel comfortable with your company is important. Scott even had a name tag tattooed on his chest so he was ready for the swimming pool.

Scott Ginsber's web site is worth checking out, it is lively and packed with short videos of chutzpah marketing ideas. (www.hellomynameisscott.com/)

Chutzpah office paper

Letterhead

Some ten years ago there was a rumor that computers were taking over and paper was going to become a thing of the past. To date, I have not noticed any decrease in my office paper consumption. The attorneys in my building seem to be hauling humongous files around, so I doubt if their paper consumption has decreased.

For the chutzpah marketer, paper is not simply paper, it is a marketing opportunity. All the paper in your office should have a "feel" to it. Your logo and marketing information go wherever your paperwork goes.

Years ago professionals would have very fine paper, usually 25% rag, printed for the official correspondence. It was expensive, but seen as professional. Today, most offices use a computer word processing program like MS Word or Apple Pages to write, and subsequently print, their correspondence. (Personally I am partial to Apple computers.)

Getting past the medical office gatekeepers

I am on both sides of this issue. I use gatekeepers to help me manage sales callers, and I also need to get past gatekeepers so I can get referrals from medical doctors, dentists, Certified Public Accountants, and attorneys.

Every marketing book I have read, and every company management course I have taken, has a section about how to get M.D. referrals. They explain the importance of buttering up medical doctors as a valuable referral source.

 One marketing guru told his audience that the "secret" to getting M.D. referrals was giving gifts to their wives and children. He explained how to gather familial information about local M.D.s and how to make sure that the M.D. knew, politely, where the gift came from. I adamantly advise against this marketing bribery. It is unethical and basically nasty.

Another marketing prophet had ten "secrets" of how to get by the gatekeeper so that you could take the medical doctor to lunch. All ten seemed like an embarrassing waste of time to me. So, you will not find any of those techniques in this book.

Please allow me to tease you for a moment.

How do I get consistent medical doctor referrals, often from medical doctors I have never even met?

I will tell you in a second, but let me continue the tease.

My procedure costs me nothing from my marketing budget.

My procedure gets the gatekeeper at the doctor's office to put "me" directly in front of the medical doctor.

My procedure is professionally and ethically correct.

 The answer is, cue the band… with two pieces of paper. That is it. I use two pieces of paper. Please allow me to explain.

If a patient on intake tells me that three or four times a week she is overcome with feelings of confusion, pressure in her chest, and experiencing a cold sweat, I am almost certain she is having an anxiety attack. It may even be fair for me to assume that I am almost 100% sure it is an anxiety attack. But, also I know that it could be something else, something outside my scope of training, such as symptoms of a heart attack or maybe a pulmonary embolism. I do know that "I don't know what I don't know," so I am clinically obligated to refer my new patient back to her medical doctor.

I advise my new patient that it is best to rule out any medical condition that could be causing her symptoms. I ask for a Release Of Information for her medical doctor, and I explain that I would like to send him a note, explaining why I am advising her to get a complete physical. I emphasis that I will help her with her emotional turmoil, but if there is a medical issue, we need her medical doctors on the team.

This referral back to her medical doctor is best for my client and it is also a way for me to put my name in front of the medical doctor. My letterhead and 3-up brochure are seen by potential referrers, placed in front of them by their gatekeepers.

I am also a great referral source for other professionals and because of my income level, I am also a target of numerous cold calls. Brokerage firms, investment realtors, and accounting companies want me to invest in their great new program.

I am polite on the phone and listen for a few minutes to their pitch:

"Dr. Copernich (they never get my name correct), we here at ABC Brokerage would like to take you to lunch and discuss our portfolio management program. Many find it the easiest way to wealth. Are you happy with your stock returns, are you making as much money with your money as you think you should be making?"

"That sounds very interesting," I say. "It sounds like you are good at managing money."

"Ahhh, well yes sir, many people, like yourself, find that we put them on the road to prosperity. Are you happy with your stock portfolio?"

"Do you personally invest with your company?" I ask.

"Yes sir, I trust my company, can I take you to lunch and meet you… and go over the ways we can help you get to financial independence?"

"That sounds very good, but first I need to know I can trust your wisdom. So, I will make you a deal, please send me a copy of your last tax return. If you make more money than I do I will happily buy you lunch. I would be very interested in what you could teach me. Do you have my mailing address?"

I have been doing this for over 20 years and I have never gotten a cold call sales person to send me their tax return. (Many have said they would, interestingly enough.) But, if one does-and I'm impressed with it, I would happily buy her lunch and take notes on everything she wanted to talk to me about.

Customer note paper

By training, I am a cognitive behavioral therapist. I tell you this because a portion of every session is "teaching" new options and interpersonal skills. To help with this "teaching" I encourage my clients to take notes during our sessions and I give homework assignments between sessions.

To help with note taking, I have clipboards with paper easily accessible. I offer blank lined yellow pads and my own "note" paper. Over the years, I have noticed that the vast majority of my patients use my notepaper over the yellow pads. I think it is because it "feels" more therapeutic to them.

The notepaper is my letterhead with the following printed on it:

Notes: Date: _____

Throughout the year, patients report that they tear the top of their notepaper off and give my information to a friend or family member. When this happens, I thank them for their trust in me and offer them a small stack of cards to keep in their purse or wallet.

If your business gives out verbal information, I advise you to make readily available note paper for your customers. Depending on your company, single sheets of paper or small ten page "scratch" pads are inexpensive and very helpful. Many printers offer 3M Post-it Notes that are easily customized.

Note cards

My mother was a lady in the true sense of the word. She had strong beliefs about manners and comportment. She believed that children should be outside playing if the sun was shinning, and inside with a book if it was not. TV was for lazy people and homework built character. She believed in hugs and using butter in cooking whenever possible. But, her number one kindness rule was, "If someone does something nice for you, you send a Thank You card."

After about age twenty-five, I started to understand the wisdom of my mother.

Thank You cards are not just an appropriate courtesy, they are a wonderful chutzpah marketing tool.

I am blessed with people around me that are kind. So, when I hear of a kindness, I send a Thank You card. You may say, "Yeah… OK so?"

"SO?" you say. Because it is rare, it gets a lot of notice. I personally like sending the note, and I also get the secondary gain that the recipient of the note likes getting thanked.

My goal is to send 10 notes per day. When I tell people this I regularly hear, "How?"

The answer is simple, people are nice to me, and I like acknowledging and encouraging niceness towards me. I have specific notes for thanks, illness, and referrals. And I have my note cards easily accessible for me to write, envelope, and stamp. One of my drawers in my desk at the office, and in my desk at home, is dedicated to note cards. (Remember chutzpah marketers are basically lazy, so we organize and prepare to make a regular task as easy as possible.)

How to make a note card

It costs me 60¢ to send a note card. At the present postal rate of 44¢, plus the card and the envelope. (The only exception is my chutzpah get well note that I will discuss later)

I use the Office Depot brand Baronial Invitation envelopes. They are 4 3/8" x 5 3/4" 24 lb. heavyweight bright white woven. They come in boxes of 100, and are on sale about every three months. I get a coupon emailed to me by Office Depot every week offering X off either $75 or $100 in purchases. (You can sign up for the email advertisements at www.officedepot.com. This is also the store that is most convenient to my office. But, I assume that the other national office store chains have similar offers.)

This basic invitation envelope works well with a card that is printed on 8.5" x 11" card stock paper. This is the same card stock I use for the 3-up brochures (chutzpah consistency).

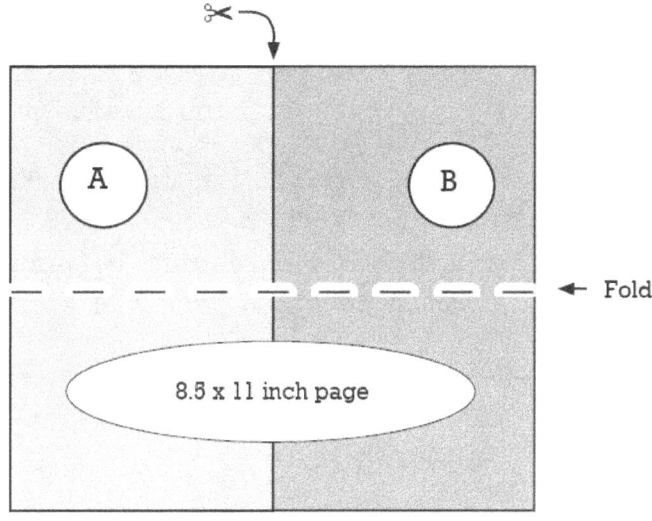

Parts of the basic note card

Each page produces two 8.5" x 5.5" sheets that are then folded into a 4.25" x 5.5" tent card. See Chapter 2: **Your Most Important Marketing Tool Costs 5¢: Getting your card printed,** concerning printing issues. This format will give you lots of printable area:

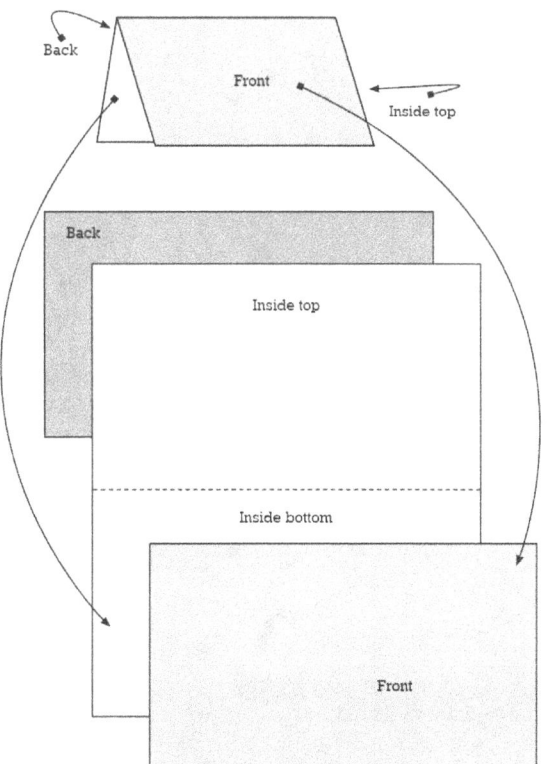

Printable areas of the basic note card

Examples of note cards

Thank you

The Thank You card is about the thanks. The cross-marketing is secondary. Feelings go on the front; no direct advertising.

Because my logo is being used, this card will be printed in color. Even without the use of a logo, I would recommend you use warm colors to connote warmth and feelings.

Example of chutzpah Thank You card (front)

On the inside of the card you have a top and a bottom half.

Advertising goes on the inside top half. The bottom half is for a personal note.

On the inside top half, stay on message concerning your business. Give your most general information. Also, please note that the message is understated for the area. The extra white space around the words soften the advertisement aspect, so as not to distract from the purpose of the card: Thank you!

Dr. Philip Copitch
Ph.D., Clinical Psychology
Marriage • Family • Child Therapy • MFT 19367

1650 Oregon St. Suite 218, Redding CA 96001

CALL (530) 244-7528

PRACTICE SPECIALIZING IN:
* Family Therapy   * Marriage Counseling
* Physical, Sexual and Emotional Abuse
* Violence in Families   * Behavior Problems
* Victims of Violent Crime

Children • Teens • Adults
www.CopitchInc.com

Inside top of Thank You card.

We will cover what to write on the bottom half of the inside later in this section.

Quite often in seminars this is the point where the question comes up, "Won't the person receiving the card think that this is just a gimmick to get your advertisement in front of them?"

I don't think so. I only send a Thank You card if I have a specific reason to thank someone. I believe that my authentic reason for sending the card is "felt" by the recipient, and I tend to get direct feedback. Often the recipient picks up the phone and calls. "I just got your Thank You card… that was so kind of you." Or I will run into someone who says, "I really appreciated your card a few weeks ago."

My mom was right, it feels good to thank people for saying nice things about me or doing nice things for me.

Two other cards I use are a Condolence Card and I heard about you… card. In both cases the card is exactly the same as the Thank You card, except for the words on the front.

The Condolence Card is self explanatory.

The "I heard about you…" card is used to send a pat on the back to someone I know.

If a friend's child is in the news for winning the spelling bee, I send the family a note. If I hear through the grapevine that a colleague just returned from a trip, I touch bases with a card.

Get well cards

My Get Well card is expensive, but it is a workhorse of a chutzpah card. It costs a dollar to mail, and the parts cost another buck and a half.

My chutzpah Get Well card is printed, in full color, like the others we discussed, and mailed in the same envelope.

Grandma Copitch always said that...

"Chicken soup will cure anything
or at least it couldn't hurt..."

So, I am sending you a little pick me up...
along with my hope that you feel better soon.

Chutzpah get well card (front and inside)

I use the bottom of the card for a personal note, and if need be, the back of the card if I'm feeling wordy. I put no advertising in a Get Well card.

What I do put in the card is a pack of Lipton instant chicken noodle soup. I'm hoping it has magical healing powers, but it couldn't hurt.

Because the soup is bulky, the postage is higher.

I get a lot of feedback from this get well pick me up, warm fuzzy, smile a lot, card.

I have had people request it. One answering machine message was,

"Dr. Phil, this is Gail, I'm in bed with the flu and thought you would want to know so you could send me your mother's soup."

I send the soup card if a customer, or anyone in her family, is laid up long enough to need it. This week my "mother's" soup has helped heal a hip replacement and three flus.

I am often told "I didn't eat the soup, I wanted to show it to people at work." (If anyone at Lipton reads this, please send me a case of instant soup for helping to cross-market your product for you!) The stick and show ability of this get well card, along with the humor, is worth the expense.

From the desk of: notes

 I use two note pages on a regular basis. The first is a small version of my letterhead that is used to send personal notes along with other papers or enclosures. The second is a more playful note page that I use when sending messages to friends who also happen to be professionals. See below.

1/2 page note page examples

If I am sending a report to another professional, I send a formal letter on my letterhead. It is better to be overdressed than underdressed, so a typed letter is best. However, if I am sending a packet of information to, let's say a county social worker or an attorney, I add a personal touch and send a hand written note.

Hi Mary,

Enclosed are the copies you asked for.
Hope all is going well for you and your family,

PC

If I know the person well, I tend to be more playful. I send the note with an appropriate message.

Hi Marge,

Enclosed are the copies you asked for.

Haven't seen you and Howard much lately. Now that Track is over, I miss running into you. Why don't you get Howard to buy us lunch... Call me when you have time.

PC

I use one of these 1/2 sheets if I even think of someone. For example, if I am reading an article in a magazine and it triggers a thought, "Michael would be interested in this." I take a moment and copy the article (or rip it out) and jot a note to Michael.

Hi Michael,

Thought you would find this interesting. Paragraph three made me think of our conversation a few months ago.

Be Well,

PC

My hobby is cartooning, so when I get bored with the informal note page, about once a year, I make a new one. I use something lighthearted, whimsical and fun. Last holiday season I used a Peace on Earth TB.

Peace on Earth TB

What to write in note cards

When it comes to chutzpah note cards the personal touch counts. I advise that you do not print a generic thank you message in your card. While it would save you a little time, it would not be personal. (My mother would not approve of an impersonal card.)

A chutzpah marketer takes the time to make a personal connection. So, I write a note in each card, and I hand write the address on each envelope. This personal touch counts.

I received a thank you note from an attorney that consisted of a nicely printed note card with a post-it note stuck to it. The post-it read: "Send T/ U to Copitch by 3/16. J." The printed card was signed by "J" but I assume in reality by his secretary. I did not feel the love.

As discussed earlier, by having all the parts readily available in one location, sending notes is pretty easy. In the old days, I had a huge Rolodex with names and addresses. Now I have a computer database which is much better. I simply search for the person I want to send the note to, and like magic, it is there.

My database is constantly being updated. A chutzpah marketer keeps track of his contact's vital information. See Chapter 6. **Advertising Part C: Chutzpah Gold Mining.**

Entrepreneurs regularly confess to me that they like the idea of writing note cards, but in actuality, they find it a little intimidating. What do you write?

First, relax. It is not like you are going to have to write a screen play or a book. It is just a note of thanks or condolence.

Second, you have to write neatly. The goal of the note is to communicate to the reader your thanks or condolences. If it can't be read, it communicates frustration. I choose to print. Only my wife and I can read my cursive. I'm not joking about this. Over the years, my cursive has become cursive short hand. On a regular basis I leave out the ending of words. I use shorthand codes even without thinking about it. But, when I print, I have to slow down and notice every letter. No --g for ing. No Tx or Hx for treatment or history, respectively. Remember, the goal of the note is communication. So, unfortunately neatness counts.

Third, the note has three parts: Hi, I thought of you, and bye. The Hi and Bye are easy, but so is the "I thought of you." Label what you know, saw, or feel. Share your feelings, but not too sappy.

Thank you examples:

I appreciate your recent referral. Your trust in my work is very important to me.

Mary told me of the nice things you said about me. Thanks! I am touched that you speak so kindly of me.

I read/heard examples:

I read in the paper that Bobby won the spelling bee. I am so impressed. In school I would get picked first in kick ball, but for Spelling Bee teams, my classmates pretended not to see me.
Tell Bobby how proud I am of his hard work.

I ran into Carl at Costco and he told me that you have decided to start teaching part time at the college. Sounds great! I expect your students will get a lot out of your classes. Good luck with all those challenging fresh minds.

Condolences:

Just heard of the loss of Egor. He was a great pup. I loved the way he slobbered and how he made you laugh. I'm sorry for your loss. I'm a phone call away if you want to talk.

I read in the paper about the passing of your aunt. I know you were very close, and I have always been impressed that you helped her so much these last few years. I am sure that you brought great comfort to her.

I have no way to help soften the pain of your loss, but just wanted you to know that I was thinking of you.

I'm a phone call away if you want to talk. Sorry for your loss.

When penning a note, be careful with humor. It is easy to accidentally offend someone. Write clearly and kindly. Writing is more powerful than speech so a little "feeling" goes a long way.

Any other mail that goes out

Any mail that goes out of a chutzpah marketer's office serves at least two purposes.

1. The reason for the mail.
2. Cross-marketing

If you have to spend a stamp to get a letter somewhere, your chutzpah 3-up goes for free. You get to put your information in front of somebody for free. Why wouldn't you? You do not know where your little seed may land, but if only one makes it back home, wow! Free becomes income.

I send my 3-up out to work constantly. And a lot have returned over the years. In every envelope that leaves my office, I add a 3-up.

Blue Cross of California has a major clearinghouse in Chico, California. Chico is about an hour from my office. My 3-up has helped individuals, friends, families, and extended families of Blue Cross employees find my services.

The hardest working 3-up that I know of was one that went to a court in southern California. It was subsequently mailed by a court clerk to her sister in San Francisco, who then bought my parenting book from Amazon.com. Two years later, the book with the 3-up (now a bookmark) was loaned to a friend in Sacramento. This friend was going through a heated divorce and gave my 3-up to her attorney. I politely turned down the evaluation consult requested by the attorney. Six months later, the attorney was asked if she knew a therapist in Redding, California. She gave my name. I got to help a family. My hard working 3-up did all that for me. Sweet!

When the Macy's Credit card bill arrives, it has cross-marketing that smells great. The phone bill has paid vender marketing from different companies. I suspect that the phone company gets a nice check from these companies for the privilege of piggybacking their advertisement in with the phone bill.

 If your friend in a non competing profession is as chutzpah aware as you are, offer to place his ad in your billing statements in exchange for your ad going in his statements. If he is not as chutzpah aware as you are, teach him. It is worth your effort. This very low cost ad seeding is powerful.

Dr Phil's thanks a million letter

As discussed above I enjoy saying thank you. Sometimes I also want to say thank you with a token of my appreciation, a gift or an incentive to keep up the good work.

 To this end I have a one million dollar thank you letter. See below. It is fun and has proven to have lots of show and stickability.

It is printed in color on 8.5" X 11" white index card stock. People seem to really like getting these thank you letters. My guess is that it is fun to hope for the big prize. I have also found that people like the lucky gold penny I send along with the letter.

Fridge Art

Fridge Art is a friendly way to get your name out. It costs pennies and children and families love it.

Fridge Art is in the form of chutzpah coloring sheets that are available in my waiting room. I tend to have 6 to 8 different types of Fridge Art for kids to color next to a big container of crayons. Often, kids ask if they can take one of each drawing home, and I happily agree. Regularly, parents ask if they can "have a few for the cousins." Again, I'm happy to oblige.

The reason I love Fridge Art so much, is because I like where they end up. On the refrigerator. I like that my company information is clipped or magnetized to the icebox. Some go to work with parents, and many go to grandma's house to adorn her fridge. A few teachers use my Fridge Art as rainy day activity sheets. I know of one cul-de-sac where all six homes have Fridge Art on their refrigerators.

I change the Fridge Art with the seasons and the holidays. Don't worry if you can't draw, you have a cousin who can. The children love to color, just give them something fun. (Teens and adults enjoy coloring in my waiting room too. And, while I think of it, they also love the Lego table and doll house!)

Fridge Art example (Reduced)

I have two Fridge Art templates. One portrait view (tall) and the second landscape view (wide). You can do this in any basic word processing program. Then, neatly paste art onto it and make copies. This pasted sheet is called a Master. Protect your masters by storing them safely, and you can make copies for years to come.

Over the next few pages you will find a few Fridge Art drawings to get you started. Feel free to put them on your own fridge advertisement, I mean art sheet. Don't forget to add your cross-marketing information. These work well whatever your business.

I also make available free PDF downloads of my fridge art at my website: www.copitchinc.com/downloads.html.

First for the little ones:

Dot to dot and color fun!
With my friend Bunny Bun.

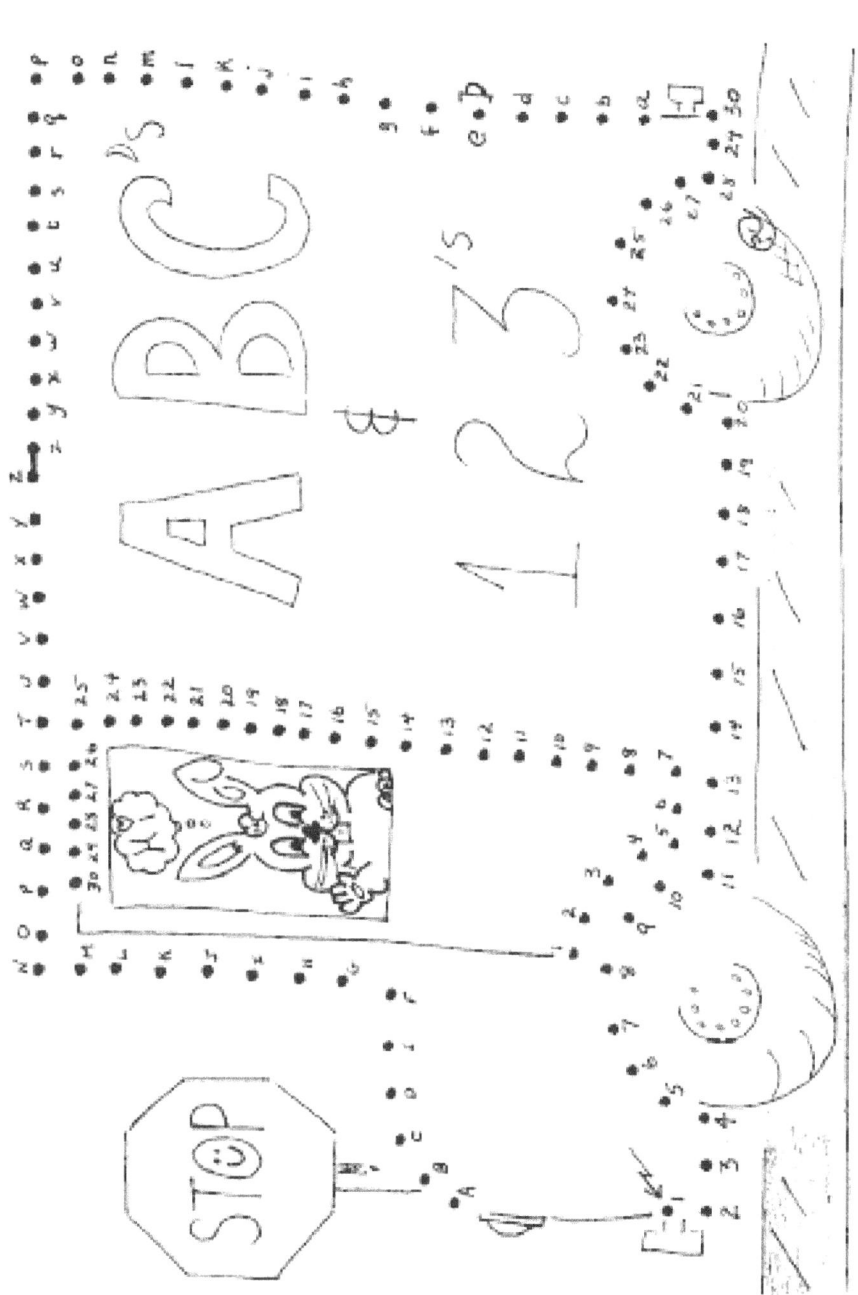

For the older children at halloween:

Around Thanksgiving:

Christmas:

When a movie comes out that the kids enjoy (me too), I often make up a "how to draw" Fridge Art. Adults often take these with them to experience in private.

For the older kids and teens:

How to draw

How to draw

The following spoof was for my friend Dr. Hanson's dental office:

Color me

"I told you to go brush!"

If you have customers that need to wait, color me, table games, and puzzle pages are great cross-marketing tools.

Business vehicles

Signs on business vehicles are nothing new. However, with the invention of special vinyls, signs have grown up in the last few years. Your choices are huge. From window tinting with a subtle message to full vehicle wraps (expensive).

Companies such as Ads on Wheels (http://www.adsonwheels.com) offer remarkable vehicle wraps that give your vehicle chutzpah wherever it goes.

Most of these wraps are over the top with too much color and too much design. As with other forms of advertising, white space counts. You want the reader to get your message.

Window advertisement has come down in price recently. You can have vinyl letters placed on your windows proclaiming your information to the world. Or, you can get custom window graphics that still allow you to see out (moderate cost).

A company named sticviews (www.sticviews.com) makes custom skins for almost anything you would like to cover, from your iPod to your fleet of vans.

As this technology gets around, the prices seem to be coming down.

A nice example of using a small space well.

Magnetic signs

A nice option to permanent display ads is magnetic vehicle signage.

Magnetic vehicle signs are vinyl weather resistant sheets mounted onto thin magnetic backing. They hold onto the car even at well over highway speeds. If you own a fiberglass sports car, the magnetic sign will not work for you. Newer magnetic signs tend to hold up well over time, but the sun will fade them at some point.

The biggest problem with a magnetic sign is that it is easily to steal. The more "cool" your sign is the more likely to have it end up in some teenager's bedroom.

You can get a full color magnetic sign in an industry standard size from $10-$20. Vista Print (www.vistaprint.com) offers to give you your first small magnetic sign for free. I have used their web site may times and I have found it very easy, but they are not always the lowest price if you are looking for quantity on an item.

Vehicle magnets can also be cut to virtually any shape to fit your needs. You can even get signs that glow in the dark or reflect light for easier night viewing.

As with all outside signage, you have to keep in mind that the viewer is many feet away. In the following example, the little car and colorful sign catches the eye, but the advertisement value is limited because the message can not be easily read.

Magnetic signs are a form of a name recognition chutzpah ad.You will often not have the space for all four major ad components.

1. Chutzpah headline
2. Chutzpah supporting information
3. Chutzpah supporting secondary benefits
        ------Name and address
4. Chutzpah call to action

(You want to avoid the 5th major component of print ads, save/stick/pass-ability, for obvious reasons.)

What tends to work best is the Chutzpah Headline (Most often your company name) which is a clear announcement that you are present with the implication that you serve this section of town or part of the county.

When you design your magnetic sign, work from the assumption that your reader will be at least 10 feet away when confronted with you chutzpah notice. Using large letters with solid contrasting colors and edges is very important.

The following example shows two clear to read magnetic signs.

This next example shows an informative chutzpah magnetic sign that can be used for a few weeks to stimulate business:

Business card dispensers

A newer item is the car business card dispenser.

I have not seen these in stores yet, but I suspect that they will show up in office supply stores soon. This chutzpah idea places your mini-billboards right next to your vehicle signage. The small water resistant boxes cost under $10 each, I have seen them for $6 in orders of 3 on eBay.

Cross marketing inside your store

Up to now we have discussed cross marketing inside your office. All that information is useful inside your store also. There are lots more chutzpah ideas ideal for store cross marketing.

The goal with in store cross marketing is to anticipate a customer's needs and present a useful and immediate answer. For example, if you sell eggs, an easily grab-able egg slicer is a nice up-sell. A small sign stating, *Bread is on Aisle 3*, is a helpful sales boost. One manager told me that English Muffins (a higher profit item) and single bananas move quickly next to the eggs. By moving ripe single bananas to the egg area he found that he could move bananas that had a short remaining shelf life.

Some items go together well such as beer and beef jerky. A sign next to the beer and jerky such as, *Nuts, Pretzels and Chips aisle 6*, encourages the beer buyer to walk through your store and see what else you offer.

Getting the customer to keep looking for must need items is important to the bottom line.

The signage industry has developed lots of ways to help you cross market inside your store. Many are low cost and reusable.

Floor and carpet graphics

Floor and carpet graphics allow you to place an advertisement or directions at every customer's feet. With multi-color large vinyl printers, most sign shops can offer vinyl floor graphics at a reasonable cost.

You can get more attention for a specific product such as these soft drink choices, or you can direct your customer to another part of your store with welcoming footprints. Many product distributors will help off set the cost of product specific signs if they don't have some already made for you to get for free.

DDI Signs (www.ddisigns.com/floorgraphicsdecals.htm) for example, offers durable and colorful vinyl products that are custom made and custom cut. You can really let your imagination flow. I like their "follow me" footprints.

Vinyl floor decals are easy to apply and removable with little fuss. Some companies offer movable and reusable graphics.

Custom design carpets are a little pricer but last a long time. Companies like The Inside Track (www.theinsidetrackinc.com) can take your message or logo and inlay it into carpet:

This is an elegant way to present your company. Inlays are an art form and become quite pricy. A lower cost alternative is having your message digitally printed onto carpet.

Matco Products (www.matcoproducts.com) offers a full line of carpet advertising choices. Their welcome mats start around $50 dollars.

"Incontinence hot line, can you hold..."

© 2010 CopitchInc.com

8. YOUR PHONE AND EMAIL ARE CHUTZPAH MARKETING TOOLS

When I was a teenager I had a boss named Vic. Vic had a love affair with his phone. At least once a day he would blurt out, "My phone is directly connected to my customers' wallets." Then he would send out the tow truck to pick up someone's disabled vehicle.

Vic owned a gas station in the posh part of town. He amassed a great fortune from this single gas station. While his competitors pumped gas, and occasionally worked on someone's car, Vic became the go to guy for the people of this upper crust neighborhood.

Vic's gas station gave full service. When a car pulled up, an attendant, wearing a clean uniform, pumped the gas and checked the fluids. At the end of each pumping, the attendant handed the driver a business card and said, "If you have a car problem, call Vic."

Vic's gas station had the highest gas prices and the most polite and helpful attendants. But Vic didn't make his fortune by pumping gas, he made it by answering the phone. If any of his customers had a car problem, Vic fixed the problem. He had two service bays at the gas station, and another four bays about ten minutes away. It was impressive how many cars Vic's mechanics (mostly cousins) worked on.

Vic taught me that people are willing to pay for service, and that the phone is a chutzpah marketing tool.

I agree with Vic, the phone is directly connected to your customer's wallet. However, I also add email to this statement. So, for me, the phone and email are my direct lines to potential and established customers. If I use this technology wisely, I serve my customers well. Well served customers keep using your services, and like to tell other people about your services.

Penelope, a fellow entrepreneur, had invited me to her office to discuss the marketing of her company.

"Excuse me Phil," Penelope said as she reached for the ringing phone.

Then she did something I didn't expect. She reached around back and disconnected the phone line. "They'll call back if it's important," she said.

"I'm sorry, if this is a bad time…" I started.

"No, not at all," she interrupted. "I hate that damn phone. Some days, it just drives me nuts."

This is a common reality for many professionals. The phone feels like a tightening noose, squeezing the life out of them. Professionals often speak of their dislike for the phone and the people who call them. This is a sign of job stress

---

The phone and Internet makes the world seem small.

A few months after the release of my parenting book, I got a phone call from a woman thanking me for it. As it turned out the caller was very concerned that she may be spoiling her children and was looking for information to sooth her worries.

After she explained her situation, second marriage to a man who works constantly along with three children from their combined three marriages, I offered to make her an appointment so we could continue exploring her dilemma. She apologized for not being able to come to my office, "I need to be in Brussels next week and I have no plans to come to the States."

As it turned out, she purchased my book from Amazon UK and was presently on her yacht off the coast of France.

At the end of the phone call she thanked me again for my book and assured me that she was giving a copy to the au pair.

and potential job burnout.

In this chapter, we will discuss how to use your phone and email to transmit and gather information: how to make your phone and email a chutzpah tool. We will discuss how to tame the phone monster so that it works for you. Hopefully, by the end of this chapter, you will be in love with your phone and email again.

Controlling the phone and email monster

Your phone and email are amazing chutzpah tools. They allow you to have easy and inexpensive contact with the world. Unfortunately, the phone and email are not respected by most companies. Thus, these ubiquitous devices often become linked in a chain of despair.

Your phone and email are amazing chutzpah tools—if they are controlled. The good news is that this monster is easy to control.

Phone machine or answering service

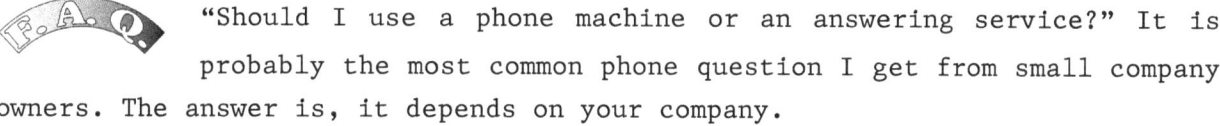 "Should I use a phone machine or an answering service?" It is probably the most common phone question I get from small company owners. The answer is, it depends on your company.

If you are an agency with sixteen architects, you will need an answering service and an amazingly well organized secretarial pool. If you are a single architect, you may need a service, but an answering machine may work just as well. There are advantages and disadvantages to both. The three "Cs"— cost, control, and competence need to be weighed out.

Answering services are expensive, but they position your company as "professional" in most areas of the country. Most entrepreneurs who I have talked to about answering services complain about the cost and incompetence. It is hard to keep control over the tone of whoever answers your phone at a service. I have heard horror stories about surly service and issues of privacy.

The problem with an answering machine is that it may seem impersonal to some callers. However, it has the advantage of being secure and private.

 One nice thing about being a small company is that you will probably not need an answering service or a secretary.

For the last twenty years, I have used an answering machine (actually two) and no secretary. I still recall the cost twenty-one years ago. My secretary cost $60,000 with benefits and taxes, and my answering service was $2,400. These figures are twenty years old, but my rough calculation indicates that I have saved, not adding inflation, $1,248,000.00! I did the math twice; I saved over one million dollars over the last twenty years.

Please allow me to explain my system. It consists of three telephone lines and two answering machines. In my office I have two telephone lines. One is my office number that is printed on everything we hand out. This line has an answering machine on it. The second phone line is the back line (back of the office). The back line is used for all outgoing calls so as not to tie up the main phone line. The back line number is not given out. The third line is in my home den. The den line has an answering machine. The den phone number is not given out.

During my work day, the office line rings regularly, and the machine captures the message. Most of the time I let the machine answer the phone for me. At the end of my work day, I transfer the phone to my den. This is done by signing up and using call forwarding, a service of the phone company. (It is explained in the front of your local phone book).

The next workday, before I leave home, I un-forward my calls. This call forward/un-forward is a very easy process. Anyone who calls always uses the same "office" number. Only I know where I am. Last summer, my family was evacuated due to forest fires. Over the hectic week I call forwarded my office phone to my cell phone in the evenings, allowing me to take care of family matters and work matters simultaneously. (Many of my patients were also evacuated and making myself available to them prevented a lot of heartache for them.)

When I am away from the office for extended periods, I can easily check my messages from anywhere in the world by calling into my machine and using my code number to access it.

When you call my office you hear the calm voice of my wife, Geri:

> Thank you for calling the offices of Dr. Philip Copitch. Please leave a message, including your name and phone number after the beep. Be sure to speak slowly and calmly, and Dr. Copitch will get back to you as soon as possible. Thank you.

I get teased regularly because of the words "slowly and calmly". When other professionals call they tend to talk very slowly and in monotone for the first few seconds of their message. "This… is… Bob… Kelsow… calling… from… Sacred… Heart... Hospital…"

The admonition, "slowly and calmly," helps excited or nervous callers leave an understandable message. Without this cue, callers tend to speed up when they are leaving their name and phone number, making the last four digits of their number come out in a gibbering whirl.

I check my messages between sessions and once or twice per evening. I only return emergency or urgent calls as soon as I get them. More on this later in this chapter.

It is important for you to have clear guidelines concerning how phone calls are returned.

When shopping for a phone answering machine, you want one that does digital recording. No tapes. Look for a machine with at least a 45 minute message capture so you are not missing calls. But, understand it will take you 45 minutes to listen to it if it is full.

I triage messages throughout the workday, between appointments. If I am on target, I get about 10 minutes between patients. My goal is to log the patient I just saw into the computer and check calls during that time. However, bathroom runs or food can often be the priority.

I do not have a phone in my treatment areas. When I am with a patient, that person or family gets my undivided attention.

Phone and email time management

I want to tell you something that you may be shocked to hear me say. I DO NOT MULTITASK. I understand the human brain and respect it by not multitasking complicated tasks. (See Multitasking And Brain Research, this chapter.)

I compartmentalize. When I am with a patient, I am 100% focused on their needs. When I return calls or check email, I do just that. One at a time for an allotted period of time. I stay focused on my task and get it done quickly, and hopefully well. As I sit here right now writing, I have no distractions, by design. The phone ringer is off, the machine will get my calls. The email program is closed. I will check my phone and email messages during my next writing break, in about 14 minutes. Unless there is an emergency, I will take 10 minutes to check messages and 15 minutes to walk and refresh myself. Then, back to writing for two more hours. By focusing clearly on one important task at a time, I get much accomplished.

I have seen skilled adults perform at about 25 percent efficiency because of unnecessary interruptions. One entrepreneur I worked with hated the idea when I suggested no Instant Messaging (IMing) in her office. "But what if my husband or the kids want to get hold of me!" she protested.

"You'll call them back or email them later," I said.

"But what if there is an emergency," she said sadly.

"Isn't that a red herring?" I asked. "Emergencies are very rare. What you are doing is adding hours to your average non-emergency day."

I continued, "When you are at work you have to leave the family distractions at the door."

The truth was that she didn't want to leave the family distractions at the door. She liked "being there" for her kids.

A graduate student I worked with spent 6-8 hours per day working at his computer on his dissertation. On most days he produced not a single page. When he removed IM and a game called War Craft, his dissertation was completed in four months and three days. What I found so interesting was that he was IMing and playing War Craft with other grad students who were "working" on their dissertations.

I tend to check my phone and email as part of opening up shop in the morning. I check my phone messages between customers, and my email midday. I schedule 30 minutes to deal with my email because I conduct a lot of business through email. At the end of my day, I check my phone and email for the last time.

Multitasking and brain research

Excerpted from:
Change: How to Bring Real Change to Your Life: The Psychology and Secrets of Highly Effective People
By Philip Copitch, Ph.D. Hutzpah Press (2008)

When it comes to the common understanding of the human brain, the public is confused. At least once a month someone tells me, "You only use 10 percent of your brain." That's simply wrong. We use all of our brain.

Weekly, a teenager in my office tells me that they are great at multitasking. This same teen tends to be a solid "D" student.

The reality is that the brain cannot multitask.[4][5][6] The brain can only focus on one activity at a time. This may seem contrary to your experience. I

---

4 Rubinstein, Joshua S., David E. Meyer, and Jeffrey E. Evans. "Executive Control of Cognitive Processes in Task Switching." Journal of Experimental Psychology: Human Perception and Performance 27.4 (August 2001): 763.

5 Stoet, Gijsbert. "Pay attention!" Psychology Review 13.1 (Sept 2007):19-21.

6 Stoet, G. & Snyder, L.H. (2007). "Extensive practice does not eliminate human switch costs." Cognitive, Affective, & Behavioral Neuroscience, 7(3), 192-197.

once saw a clown juggle while playing a harmonica. You are reading, and breathing, and digesting, and scanning your environment for new sounds. All that is brain multitasking. But, the brain cannot pay attention to two things at one time. For example, do homework and watch TV. The TV may be good background noise for you to study by, but if you know what is going on, on the TV, you are watching TV. If you know what is going on with your homework, you are doing homework. The learning part of your brain is an amazing single task organ.[7] [8]

When a person is "multitasking" the brain takes a few hundredths of a second to switch to the next task that it then focuses on. Each refocusing takes a few hundredths of a second. That is very fast, but it has its drawbacks. If the refocusing uses different parts of the brain, then each switch also means that the brain needs to re-access the rules for dealing with each task. The part of your brain that you use for math is different than the part used for feelings. Often, it takes minutes to get back up to speed when switching between intensive tasks. If this isn't inconvenient enough, your memory also gets affected.

One evening, my wife and I were cooking dinner together and having a very pleasant conversation. Our five-year old son ran into the kitchen and interrupted us. He excitedly exclaimed, "On Tuesdays you get mashed potatoes and aardvarks!" He laughed in our general direction and ran off.

We looked at each other and attempted to go back to our pleasant conversation. Neither of us could recall what we had been talking about. We both knew we were enjoying the conversation, but never remembered what we were talking about. Our son's forced refocusing of our attention wiped out both of our working (short-term) memories.[9] [10] [11] (Kids have that effect on their parents.)

If you are switching between known tasks, like washing the dishes, listening to the radio, and watching the kids do their homework in the next

---

7 Duncan, John J., Jr., and Adrian M. Owen. "Common regions of the human frontal lobe recruited by diverse cognitive demands." Trends in Neurosciences 23.10 (Oct 2000):475.

8 Stoet, G. & Snyder, L.H. (2007). "Task-switching in human and non-human primates: Understanding rule encoding and control from behavior to single neurons" In S.A. Bunge and J.D. Wallis (Eds.), pp. 227-254. The Neuroscience of Rule-Guided Behavior. Oxford University Press.

9 Tulving, E., & Watkins, M. J. Structure of memory traces. Psychological Review, 1975, 82, 261-275.

10 Bobrow, S. A., & Bower, G. H. Comprehension and recall of sentences. Journal of Experimental Psychology, 1969, 80, 55-61.

11 Craik, F. I. M., & Tulving, E.. (1972). Depth of processing and the retention of words in episodic memory. Journal of Experimental Psychology: General, 104, 268-294.

room; you can easily switch focus from task to task. But, if you are trying to learn something new, like how to calculate mortgage amortization while listening to the radio, and watching the kids do their homework in the next room, you're setting yourself up to do each poorly. Also, you are likely to become short tempered.

Return calls and email in bunches

I recommend that you deal with the phone and email in batches. I find that I can get a lot done in 15 minutes. All things being equal, I like to use email. So, whenever possible, I use it. When it comes to email the clock is not that controlling. I can respond at 2 P.M. or 2 A.M. without bothering anyone. I tend to be in my office late, so I often have an issue of "when do people go to bed?"

My rule of thumb is, if it needs to be dealt with in the next 2 minutes-call. If it needs to be done today-email.

I have noticed that when someone calls, the reason for the call is the third thing they say.

1. "Hi Dr. Phil this is Eustace Tilley."
2. "How are you doing?"
       "Marvelously, may I help you?"
3. "I was wondering if…"

When it comes to email. We get to skip directly to number three. This saves time, which I have very little of. However, I have noticed one major drawback to email. If you request multiple tasks, often only one will get accomplished.

To help with this I started numerically listing what I wanted:

There are three parts to this task:
1. xxxxxxxx
2. yyyyyyyy
3. zzzzzzzz

Please apprise me as each part is accomplished.

I have noticed if I get past three specific requests in one email, balls start to get dropped.

It is common to leave off the greeting and the closing to email. I do not allow myself to do that. My email always start with "Hi Joe," or "Dear Jane," and I close with "Thank you," or "Be well,". I see it as the base of common courtesy. I receive responses to email where the answer is in the subject line and the email is blank. I recommend against this because it seems rude, but more importantly, it can lead to confusion.

When responding to an email, it is helpful to indicate what you are specifically responding to. Most email programs will set this up for you when you hit the email reply button by giving you a new email window starting with:

> On Feb. 13, 2009, at 10:52 AM, Eustace Tilley wrote:

> Followed by a copy of the email highlighted and indented.

You can also cut and paste a part of a longer email, followed by your answer.

A few warnings about email:

- Your email will be stored somewhere forever. Do not email any message you would not like quoted in open court.
- It is common, and often recommended by counselors, to write a letter that you would never send to help you emote or cope with your feelings. This is a great idea, but not in an email program. Twice this year I have been told by astonished individuals that they accidentally sent an emotive email instead of deleting it. (One was an entrepreneur cussing out her boss.)
- Humor can be dangerous in email form. Be very, very careful.
- No matter how careful you are, someone will take offense at something they misunderstood or took out of context. Be prepared to apologize.
- Discuss no confidential patient, client, or employee information by email unless you understand and use a secure server.
- If sending a picture, keep the file size small. 5k to 30k is nice. If you send a huge picture, 250k or larger, it will be a bugger to download, and the recipient will not appreciate you.

A few helpful hints about returning batch phone calls:

- Be prepared before you call. Have your information organized and in front of you. Write out the questions you need answered and tick them off as they are. A two minute call can become a ten minute call if you have to look for something.

- If you are calling back customers in batches, you will often have numerous files in front of you. Only open one at a time. Avoid compromising the files. A misplaced paper can become an unnecessary liability.
- When leaving a message, protect confidentiality. Do not assume that a message machine is private. You do not want a child, roommate, parent, or spouse learning something confidential from your message.
- Use a quality headset. Over the course of time your neck will thank you.
- Keep track of your calls. You will drive yourself nuts trying to remember if you called or didn't. Log calls appropriately.
- Avoid using the hold button. If you must, 20 seconds is the maximum. After 20 seconds, the person on hold starts to notice, and often becomes resentful. It is better to call someone back rather than to put them on hold.
- At the beginning of the call, set the stage: "I don't mean to be rude, but I only have three minutes before my next appointment. How may I help you?"
  - I find that people are very understanding of my request.
  - If the call will take longer than say, 5 minutes, I set a phone appointment so I can assist the person appropriately.
- If I am initiating the call, I always start off by asking if this is a good time for them :
  "Hi Mr. Bogg, this is Dr. Phil, is this a good time for me to interrupt you?"

By asking permission, I am showing respect for the person I am calling. If this is not a good time, I ask if we can set a phone appointment. Again, my mother's insistence on manners has served me well.

I do not mix business with pleasure. If after we are done with the business of the call, a colleague wants to chat, I politely suggest, "We need to catch up, want to buy me lunch next week?"

A chutzpah professional does not take away from the money making part of the day for personal time. When I am at work, I stay focused on work. Conversely, when I am playing, I do not think of work.
- If I have to leave a message with a person, I control the conversation with the following statements:
  "Do you mind taking a written message?"
  "Thanks, do you have paper and a pen?"

I leave a short message. Always saying my phone number slowly twice. Then I ask,
  "Do you mind reading that back to me?"
- Switch from phone to email if appropriate.

"That sounds exciting Barry, if you don't mind, can we go over the particulars by email?"

I like to keep control of the movement of a project. So I offer to initiate the email correspondence.

"Give me your email address and I'll send one to you right away. That way I'll make sure I have your email address in my computer correctly."

By taking responsibility for the next action, I know it will get done. I have no control over anyone else, so hoping that they will keep the ball rolling is a giant chutzpah mistake.

A few helpful hints about returning batch email:

- One aspect of email that I really like is that if I have to do the same task repeatedly, my computer will allow me to automate it. I have written nine books to date (You are reading number 10. Thanks!). So I get email daily concerning them. I read and answer every one. My goal is to answer my email the day it comes in. When I notice the same question popping up, I write a template answer and cut and paste it into the email reply. It is a written form of a 9-second speech.
- I recommend that you do not give any confidential information in an email.
- If you are setting or confirming an appointment, always write the day and the date, such as Monday, 02/06/02. The day will help catch if the date is wrong, or vice versa. Patients who normally come in on say, Thursday, often need a reminder if the date and the day have changed.

Email cross-marketing

Most email programs allow you to put predetermined text at the bottom of every email you send out. Most mail programs referred to them as signatures.

These signatures can be anything you want to make people aware of. You can have lots of signatures and change them depending on the email you are sending. Not only is this a great time saver, but brilliant chutzpah marketing as well.

Are you doing a talk? Add the contact information to a signature on all outbound email for the month prior to your date. Have a web site with amazing content? Put it in a signature!

A signature can also have graphics!

The sidebar is my basic email signature. Wherever my email goes, this advertisement goes with it. The graphics and the underlined words are hot linked. So, if someone clicks on a book in my signature, their computer automatically opens an Internet window and takes them to this book's page

at amazon.com. Google's free email service, Gmail, sends a signature promoting Gmail on every email. A link invites readers to try Gmail. This no-cost viral advertisement is one of the reasons that Google has more money than we do.

Note: These are tiny 2k graphics. I made them in Adobe PhotoShop specifically for quick web loading.

If you put a large graphic (10+k) into your signature the email will upload and download slowly and you will upset your recipient.

When developing your signature graphics you want to catch the eye, but be very careful that your graphic is minute (under 5k). Larger graphics will clog email servers, so many service providers will not

allow email greater than 100K total to pass through their system. Some service providers will simply strip the offending graphic and replace it with a broken link symbol (lk) while others will reject the email completely and send it back to you with a nasty system error or no spam note.

Gathering statistics

It is imperative that you know how people find you. Not just generally, but exactly. Most of this information is easily gathered at the first contact with a potential customer.

Ask the question:

"How did you find me/us?" (Then wait for an answer.)

"Thanks! I/we just like to keep track of how people find me/us."

I clearly log the answer in my phone message book. At the end of each week, I transfer the accumulated information to a running log. Because I have kept this information over the years, I know a lot about my market area.

The telephone transmits feelings

When you or your staff answer the phone it is a chutzpah imperative that the highest amount of professionalism be maintained.

Probably once a month someone on the phone will compliment me on my phone etiquette. I do not think this says as much about me as it does about how other businesses treat customers on the phone. Compassionate politeness should be the norm. Chutzpah politeness is what I choose to offer.

On my way into work today, I stopped by a pharmacy to buy some Sudafed. Because of the fact that a minuscule percent of our population use Sudafed to make methamphetamine, I had to wait in the pharmacy line to buy over-the-counter decongestant. While waiting, the phone rang and I watched the pharmacy assistant answer it. "Thank you for calling Longs, your neighborhood pharmacy, can you hold?" Instantly she placed the caller on hold. There was no way she heard the caller's answer.

Ten minutes went by until it was my turn, and another two minutes for my transaction, when I said in a low voice, "You left someone on hold."

"Oh my gosh," she said. "I forgot all about her."

When you, as a business owner, look at this situation you have to question if the statement, "Thank you for calling Longs, your neighborhood pharmacy" comforted the person on hold for twelve minutes. The pharmacy assistant was very polite to everyone I saw her have contact with, and I assume she truly made an honest mistake. But was it avoidable?

What are the phone policies of the pharmacy? Do they account for busy times with two lines of customers waiting to pick up medications? Are you supposed to get permission from the caller to put them on hold, or simply ask for permission?

The phone transmits feelings. To help transmit positive feelings, I recommend three basic rules before anyone in your company answers the phone.

1. Only trained personnel answer the phone.
2. Before the phone is answered the trained personnel places a huge smile upon their face.
3. Place a small mirror by the phone. While on the phone all trained personnel should check their face to make sure that they are presenting themselves as happy and professional.

I want the mirror neurons in our brains to fire positive neurochemistry.[12,13] Then, I want this positiveness transmitted through the phone line. I take this chutzpah seriously. When someone calls my office, I want them to know that my company works for them. I want them to know that they are important.

Anyone who answers your phone represents you

For those of us who are Star Trek fans, we understand the importance of first contact. In your shop, restaurant, or office, every contact is first contact. As a chutzpah marketer, I am always aware that my customer is constantly evaluating my services and then reevaluating them again.

If you are spending hundreds of dollars to have an amazing meal, wouldn't you scrutinize the taste, atmosphere, and service? And wouldn't you scrutinize through a filter of "damn this is expensive!"

You should expect your customers to do the same. If you consistently pass the test, they will tell lots of people, and that will be good for your business. Conversely, if you start to slip, they will tell even more people, and that will be bad for your business.

For example, in the last few pages I told tens of thousands of readers

12 Rizzolatti, G., Fogassi, L., & Gallese, V. (2006, November). MIRRORS IN THE MIND. (cover story). Scientific American, 295(5), 54-61.

13 Schulte-Rüther, M., Markowitsch, H., Fink, G., & Piefke, M. (2007, August). Mirror Neuron and Theory of Mind Mechanisms Involved in Face-to-Face Interactions: A Functional Magnetic Resonance Imaging Approach to Empathy. Journal of Cognitive Neuroscience, 19(8), 1354-1372.

about my pharmacy experience. But, I'm not as inclined to tell a story about routine, proper, phone etiquette.

Phone scripts keep your company consistent

In addition to the three rules already stated, chutzpah marketers use their phone wisely.

A chutzpah phone script is one form of the 9-second speeches that are provided to all personnel that answer your office phone. (A copy should be by each phone.[14]) Unlike the 9-second speech where the answer is personal to you, the chutzpah phone script is a collection of the best responses to common questions that are asked over the phone. If you answer your phone regularly, you probably know most of the questions. If not, you need to start a running log of questions prospects ask. Within no time you will have a decent list.

Please note: In this section I will discuss only questions associated with marketing, but you will also want to develop scripted answers associated with commonly asked business questions.

The goal is to quickly get to the answer you need while talking on the phone. There are three common ways to display your chutzpah script.

1. Print the questions and answers on three hole paper and place the paper in a binder. Organize the pages by common questions. Colored card stock may be helpful in locating questions in a hurry.
2. Print the questions and answers on 3" X 4" paper. Place the paper in an organized fashion in a clear 3" X 4" plastic sheet photo album. This way you will easily see six Q&A sheets per plastic page. This is also a good way to develop your scripts, allowing you to move parts around as you build your questions and answers.
3. The most professional display is to make a set of flip cards. Each topic card has commonly asked questions on it. Your employee simply flips to the topic and can see each question and answer. The pages are spiral bound and the number of pages is

---

14 I have developed phone scripts for, and with, a variety of professionals. These documents take a lot of man hours to develop. I know of two different times when the document was pilfered. One was stolen by an employee of a chiropractor and given to her boyfriend, a competing chiropractor. The second was liberated by a part-time attorney when he left to open up his own private office.

individualized to your needs. Each page is made of card stock so it will hold up for a long time. See below.

Chutzpah flip cards.

No matter the format, the goal is the same, to make it easy for whomever is authorized to answer the phone to represent your company well.

Whether you are a new company or a seasoned professional, I advise you to develop phone scripts. This way you will have the best answer at your finger tips when you are on the phone. In time, you will memorize your well developed scripts. But, given enough time, we all get sloppy and a refresher course is then only fingertips away.

Let's look at some common phone questions:
- What are your hours?
- Is the owner there?
- Are you hiring?
- What kind of certification/bonding/license do you have?
- Do you take Visa, Master Card, American Express… ?

- Do you accept checks?
- How long before you can help me?
- How much will it cost?

Avoid the hold button

The hold button should be avoided if at all possible. However, sometimes it is unavoidable. A few hints on how to use the hold button when it is unavoidable. By following these tips, your company will shine in customer service.

1. Do not answer the phone unless you have a few minutes to handle the call. Let the machine or service take the call if you are not in the frame of mind for customer service. Have the phone area conducive to helping callers - have paper, pens ready and keep the area free of clutter. Smile.
2. Always ask for permission, and wait to hear the answer. "May I put you on hold so I can get your file?"
3. Follow the 20 second rule. Never leave anyone unattended for over 20 seconds. People start to feel negative about your company at about 30 seconds. When you return to the caller, call them by name and thank them for their patience. "Hi Mr. Reredos, thank you for your patience…" By treating the caller's time with respect, you are showing care for the caller.
4. If your task will take more than 20 seconds, ask the caller if you can call them back in a few minutes. "It will take me a few minutes to research your question, may I call you back in less then ten minutes with the information you are requesting?" Then wait for an answer from the caller.
5. Just before you reestablish contact with the caller, smile. Remember, you are answering the phone to bring service to the caller. (The caller doesn't and shouldn't know that you spilled coffee on yourself while reaching for their file.)

As Vic, the extremely profitable gas station owner, taught us at the beginning of the chapter, the phone is directly connected to your customer's, and potential customer's wallets. How you use your phone and email, directly influences your company's bottom line.

9. EMBRACING THE MEDIA WITH A CHUTZPAH HUG

F.A.Q. I am frequently asked by other professionals, "How do you get on the news or quoted in the paper so much?" In this chapter I explain how to get "free" media attention. But, before I start I want to let you know up front that media attention is far from free. It doesn't cost money, but it does cost time.

Early in my career I did not know this, so I built relationships with on-air and print reporters. I found it fun to get interviewed. I enjoyed my very small amount of celebrity. Please let me explain the cost of "free" media.

I was invited onto *A.M. San Francisco* to participate in a panel discussion on child abuse and its influence on society. In the 1980s, *A.M. San Francisco*, the local morning news show, followed *Good Morning America* and was hosted by Fred LaCosse and Terry Lowry. It was a highly watched show as I was later to learn.

I got to the show early and went to make-up. The show was aired live from 9:00 -10:00 AM. It was sweeps week, and for days the issue of child abuse had been getting lots of attention from this ABC affiliate, KGO-TV. The first 45 minutes of the show was a serious look at the issue of child abuse. The last 15 minutes was more relaxed, a piece on the local firefighters' chili cook-off to raise funds for needed services.

Early on I was asked by Terry, "Give a brief overview of the 3 forms of child abuse." I happily explained that there were actually 4 forms of child abuse—physical, sexual, emotional, and institutional, and proceeded to quickly define each form. During the first commercial break, Terry told me that she liked my enthusiasm, and asked if I was up for more questions. I told her I was happy to oblige. Over the next thirty minutes I answered question after question. The hosts, or members of the audience, would start their question, "Dr. Copitch, what do you think about…" or "Dr. Copitch, would you explain…"

During the second commercial, Terry leaned over with kind words of encouragement. At that very moment the makeup lady sprayed a cloud of hair spray to control an errant hair on Terry's perfectly manicured coif. I got a mouthful of hair spray.

During the last 15 minutes of "my" part of the show, firefighters in the backstage area were heating their chili. The aroma was amazing. It quickly filled the studio. It didn't mix with the hair spray so well, but I happily answered questions, even as my mouth watered.

After the show there was a few minutes of congratulations and thanks for all involved. I had a flight to catch, and as I was leaving, another panelist from the show stopped me in the hall. She was furious with me and explained that I had hogged the spotlight and wasted her time. I tried to apologize, and explained that I just answered questions that were posed to me, but she wanted to hear nothing from me.

I left and went to the airport for a flight to the east coast. When I got seated, the elderly lady next to me was excited about the show she had just watched. As it turned out, the flight crew were avid viewers of *A.M. San Francisco* and were extra attentive throughout the flight. From San Francisco to New York, I was constantly questioned about family issues. People bought me drinks, even though I don't drink, and by time we hit the Midwest, the elderly lady next to me, who was happy to drink the free offerings, was feeling no pain. The last two hours she snored and drooled. It was a long flight.

When I returned from my trip, I found lots of invitations to be on other

TV and radio programs. I also got many letters. Some from inmates asking for my help for themselves or their children. Some from distraught parents wanting me to help them get their children back from Child Protective Services or the Foster Care system. I also received three letters from angry professionals that thought that I should have slipped in the name of their program.

The reason I tell you this story? For all the time and energy that show took, I got no new clients. Zero. Goose egg. Nada!

It is very important to know what you want out of your media appearances. I'm going to explain how to get media attention, but you must understand that you cannot control what the media does with you. If you purchase an ad in the paper, you have a lot of say about the presentation of your ad. But, if you are interviewed by a newspaper reporter you have no say about how you will show up in print. The same is true for TV and radio advertisements versus interviews.

The media doesn't owe you anything

I often consult with entrepreneurs who are upset that the media outlets in their community are not featuring their story often enough, or at all. Frequently, these complaints are due to unrealistic expectations of the local media role in our community.

It is imperative that you understand that the business of the media is to keep viewers or readers. The more viewers or readers, the more the media can charge for its commercial spots or advertising space. The basic goal of the media is to keep and expand their audience (market share). If your story will not help them do that, you will not get coverage.

This information is the key to your media success. You need to offer the media an eye capturing story that, in the chutzpah words of **The Godfather**, they can't refuse.

There has to be a Wow! factor to your story. Something that they can say just before going into commercial, or use as a headline, that makes the viewer or the reader say, "Wow, I want to know more!"

I once was tasked with the responsibility of organizing a charity softball game. It was an annual fundraiser that brought in a nice chunk of change. My goal was to sprinkle chutzpah onto a good fundraiser to make it even better.

In the past the softball teams were gathered from the public: local business playing local business. This was nice but generated little media attention. And without media attention, getting the word out about the event cost money (paid advertising). I changed the teams to San Francisco Bay Area police department softball teams and Bay Area media softball teams. It was great fun and garnered lots of media attention. We got lots of free publicity as well as fun rivalry. My favorite part of the whole event was when the Chief of Police from Fremont California, who graciously agreed to be the Chief Umpire, announced the rules at the beginning of the day long event. "The rules are simple," he bellowed from behind home plate. "The umpire is always right and the umpire is wearing a gun." It was great fun for all and no one argued with the umpire.

In addition to the "Wow Factor," it also helps if your Wow story is unique. If you have a great Wow story, but the same story was done 4 weeks ago, your Wow story becomes old news.

It becomes your job to make a Wow story.

Wilson was a retired entrepreneur who organized a small after school homework program at his church. He also was involved with a therapy program that took companion animals into nursing homes and hospitals. The companion pets were all adopted from the local animal shelter. By combining these two interests he got media attention for both charitable endeavors: the after school program and the local animal shelter.

Wilson organized a blanket drive at his local church. The kids in the after school program provided the muscle, by boxing and delivering the blankets to the animal shelter. This activity, underprivileged kids giving charity to sad eyed pets, was overflowing with "Wow." If the media had been invited to either one of the important daily activities of either charity program, I suspect there would have been no coverage.

It is important that you think of the visual of your media story. When planning an event, it is imperative that you show the story, not simply tell the story. Kids carrying boxes, and puppies with big eyes and damp noses, are a visual. Show don't tell.

Getting noticed as an expert by the media

Often professionals are surprised when I tell them that it is easy to get media attention. But it is! Everyday the editors of the newspapers and the producers of local TV and radio have a lot of space or time to fill. And once the paper is put to bed or the show is over, the process starts all over again. The media is hungry for interesting stories to tell.

Reporters tend to be ambitious professionals. They have high expectations for themselves and tend to work long hours with limited resources. This has become more true in the last five years. All media outlets are cutting back. Less money, less support staff, and less editorial staff. But, the newspaper still needs to be put to bed every night by 3:00 AM so it can be on news-stands at 6:00 AM. The news program needs to be ready for air every weekday at 5:30, 6:30 and 11:00 PM. And then again at 6:00 AM. In the news business the clock is always ticking and the clock is always the unforgiving enemy.

Every reporter has some sort of database where they keep track of their contacts. Reporters guard their contacts because it is a dog eat dog media world. Reporters keep their contacts broken down into subject categories such as, housing, emergency medical, mental health, or automobile repair. The reporters I know have hundreds of specific categories. If you got to look at these treasuries, you would see the unpublished contact numbers of politicians, doctors, lawyers, and the director of the waste management district.

Reporters like to have at least four numbers under each category. Let's say the reporter is doing a piece on the homeless sleeping on the benches in Municipal Park. After three days of constant interrupted writing the reporter is told by the editor, "Yeah, get a few quotes from someone concerning why the people are homeless!" The reporter has 24 minutes to finish the article and get back to the copy editor for proofreading.

Our mild mannered reporter goes back to her disheveled desk and gets back on the phone. She calls likely sources like the director of the local homeless shelter and the director of county mental health. She leaves messages. She knows she has 17 minutes. She starts racking her brain, who would know about why people are homeless? "I need a shrink!" she tells herself, and then checks that category in her database. She calls her local shrink source -me, on my back line. I answer it. She explains her predicament. I spout a few quotes. She thanks me and hangs up. The next day I am quoted in the paper, "There are many reasons why people are homeless, one major one that is not well understood, is the role of drug abuse and mental health disorders in our growing homeless population."

Was my quote earth shattering? No, but was it colorful, and maybe a little controversial, yep. Colorful and a little controversial will get you quoted in the media.

So, how did I get my back line phone number into the reporter's "experts" database?

I asked her to put me there, kind of

The best way to get into a reporter's database is to have short contacts with her over a few months. Remember, reporters are very busy, and you don't want to waste their time, not even a few seconds.

Read the local section of your newspaper. Over the course of a week or two, you will be able to get a list of the reporters that "need" quotes from you. To begin, pick one of these.

Once you have read a few articles, drop her a written note commenting on a recent one. "I found your article on the volunteers at the Human Society warm and inspirational. Thanks for your concern for the common person who makes our community so vibrant and caring." Add your card.

A few weeks later, comment on another article. A few weeks later, do it again. After four or five notes to the reporter, add to your normal note, "If I could be of any help in your work, please feel free to contact me. My private contact number is: 123-1234." This time add your business card, and your business brochure - if you have one.

I have been called after the first note, I simply lucked out and filled a reporter's needs. "I received your kind note today Dr. Copitch. Thank you very much, I really appreciated it. If you have a minute, can I tell you about an article I am writing on…"

I have also had reporters call and ask if they can give my name to another reporter. "He's doing a piece on children and pets, do you mind if I give him your contact number?" I have found over the years, that reporters are very respectful of my contact number. I have never had my back line number or cell phone number used inappropriately by a reporter.

Getting press will get you more press

Once you get known as a professional who is easy and quick to work with, you will get lots of attention. Earlier, I told you about getting called for a quote concerning homeless people in Municipal Park.

A few months later, a reporter called my office wanting to interview me concerning a local issue. When I asked how she got my name, she said, "I searched the paper's database. I liked your quotes on the homeless."

If a reporter has too few contacts in any particular category of her database, she will search her own paper as well as the competition and add you to her database. Getting press gets you more press. I have even had a reporter confess to finding my name in the Yellow Pages. She wanted a quote concerning children and the importance of sleep; she was minutes away from going to press and was frantic. I had to wait until the paper came out to find out what her name was.

Controversy sells

At this point you may think to yourself, "Dr. Phil, what a kiss ass!" Please allow me to assure you that I am often referred to as a "pain" but never as a "kiss." Keep in mind I was building a relationship with a reporter whose work I liked. If I didn't like the reporter's work, I wouldn't have continued reading her articles in the first place. Remember, I have chutzpah, I don't waste time lightly.

There are times to be opinionated. When it comes to the media, the correct time and place is in the Op-Ed section of the newspaper or broadcast.

Traditionally in newspapers, the Op-Ed page was printed opposite the editorial page. Over time, Op-Ed has been generalized to being *another point of view*, not necessarily an opposite point of view to the editorial point of view. Depending on the paper, there may be a clear editorial point of view, for example, clearly right leaning or clearly left leaning. Most smaller newspapers tend to be very pro local community. They may tell the national story on the front page, but they know that to sell papers they need to extoll the virtues of the local community.

If you read an article that you disagree with, it is perfectly OK to write a letter to the editor and criticize the article. For the purpose of chutzpah marketing, I advise you to follow a few rules.

- Complain about the facts of the article, not the reporter or the newspaper.
- Avoid inflammatory comments, clearly present your opposing opinion.
- Do not exaggerate to prove your point, that will get you labeled a crack pot and keep you from being published.
- Give clear facts which you have based your opinion on, if you have them.
- End your letter cordially, "Thank you for the opportunity to voice my opinion. I appreciate that the (name of paper) encourages thought and conversation."

When your letter to the editor is printed, drop a nice thank you note to the editor. After the third letter to the editor is printed, add to your nice note, "If I could be of any help in your editorial work, please feel free to contact me. My private contact number is: 123-1234." This time add your business card and a business brochure if you have one.

Once I read an article in the newspaper concerning date rape. This is a pet peeve of mine, I find the label "date rape" inappropriate. So I wrote a letter to the editor, following the rules above, and voiced my opinion. "Date rape is a misnomer, it is simply and more accurately, rape."

A few days later, a reporter from the paper called wanting to do a story on the controversy concerning the term "Date Rape."

The following week, I was interviewed by the local TV news concerning the "controversy." The first question from the television reporter was, "Do you think that by calling sexual assault between people that are dating, date rape, it makes it harder for the victim to get help?" As we discussed before, the media "steal" from each other. Once you get press, you tend to get more press.

For months after the article and news story, I was told by a colleague that they couldn't hear the term "date rape" without cringing.

Don't confuse editorial coverage with advertisement

Please allow me to share this admonition. At some point if you advertise at all you will want more for your advertising loyalty than just your ad. You may find yourself saying, half jokingly to the ad sales person, "Are you guys ever going to do a story on my _____?"

If you are dealing with a legitimate news establishment, the sales person will laugh it off and gently teach you that the ad department and the news department are completely separate. If you voice it to an editor, let's say at a party, "I advertise a lot with your paper, how come you haven't done a story on my _____?" The editor may bite your head off. (Editors have a reputation for being verbally combative.)

There are some "newspapers" that blur the line between ad content and news content. An example would be a monthly curricular that allows an article on flea care, written by a local veterinarian. The vet's advertisement directly follows the infomercial.

Before you participate in this type of enterprise, consider the reader's view of your info-article and subsequent advertisement. Even a well written article may make you look less professional. I also give this warning advice against producing ad copy that is made to look like a news story. I advise against spending money to make yourself look questionable, or even worse, unscrupulous.

Writing a press release

The process of writing a press release is easy, in a moment I will explain how to do it. The problem with a press release is getting the media to notice your press release.

There is no conspiracy, just simple numbers. The editor of the newspaper may get hundreds of press releases sent to her every day. In the old days, a press release would have to be mailed. Nowadays most media accept, and even encourage, email press releases. This encourages press releases from around the world.

The public relations engine of every medium to mega corporation is pumping press releases out all day, every day. If one happens to stick, great—free publicity. With email submissions, the cost of the release is almost zero.

Don't despair, you have chutzpah on your side so you can greatly increase your odds of getting noticed.

First, we will go over the common types of press releases: general and specific. Then I will explain the 4 rules you have to know to write a press release that will get noticed. Finally, I will show you a few press releases. You are a few minutes away from being a press release chutzpah star.

There are many different types of press releases. The major type of press release is called the General Press Release. The rest are simply variations on the general, depending on what you want the press release to do for you. They are all written about the same and there is no consistency in the public relations business on what the types are called. Actually, the names are irrelevant since you never need to label your press release with a name anyway.

A general press release is the workhorse of business to media communication. It is a simple format that allow businesses, profit and nonprofit, to give information to the press. Often this information is not great journalism. It is just information that a company or agency wants everyone to know about without having to pay for media space or air time. The media tends to call this information, filler. If there is room, they use filler to complete the paper or round off a TV or radio news show.

If you want to get your information into a specific part of the newspaper, say the **Weekly Business Journal**, a feature specific to your local paper, you will need to modify the general news release to mimic the format of your target. For example, if the **Weekly Business Journal** lists the comings and goings of middle and upper level employees in your community, you may wish to get recognition for your new hire.

What most people do not know, shush ... this is a secret ... the media will often print or read a press release exactly as you wrote it. This is why it is imperative that you study your target carefully. This is especially true for fillers, if your release mimics the media's style, you greatly increase your likelihood of being "picked up." Don't let the word "filler" hurt your feelings. The square inches in a paper that a fill takes up would cost you hundreds to thousands of dollars to buy. Plus, you can't buy it. Fillers go in the news part of the page, whereas all you and I can buy is ad space.

There are a 4 chutzpah press release rules that you must follow to maximize your effort:

1. Aim
2. Spell
3. Wow
4. Follow up

Aim

You have to aim your press release at the correct editor. I am not talking hand grenade type of aim, I am talking precision scalpel type of chutzpah aim.

Six months ago, when I outlined this chapter, my plan was to go to the Los Angeles Times web site and the Redding Record Searchlight web site and compare large city to small city newspaper editorial staff.[15] I wanted to reprint the complete list of the LA Times editorial staff to elucidate my point on the need to aim your press release precisely. The list was massive. Even when I changed the font to 6 point, super tiny, the LA times editorial list filled seven pages. I tend to like to *Show Not Tell*, but seven pages is too much. However, it does prove the need for the precision aim of your press release. If it goes to the wrong person, it will be lost forever.

The next question is, which editor is the correct editor for you to aim your press release at? We will cover this under #3 Wow.

Spell

When your press release gets to the editor's office it has to be sorted. The first sort is the one you can protect yourself from.

Many editors believe if you do not know where you are sending your press release, you can be ignored. Thus, it is common for the first sort to be the name and title you address your press release to. Make sure you spell the editor's name and her title correctly.

> Bod Smith, city editor, is not the same as Bob Smith, City Editor.

---

15 To see the complete list:
http://www.latimes.com/services/newspaper/mediacenter/la-mediacenter-editorialstaff,0,1090476.story

You want to make it through the first culling, spelling counts!

Wow

Congratulations, your press release is in front of the correct pair of eyes. An assistant to the editor or producer, commonly an intern, is reading your work. You have seconds to Wow her or your press release will be tossed in the circular file or deleted from the assistant's computer.

No pressure, all you have to do is get her interest, get her to pass your information onto the editor. You have to Wow!

This is where your chutzpah training comes in. When you develop your press release you do it the same way you did your business card, ad copy, and 9 second speeches. You write your copy speaking to the editor's needs. Not your needs, her needs. You solve problems for the editor. You help her put out an amazing newspaper or news program that will help her get market share and the recognition of her peers.

When writing Wow copy you need to solve the reader's needs. If you are aiming to get your press release in the city section of the paper, pump up the local, city angle of your release. If you are aiming for the business section of the paper, extoll the local business angle.

For example, when I write a press release for the book you are holding in your hands, I will tailor it to the editor's needs.

City editor:

Dr. Copitch's book, **Small Business Chutzpah Marketing: Simple and Low Cost Ways to Build a Fortune**, was written in northern California. When asked why, Dr. Copitch said, "My wife and I moved to Redding to raise our family: with good schools, amazing vistas, and a low crime rate it was ideal for us. After living here for over 20 years, we can't imagine living anywhere else."

Business editor:

As the economy forces every small business to maximize productivity, Dr. Copitch's latest book, **Small Business Chutzpah Marketing: Simple and Low Cost Ways to Build a Fortune**, shows small business owners how to compete in an ever changing business environment.

When asked why he wrote **Small Business Chutzpah Marketing: Simple and Low Cost Ways to Build a Fortune**, Dr. Copitch said, "By taking my training in psychology and my understanding of business, I knew I could teach others how to have great success in business. This is good for the business owner, their family, and their community. After thirty years of experience I finally tell all the secrets of how to market a small business."

When writing your press release make sure you "show" how the article or interview can be presented. Give it your Wow slant!

I have had editors and reporters "lift" my quotes right off the press release and place it in their article. It is common that the questions from a TV reporter will lead you directly into the quote that they have read in your press release.

"Well Dr. Copitch, why did you choose to write your latest book in Redding, California?"

"With your training in psychology and thirty years of experience in business, do you have secrets to share about how to market a small business?"

This doesn't mean the reporter is lazy. It means that she liked the Wow slant.

Follow up

A few days after you have mailed or emailed your press release you need to call the editor's office and follow up.

Remember, editors are busy. The reason for your call is to confirm that they got your release. Don't waste their time, just simply ask, "Good morning, this is Dr. Philip Copitch, I sent you a press release concerning my new book. Did you get it?"

Then answer any question the editor may have. Do not ask another question. You need to truly respect the editor's time. Editors are under astronomical time sensitive pressure.

If the editor says, "No, haven't seen it yet." You politely say, "I understand you must be very busy. Would you like me to send you another copy?"

If he says "Yes," you say, "I'll be happy to. Goodbye." Then softly hang up the phone. You then send another copy by express mail ($10), directly to the editor. On the outside of the envelope write, "As requested via phone at 10:42 AM" and the date.

If the editor says, "I haven't had a chance," you say, "Thank you for your time, sorry to interrupt your day. Bye." Then softly hang up the phone.

I understand that this is difficult for most people. You are having to verbalize, "Pick me, please, please, please, pick me!" But with such chutzpah comes great rewards.

As you read these conversations, I want you to understand the editor's world. You may be the only polite and respectful voice she has heard in hours. It is not uncommon for editors to get cussed at or have the phone slammed down in their ear. You were even aware of that, and placed the phone on the cradle gently. (Not a problem with cell phones.) You were pleasant to have contact with. You respected the editor's time. Personally, I think your kindness should be normal. However, your kindness is <u>abnormal</u>, making it the exception. This makes you stand out in a positive light.

I have been thanked by reporters and editors for my phone etiquette. This actually says more about society than it does me. My mother would not have expected anything less.

The parts of a press release

A press release has the following parts. The order counts, you want to put the information the editor, reporter or production assistant is looking for where they expect to find it.

Date:
This is the date you would like the information to be made public. It is common to write in all caps, FOR IMMEDIATE RELEASE if that is what you want. (12 point Times[16], plain text.)

If you are attempting to get attention for a big event, you may need to start a month ahead of time to land a feature article. It is common that there are press releases at different stages of an upcoming event. Sometimes, even after the event to generate a mention about crowd size, or tax dollars generated, or who won the grand prize in the drawing at your wonderful event.

Contact:
This is the contact information. Give the company's name, the spokesperson's name, their position along with their business address, phone number

---

16 Why Times? Because it is easy to read and a common font found on most computers.

and email address. (If you have a professional web site, give that information also.)[17] This phone number must be answered. If the reporter calls, she wants to talk now. People in the media are <u>always</u> on deadline. If your name is not easy to pronounce, help them out with a pronunciation key. For example, Dr. Philip Copitch (like a police officer with poison oak, cop itch) or (cop·itch). (12 point Times, plain text.)

If you are granting interviews, giving a press conference, or promoting an event, a brief overview of that information also goes here. You will have room to expand on this information in the supportive information later in your press release.

Title:
This is your proposed title for the article or interview.(12 point Times, bold text.)

Sub title:
This is a short compelling statement that supports the title. (12 point Times, bold text.)

Supporting information in paragraph form
In this section you give a few snappy paragraphs supporting the title. Don't be modest. Start with your best idea, then your second best, and so on. Make sure you answer the who, what, where, when, and why questions. Reporters in all forms of media are trained to answer the who, what, where, when, and why's of every story.

Paint pictures with your words, clearly explaining the <u>benefits</u> to the reporter's audience.

At the end of your press release you need to indicate that you are done. By placing three pound symbols (###) at the bottom of your press release you are letting the reporter know that she has all your information. This as a quick way to let the reporter know that she hasn't misplaced the next page.

Sample press releases

This first example is a press release requesting a feature story. It may also get picked up as a filler:

---

17 A reporter will always check on a source. It is common for them to Google the company and the spokesman. If you do not have an impressive web presence, you should. See the accompanying white paper, Chutzpah Web Site Marketing for Professionals.

FOR IMMEDIATE RELEASE

Name of Editor, media name (triple check spelling and title.)

Sensei Sheryl Hager, 6th degree black belt
School Head
Redding Jujitsu Academy, Inc.
3092 Bechelli Lane
Redding, CA 96002
(530) 223-2435

Interviews with Professor Carr are available by calling: _____.

Lively photo opportunities are available with diverse classes: pre-school children, elementary age children, and adults. All classes are co-ed.

LOCAL MARTIAL ARTS INSTRUCTOR EARNS NATIONAL HONOR

PROFESSOR JANE CARR, FIRST WOMAN TO BE SO HONORED

REDDING, CA — Redding Martial Arts Instructor inducted into National Martial Arts Hall Of Fame.

Professor Jane Carr of Redding was inducted into the Danzan Ryu Jujitsu Hall of Fame for her 45 years of dedication to teaching martial arts throughout the United States. Professor Carr is the first woman ever to be honored by the Danzan Ryu Jujitsu Hall of Fame.

Established in 1991, the Danzan Ryu Jujitsu Hall of Fame honors those individuals, living and deceased, who have made significant contributions to the Jujitsu community of the United States of America. Inductees to the Hall of Fame are selected without regard for organizational affiliation, rank or title.

Professor Carr is an 8th degree black belt who presently sits on the Governing Board of the American Judo and Jujitsu Association, the nation's largest Danzan Ryu organization established in 1958. She is a sought after instructor and Jujitsu ambassador propagating the spirit and science of martial arts throughout the country.

Throughout her four-decade carrier, Professor Carr has been dedicated to maintaining martial arts traditions while opening doors for all Americans in the international Jujitsu community. Professor Carr has been teaching martial arts at Redding Jujitsu Academy for over 40 years. The Redding school was established in 1961. The RJA is a nonprofit organization.

###

This press release is a typical filler:

FOR IMMEDIATE RELEASE

Malcom Forbes, Business Editor
Anderson Business Review

Robert Thompson
Managing Editor
Radcliff Lillie Publishing House
1 Radcliff Lillie Drive
Redding CA 96001
(530) 555-1298

KATELL FILLS SENIOR EDITOR'S POSITION

GERALDINE KATELL JUMPS FROM REGARM HOUSE TO RADCLIFF LILLIE
PUBLISHING HOUSE

REDDING, CA — In what was seen as a board room coup d'état, prize winning editor, Geraldine Katell, has accepted the position of Senior Editor at Radcliff Lillie Publishing House. Contract details were not disclosed.

Geraldine Katell, best known for her ability to develop talent, is expected to bring well known authors to her new publishing house.

This press release is aimed at a specific location, the Business Happenings log in a specific newspaper. This press release mimics the style of the short business blurb that is typical of this section.

The future of press releases

The future is now. With the 24 hour news cycle and the lower cost of digital video, chutzpah press releases are going high tech.

 If you want to get attention for an activity that is visual in nature, for example a non profit martial arts school, you can add excitement to your press release with a small video clip.
This is simple to do. With a quality video camera ($250 and up), take exciting footage of your activity. Edit this down to :30 to

:60 seconds (no more than 5 minutes) of amazing footage and upload it to You-Tube (http://www.youtube.com/). It gets stored there for free.

All you need to do now is add the link to your chutzpah footage to your press release. If the editor is interested, one click and you're showing moving pictures inside your press release. If you are over 25, this may sound complicated or even hard. But it isn't. YouTube will teach you how (http://www.youtube.com/youtubeonyoursite):

> Whatever presence you have on the Internet—a large website, a blog, a social network page, or pretty much anything else—there are many ways to integrate YouTube into it. From simple video embeds, to our full-powered APIs, you can integrate video at all levels of technical expertise.

> The Basics
> • How do I add a video to my blog or web page?
> • How do I add a playlist to my blog or web page?
> • How do I add a video to my social network page?

The same process that you used to add video content to your blog or web site, works for your email press release. If your subject is visual, this is your press release future. And don't forget, YouTube is completely free!

Want my opinion?

After you have gone through the process of developing your press release I would be happy to give your copy a free once over. Send it to me by Email PDF attachment. Please don't send me 10's of pages. Please limit yourself to 2 or 3 of your best.

Email: DrPhil@CopitchInc.com

> The smallest act of kindness is worth more than the grandest intention.
>
> Oscar Wilde

"Oh ... I motivate the kids by waking them up early and
telling them that they can't pee until their chores are all done."

10. GETTING YOUR STAFF AND FAMILY INTO CHUTZPAH MARKETING

A common business saying[18] is:

A camel is a horse designed by a committee.

Which means that even with the best of intentions, often a group can lose track of its goal.

Over the years, I have worked with a lot of mom and pop owned companies where both Mom and Pop are entrepreneurs, doctors, or lawyers. More often, I have worked with an individual professional and a passel of family support

---

18 Proceedings Regular Meeting, Ohio Valley Transportation Advisory Board, Pacific Northwest Advisory Board, 1952 pg. 24:
"A camel is a horse designed by a committee, so we hope that this committee will—and I think it will—function appropriately."

staff. Typically, a family member runs the reception area, bookkeeping, or accounts receivable part of the company.

In both situations, the company can grow and thrive as long as the business plan is followed.

The biggest problem with most family run companies is that they do not develop, and follow, a chutzpah business plan. They have the best of intentions, but feelings get in the way. Often family members present feeling and/or opinion as fact and derail the business goal before it is even started. Other times, family members use the business as a fix for family conflicts.

Dr. Tom Marrow called and wanted an urgent get-together. "I need your help right away, my daughter is killing my business." Tom and I had developed a solid business plan about a year prior, so I was curious about how his business was "being killed."

When we got together, he showed me the books. He was so upset he was fighting tears. The books were miserable, income had steadily dropped off over the last six weeks. This six week observation is typical. Usually, it takes about this long for a change to show up in the books, whether positive or negative.

"So Bob," I asked, "what changed about six weeks ago?"

Bob grabbed his stomach and leaned back in his chair, "I hired Elizabeth!"

"Your daughter?" I said. "To do what?"

"She is supposed to be calling the next day's patients and confirming their appointments," he said as he slumped further into his desk chair.

"And?" I asked.

"She says she has been doing it, but I don't think she has. She shows up when she wants and…"

"When is she suppose to be here?" I asked.

He sat up, "Now actually."

"Great, where is she?" I asked.

"Ah…," he fumbled with his pen. "She came in a half hour ago and took $20 out of the cash drawer and went to Starbucks."

"What's going on Tom?" I asked.

"She owes her mother and me $6800 for damage to the car, so I'm trying to teach her responsibility."

As it turned out, Tom's back office staff was one person short due to maternity leave. Tom and the office manager were spreading the work among the other employees. When the car problem arrived, it seemed like a good idea to give Elizabeth the re-care call job. The problem was that Elizabeth was not qualified to do the job. After $18,000 in lost income, Tom had to fire Elizabeth.

The biggest problem with employees (and family members) is that they are people.

Change is difficult for employees

WARNING REALITY CHECK AHEAD: Most businesses that reinvent themselves, and strive towards being professional and profitable, will lose many of their employees during the first year.

The reason is, the employees were comfortable doing things the old way. They came in, did their work, and went home. Every two weeks they got their paycheck. The employee may have asked for a raise, but they were not asking for change. The owner of the company was motivated toward change. This motivation was probably because her paycheck was too small, and her hours were too long. Remember, everybody: employees, vendors, and the tax man get paid first. The owner gets whatever is left.

Employees and family members have different motivations than the owner.

I tell business owners regularly, "You are not a real adult until you have had to make a payroll during a bad quarter." It is lonely at the top.

It is lonely at the top

One nice thing about being the boss is that you are the boss. One really bad thing about being the boss, is making yourself follow the business plan.

Let me tell you another story about the six week rule.

I was contacted by the secretary at a large wellness clinic. I had not worked with this group for over five years, and was startled to find out that they were hemorrhaging money.

When I was escorted into the owner's office, I was surprised to see him dressed as a sea captain: white shorts, white shirt, and a captain's hat.

"I just got here myself," he said as he shook my hand. "Glad you could come in on such short notice."

He walked me over to a wall in his office and started explaining the pictures.

"Isn't it a beauty?" he said, pointing to the center picture of a huge boat.

For the next ten minutes he pointed out boat parts and tossed nautical jargon at me. I had no idea what he was talking about.

Finally I interrupted him, "I thought there was a problem, what's going on?"

Over the next hour, Dr. Magellan ran down a litany of concerns. We looked over the profit and loss statements, and scrutinized receivables. Then Dr. Magellan looked at me and said bluntly, "How come your business plan ain't working anymore?"

"How long have you had the yacht?" I asked.

"I ordered it about two years ago, just got it delivered last month."

As it turned out, the captain and his wife had spent most of the last six weeks enjoying their new dream boat and hiring a staff of five to maintain it. That is all fine and dandy, but the captain's wife had abandoned her post. Madge was an amazing lady, she worked for a government agency as a comptroller, and managed the books for the captain at night and on the weekends.

For twenty years, as they grew the business, Madge had tenaciously billed everybody.

After a little investigation, Madge figured out the problem. No one was reconciling the dailies. The wellness clinic was running smoothly, but the receivables were not being logged correctly, so they didn't show in the receivables column. Since they weren't in the receivables column, no billing statements were being mailed. Thus, the only income was from the computerized insurance claims. The business income was down almost fifty percent.

I have seen this type of problem a lot. When the business has matured and is finally bringing in real money consistently, the owner starts what I call an "I deserve" project.

An "I deserve" project can be building a dream home, extensive traveling, painting, woodworking or an affair. All the energy that used to go into the business, is now going elsewhere, and as a result the business suffers.

So beware of the "I deserve" project. Remember, as the owner you are the number one employee, cheerleader, and all around bottle washer.

If they could do it they would be your competition.

Employees need constant nurturing. When I say this to business owners many argue, "Not if you hire the right employee."

This sounds good, but I haven't seen it in the real world. Employees need constant support and training. They need motivation and reminders. If they didn't they would be your competition.

It is the responsibility of the business owner to give a foundation to the business. When this isn't understood, major problems occur.

Please allow me to share an example. I will often suggest to a entrepreneur that they keep close control of the receivables. If a customer is past due, action should be taken to correct the lack of payment professionally. When I suggest the best way to rectify payment issues is to contact the patron personally and ask for payment, many entrepreneurs respond with, "Yeah, that sounds like a good idea. We should implement a plan. I will have the receptionist call outstanding customers, Ah… every Friday?"

When I suggest, "How about you call any customer who is ten days overdue?" many entrepreneurs have lots of reasons not to make that call. You may be thinking of some of them right now.

Because you are the boss, it is easy to pass the job onto someone else. That doesn't always mean that it is passed on to the correct person.

It is lonely at the top.

Staff and family should be your best cheerleaders

Your goal should be to make it easy for your staff and family to refer patients into your company.

Dr. Hanson, my friend the dentist, thought nothing of saying, "Open up, let's take a look," to people he ran into. He peered into mouths at restaurants, or while waiting in line at Costco. Once, while waiting in line for popcorn at the movies, he explained to me, why a lady's back molar was so troublesome.

This middle aged woman contorted herself so he could peer way back, and she held that position while he showed off his work to me. Then he said, "You should call my office first thing Monday, I need to take a better look at that." The woman went off to the movie feeling well cared for by her dentist.

After she left, Dr. Hanson said with a twinkle in his eye, "Those Milk Duds cost her a thousand dollars, her bridge will have to be rebuilt."

In this situation, the dentist self referred.

Theoretically, staff and family members should be referral sources for your company. If a dentist's wife hears that her friend's sister has a toothache, she can simply say, "She should go to see my husband." This suggestive referral is comfortable for all concerned.

Help with the name game

Encourage your staff and family to shout the name of your company from every corner of your community. A few ways to encourage this:

4. Ask. It may sound simple, but simply asking staff and family to talk about where they work will get your name out.

5. Give each employee their own personal chutzpah business card with all of your company information, along with their name and job title.

6. Teach staff and family 9-second speeches about your company.

   • "I am the office manager for AAA Plumbing. If you ever need a plumber give me a call, I'll take good care of you." (Two cards are handed out.)

   • "My husband is a doctor who specializes in pain management. Here is his card in case you would like to contact him." (Two cards are handed out.)

   • While waiting on line at the grocery store, "Excuse me, I couldn't help but overhear, (as you hand cards to the woman in front of you) I work for a Tehama Bridal. Our web site has lots of information concerning weddings and such. There's lots of information, and it's all free." (Two cards are handed out.)

   • When you are involved in a public event, give copies of the event flier to each staff and family member. Ask for help: "Could you give these fliers out to your friends and family? I'd love for them to attend.

   • If the event is public and fun, you may wish to add an incentive for the employees.

5. Name tags and company imprinted shirts and/or hats.

 One entrepreneur I worked with liked having low cost raffles at public events. (Health fairs, book readings.) Her goal was to capture potential customers' home addresses. She would raffle off an item worth around fifty dollars. (A nice radio or lunch for two.) Her employees were encouraged to write their name on free raffle tickets that they could distribute to friends before the event. The employee with the most returned tickets also got a prize (Paid lunch for two or Friday afternoon off with pay). As her company grew, she started to offer first, second, and third employee prizes. She kept the whole thing very uplifting and fun.

Chutzpah show and tell

The enthusiasm for your company must flow from you to your staff and family. You are the leader, and as the leader, your staff and family look to you for social interaction cues.

This may sound basic, but it is a fact often missed by professionals I work with. If you walk around with your shoulders slumped, your staff will emulate you. If you smile when you answer the phone, your staff will see that as normal and copy you. If you shine at public events, your staff will reflect your shine.

So, I share with you this professional admonition: Do not talk negatively about your company. You may say something as innocuous as, "Man, I hate the Yellow Page bill!" and your staff hears/feels, "I'm on a sinking ship… how will I pay my rent… what about summer camp for the twins? I can't afford to lose this job."

As the leader, "Blossom where you are planted."

"Not a bad turnout for our first."

11. CHUTZPAH PRESENTATIONS, SPEECHES, AND TRADE SHOWS

In this chapter we are going to look at using low cost presentations, speeches, and trade shows as a chutzpah company growth tool. I will focus on techniques for getting attention for you and your company or charity. Then I will teach you how to translate this attention into new customers.

When I bring this subject up in seminars I tend to look out onto a sea of bewildered faces. These are the faces of well seasoned business owners who are getting ready to hyperventilate. I imagine that they are thinking scary thoughts such as:

- "I tried a seminar once and it was a disaster, I lost thousands of dollars."
- "What if no one comes, how embarrassing."

- "I guess I would like to put on a seminar, but what would I talk about?"
- "I can't speak to a group!"

Relax, we'll talk and you'll see how to do it.

"I can't speak to a group!"

Glossophobia (speech anxiety or stage fright) is the fear of public speaking. Glossophobia comes from the combination of the Greek words, *glossa*, meaning tongue, and *phobos*, meaning fear or dread.

Mild to moderate forms of speech anxiety are very common. On a positive note, most adults can teach themselves to feel comfortable in the role of public speaker.

In the rest of this chapter I will assume that you are comfortable giving public talks. If this is not a fact for you, I highly recommend Toastmasters International. (www.toastmasters.org) I have seen many nervous speakers build solid skills in the encouraging environment of the Toastmasters club.

In their own words:[19]

What is Toastmasters?

No, we don't make toasters!

From a humble beginning in 1924 at the YMCA in Santa Ana, California, Toastmasters International has grown to become a world leader in helping people become more competent and comfortable in front of an audience. The nonprofit organization now has nearly 235,000 members in 12,036 clubs in 106 countries, offering a proven — and enjoyable! — way to company and hone communication and leadership skills.

Most Toastmasters meetings are comprised of approximately 20 people who meet weekly for an hour or two. Participants company and learn skills by filling a meeting role, ranging from giving a prepared speech or an impromptu one, to serving as timer, evaluator or grammarian.

---

19 http://www.toastmasters.org/MainMenuCategories/WhatisToastmasters.aspx

There is no instructor; instead, each speech and meeting is critiqued by a member in a positive manner, focusing on what was done right, and what could be improved.

Good communicators tend to be good leaders. Some well-known Toastmasters alumni include:

- Peter Coors, of Coors Brewing Company
- Debbi Fields, founder of Mrs. Fields Cookies
- Tom Peters, management expert and author
- Linda Lingle, Governor of Hawaii

---

10 Tips for Public Speaking

Toastmasters International

www.toastmasters.org

Feeling some nervousness before giving a speech is natural and even beneficial, but too much nervousness can be detrimental. Here are some proven tips on how to control your butterflies and give better presentations:

1. Know your material. Pick a topic you are interested in. Know more about it than you include in your speech. Use humor, personal stories and conversational language – that way you won't easily forget what to say.

2. Practice. Practice. Practice! Rehearse out loud with all the equipment you plan on using. Revise as necessary. Work to control filler words; Practice, pause and breathe. Practice with a timer and allow time for the unexpected.

3. Know the audience. Greet some of the audience members as they arrive. It's easier to speak to a group of friends than to strangers.

4. Know the room. Arrive early, walk around the speaking area and practice using the microphone and any visual aids.

5. Relax. Begin by addressing the audience. It buys you time and calms your nerves. Pause, smile and count to three before saying anything. ("One one-thousand, two one-thousand, three one-thousand. Pause. Begin.) Transform nervous energy into enthusiasm.

6. Visualize yourself giving your speech. Imagine yourself speaking, your voice loud, clear and confident. Visualize the audience clapping – it will boost your confidence.

7. Realize that people want you to succeed. Audiences want you to be interesting, stimulating, informative and entertaining. They're rooting for you.

> 8. **Don't apologize for any nervousness or problem** – the audience probably never noticed it.
>
> 9. **Concentrate on the message – not the medium.** Focus your attention away from your own anxieties and concentrate on your message and your audience.
>
> 10. **Gain experience.** Mainly, your speech should represent you — as an authority and as a person. Experience builds confidence, which is the key to effective speaking. A Toastmasters club can provide the experience you need in a safe and friendly environment.

Why bother with doing presentations?

The chutzpah purpose of a presentation is to get listeners to go from being a listener to either customer or referral source. That may sound self serving, which it is, but that is the goal, plain and simple.

The process is quite simple. A person is interested in your topic, they hear you speak, they learn, they laugh, and they think of you as knowledgeable in your subject area. That same person still has more needs in the area you are offering assistance in, so now that he knows you, he is a smidgin more comfortable calling your office for an appointment.

I was having a discussion with a new mom concerning childhood vaccinations. She explained that she was unsure about giving the vaccinations to her baby because of the dangerous side effects. When I gently pushed for facts, she said, "I saw Jenny McCarthy on TV. She said that vaccines were very dangerous."

"Who is Jenny McCarthy?" I asked.

"You know, the TV star!"

"Sorry, don't know her," I said.

"Sure you do, she is almost married to Jim Carey. She is like this fitness health nut."

"Is she a scientist?" I asked.

"No, she is on MTV. She has a dating program, advice and stuff. She's on magazine covers," she explained.

The point of this story is that this new mom trusted Jenny McCarthy and she felt comfortable taking her vaccine medical advice from Jenny McCarthy.

When you are in public, presenting yourself as a caring and knowledgeable entrepreneur, people will be more comfortable coming to you or referring to you. The simple fact that they know you, makes you less fear provoking.

Who wants to hear your talk?

Most professionals start at what is affectionately called the "Rubber Chicken" meetings. These are often breakfast, lunch, or evening meetings of community service organizations. You may have noticed Rotary, Optimist, or Eagle plaques adorning the entrance walls of many family style restaurants throughout the country. If the restaurant has a meeting room, it probably hosts at least one service club meeting per week. I have been to a few service clubs that have had fifty plus year relationships with a restaurant.

Some clubs have their own building. Many Moose, Elk, and Eagle orders are well established and own their own halls, recreation, and meeting areas.

Most of the presentations that you will be asked to do will be in front of small to medium size groups (10-50 people). These types of groups bring together like-minded individuals with a common purpose. A 35 minute talk to an Optimist Club or the local Elks can get your name around the community in short order.

Service organizations by their nature are community oriented. Part of the draw for the members is the camaraderie of the meetings. Each group has its meeting rituals. Many of the groups have rituals that are interesting, to say the least, to observe. Laughter and inside jokes are common. I am always impressed with how welcoming these groups are to me when I have been invited to speak. The food tends to be basic, but the friendships of the members are intoxicating. These are caring people, community minded, with a solid sense of God and country.

Most groups try to have a weekly speaker. The goal is to have an interesting topic for the members to experience. Well, as you can imagine, it becomes difficult for the speaker coordinator to find forty to fifty amazing speakers every year. This is where you come in. If you have a topic that the speaker coordinator thinks his fellow members will be interested in, he wants you.

Many members of one club are also involved or are friends with members of another club. After talking to a few clubs, where I initiated contact, the speaker coordinators of other clubs started to call and request my talk.

The 60/40 rule of presentations.

My goal is to inform and entertain. The 60/40 rule is 60% entertainment and 40% information, often referred to as infotainment. The infotainment needs to be uplifting and hopeful, along with some substance.

Many people misunderstand this 60/40 to mean: entertain (60%) and talk about your product (40%). I suffered through this type of a program recently. The guest speaker, an accountant, told a few old jokes and explained tax law for small businesses. I kid you not, six times in thirty-five minutes he said, "The new statute reads as follows..." Then, in a monotone, he read the IRS statute. At the end of each statute, he explained how he would make sure that, if you came to him, your tax return would be completed correctly. What a self serving snooze.

For a chutzpah marketer, the 60/40 rule looks like: 60% entertainment; 39% usable, powerful, amazing, wowing, spectacular, informative, life changing, and life affirming information; and 1% I'm here to help. Here is how you can get hold of me.

60/39/1 lets people get to know you, as a person, and as a professional. And, as we have discussed before, if they like you they will call for your help or refer to you.

My chutzpah goal is to let the group see me as a valuable resource, who is simply a phone call away.

April is...

F.A.Q. Often I am asked, "But what do I talk about?" This is not really the correct question. The correct starting question should be, "What does the group want to learn about that I already know a lot about?"

Please let me explain. I only know a lot about two subjects, suffering and Chinese food. If you ask me a question about human suffering (psychology stuff) or what I want for lunch, I feel pretty confident that I can answer and even impress. The problem is that if you ask me about something in any other of the billions of knowledge categories, I'm liable to show you my cognitive limitations. So, I want to talk to a group about psychology stuff (preferably while eating Chinese food out of paper containers).

I am also basically lazy, so I don't want to invest a lot of time studying and rehearsing my talk. Therefore, I talk about things I already know and mold my presentation to the group I am talking to.

April is National Child Abuse Prevention Month. I know a lot about the subject of child abuse, so I offer groups talks concerning child abuse awareness, prevention and community support programs. I tailor my presentation to the group. If it is a church social club, I present a "this is how you can help" talk. If it is a police officers' association, or the nursing staff of the emergency room, I present a wound identification slide show. ("This household gadget leaves a wound that looks like…") I am comfortable with presenting either level of presentation with little prep time. With both groups I would talk about mandated reporting laws, one in passing, while the other in explicit detail.

In both of these examples, I follow the 60/39/1 presentation rule. Even the presentation to the police or nursing staff is in the infotainment format. How, you might ask? It is through the stories. The police and the nurses have seen a lot, so my stories are more graphic, but my message is of uplifting hope. With the church group I talk about how to get help for a child that may be in need. For the professionals, I talk about how to document correctly, present professionally, and how to be a part of the help team.

Autumn is a fitness instructor who prefers to work with employees concerning stress management. Autumn is comfortable talking to small groups, and by nature a calm individual. She confided in me that her biggest concern about giving a talk was "boring" the attendees.

"Autumn," I asked. "If you could give a little bit of help to each attendee, what would you want them to learn from you?"

"The importance of having personal moments throughout your work day," she said.

"How would you teach that to a small group?" I asked.

"I would teach them a simple calming mantra that they could do at their desk. A 5 minute healing mantra," she said.

"I think a lot of busy people are service club members. You could help a lot of people," I said.

Autumn offered her "Five minutes to a calmer you" talk to local groups, and she was warmly welcomed.

What small gift of help can you offer in a talk?

February is National National Awareness Month Awareness Month

According to the fun loving folks at "easilyamused.org" February is National National Awareness Month Awareness Month. Their web site has a long list of real national awareness programs. (See: www.aware.easilyamused.org) Each awareness month listing is linked to the organizer's web site. A wealth of ideas.

The Centers for Disease Control and Prevention offers a web page, CDC Calendar of Conferences & Events. On this page you will find a link to the

National Center for Health Statistics (NCHS) Upcoming Releases. This page lists the CDC events over the coming year. Often, a national conference garners a lot of press. Being aware of this expected press months in advance will lend insight into topics that local groups will be interested in, say next March. (See: www.cdc.gov/about/newsEvents/events.htm)

Other commemorative list makers that you may find helpful:

- Alphabetical List of Recognition Days, Weeks and Months (pohly.com/dates_alpha.shtml)
- The ePromos Promotional Calendar (www.epromos.com/calendar/promotional-calendar.html)
- Awareness Celebrations (www.menstuff.org/calendar/workshops/awareness.html)
- Full List of Awareness Dates (www.awarenessdates.com/2007/01/full-list-of-awareness-dates.html)
- Crime Awareness Months (www.selfdefenseresource.com/general/articles/crime-awareness-months.php)

Finding local groups

Your local Sunday newspaper tends to be a grand resource for finding group contact information. Often there is a list of the meeting times of local groups and contact information.

A partial list of national/international service clubs:

- Kiwanis International (www.kiwanis.org)
- Fraternal Order of Eagles (www.foe.com)
- Benevolent and Protective Order of Elks (www.elks.org)
- Knights of Columbus (www.kofc.org)
- Lions Clubs International (www.lionsclubs.org)
- The National Exchange Club (www.nationalexchangeclub.org)
- National Grange Of The Patrons Of Husbandry (www.nationalgrange.org)
- Optimist International (www.optimist.org)
- Soroptimist International of the Americas (www.soroptimist.org)
- Rotary International (www.rotary.org)
- Ruritan National (www.ruritan.org)
- SERTOMA (www.sertoma.org)

In addition to large service clubs, you will find small groups in your community doing marvelous things. Many local professionals have organized clubs. Realtors, teachers, and university women's clubs are common. Many high schools work with local professional groups on activities like, Mock Trial,

Model United Nations, and National Science Bowl. Often these groups are interested in outside professional speakers. My local high school has a Future Health Professionals Club that invites health care professionals in regularly to discuss local health care issues. Parents, many of them local health care professionals, participate in the club's activities making this group highly desirable for a chutzpah mental health professional.

Check your local high school or college web site under activities or clubs.

Many local churches, synagogues, and mosques have service and youth clubs.

Contacting local groups

As we discussed before, the service clubs need speakers. The goal of the speaker coordinator or faculty advisor is to bring in valuable information for the members. The speaker coordinator has openings, and you have valuable information. You both are a match made in chutzpah heaven. But, the speaker coordinator doesn't know of you, yet.

It is a simple task of introducing yourself to the speaker coordinator. By writing a letter to them, offering your services, you start the ball rolling.

It is imperative that you contact the appropriate person and that you spell that person's name correctly. This is done with a simple phone call to the group's contact person. All you have to do is ask, then repeat the information back making sure you have it 100% correct. Often when you call the contact person will be happy to give you the speaker coordinator's phone number. You want that, but you also need the address and name spelled out. I like to send a letter first, then call in about a week if I have not heard from the coordinator. I want the speaker coordinator to have my "packet" that presents me as a professional, prior to talking to him on the phone.

Over the last few years, I regularly hear from speaker coordinators, "I Googled you and would like to see when you are available." (This shows the importance of your web presence.) This way, I don't have to ask to be invited, I show my willingness, and they invite. Everyone wins.

First contact letter with the speaker coordinator

I recommend you send a simple packet of information about yourself directly to the speaker coordinator. The packet should consist of:

1. A cover letter
2. Ten business cards
3. Your company brochure
4. A photo of you talking in front of a group
Plus, resume and copies of news articles if you have them.

All this gets placed into a nice crisp 8.5" x 11" envelop, so when it gets to its destination, it presents you well.

Your chutzpah cover letter

On your letterhead you write a short and sweet letter explaining that you are in the process of getting to know your community better. After hearing about the fine work that their group does, you think that you can present some new and exciting information that will help them in their charity work.

Please note, you must explain how your talk can help them. It is all about them and their needs. Your desire needs to be to meet them and help them.

Know your group

Your offer needs to be specific to the general tenet of the group you are hoping to talk to. If your club tends to do child advocacy work, your speech needs to be about children. If the group is veteran centric, your speech needs to be about veterans' issues.

 Often an entrepreneur asks, with fear in their voice, "How can I get my company/specialty to fit a group's needs?" The answer is simple, the group is made up of people, who are just like your company or area of interest.

Let me give you some examples. My area of interest is child abuse prevention. I have a basic speech that is my framework. I then add a few talking points — stories or examples — that are of interest to my audience.

If I want to talk to a veterans group I offer talks on subjects like:

- Helping returning vets go from soldier to Mom or Dad
- Talking to the children of active duty personnel about their fears
- Helping a family without pushing them away: Helping the children by supporting the parents

If I want to talk to a service organization like Rotary or the Optimist:

- What is the latest research on pedophilia: What every parent should know
- What are the warning signs that a child is in danger

If I want to talk to a sales organization such as a realtor association or a Chamber of Commerce:

- How to deal with family problems at work
- How to deal with anger in the workplace

No matter the group, during the question and answer part of my talk, the questions will inevitably be personal to the person asking:

- "My daughter has a five year old who is still afraid of the dark, is that OK?"
- "Do you work with children whose parents are not in the military?"
- "I have a coworker who is vindictive, how do I deal with that?"

Your audience will always be made up of real people, first and foremost. Whatever you are talking about, they will hear it as personal to them.

Examples of first contact letters

Please, please, please, do not over think the first contact letter. The person you are writing to is motivated to use you. He has a lot of slots to fill over the course of the year. Thus, if you are offering something interesting and professional he wants you. You are solving a problem for him.

Your first contact letter should be short and sweet. No need to oversell or exaggerate. Simply make your offer and show a reasonable benefit.

For example:

Dear Mr. Mark Harold,

I have heard wonderful things about the Greater Bay Rotary Club. I have a 20 to 30 minute talk concerning children in our community entitled, What Are The Warning Signs That A Child Is In Danger? I thought your club would find this information helpful in your work.

Please contact me at your earliest convenience. My office phone number is 555-1234.

Thank you,

When Mr. Mark Harold calls, you simply chat about how you are interested in sharing this, or similar important information. Remember that part of your package is material that explains how wonderful you are and how professionally talented you are. Expect that the speaker coordinator has read over all your enclosures and looked over your web site. He probably Googled you also. It is his job to do due diligence and only invite vetted individuals into his speakers program.

 So, what do you do if the speaker coordinator calls and starts off the conversation with, "I really appreciated your offer, but just last month, Mary Smith did a very similar talk."

At this point, you find a need.

"That sounds wonderful, I'm so glad that your club is so well informed. Are there any topics that members are talking about where I may be helpful?" you say.

"No, not really," Mr. Harold says.

"Nothing in the news or concerning children that people are talking about?" you ask.

"Well, kind of… I think people are concerned about 'How come people hurt children?'" he speculates.

"That is a very common question, I have a short talk called, What Is The Latest Research On Pedophilia: What Every Parent Should Know. I go over the latest research and leave lots of time for Questions and Answers. Would that be helpful to you?

Honorarium

Some larger groups offer honorariums ranging from a few dollars to offset your gas, to thousands of dollars. Many of the smaller groups are uncomfortable with this whole honorarium thing. So don't be surprised if a speaker coordinator gets nervous and asks about your honorarium or speaker's fee. This is where you need a nine-second speech. Mr. Harold says, "Ah, you know we are a small group and we really can't afford speakers… we tend to buy you lunch…"

"It is always my policy to donate back any honorariums so your club can continue your important work. Is that OK?"

I have had clubs that never pay for speakers, give me an honorarium just so I can donate it back to them. It is a wonderful moment at the end of my talk when the president of the club stands up and makes his closing remarks.

"I wanted to take this opportunity to thank Dr. Copitch for his enlightening speech."

"And as a gesture of his commitment to our charity work in the greater Shasta County area," the president says while holding up a large check for $1,000.00, "Dr. Copitch has kindly donated his honorarium back to us. Thank you Dr. Copitch and thank you all for your hard work in our community."

We all applaud each other.

Chutzpah low cost trade shows

Next Saturday there will be 1500 people walking around your local mall. On a typical Saturday there are only 420. But this particular Saturday there will be 1500 because the mall has been advertising their annual Health Fair. It has been on TV and the radio for the last ten days. Some ads push the "Free Cholesterol Screening". Other ads promote the offer of a "Free Diabetes Screening". One ad explains how important the Health Fair is by gloating, "Over 80 booths! Free admission."

Other weekends your community has the Home and Garden show at the Fair Grounds, and the junior college hosts a Job Fair, "Over 60 employers."

These are a few examples of Trade Shows. Trade shows are highly effective ways to get like minded individuals to congregate.

Some are huge, like the Macworld Conference & Expo that brought 44,000 Apple Computer enthusiasts together in San Francisco for five days during January 2009. There were 400 exhibitors showing their products. According to the press, the numbers were down because of the unstable economy.

Other trade shows are small, not much more than a dog and pony show. In the beautiful and historic community of McCloud, California, there is just such an event, the Dog and Pony Show Parade. Gene Eagle[20] of the Mount Shasta Area Newspaper wrote:

> Most of the more than 30 pets and their owners wore colorful costumes during the 2nd annual Dog and Pony Show Parade Saturday in McCloud.

---

20 www.mtshastanews.com/archive/x415862849/Pets-join-the-parade-in-McCloud

Dogs, four horses and a kitten strolled down McCloud's Main Street in ideal weather for a late November outdoor event.

Many of the smaller dogs wore brightly colored bows, and all participants received either a medal or a ribbon.

As you have probably gathered, I am using the term Trade Show very loosely. Depending on your company or organization's needs a "trade show" can be a chutzpah gold mine.

In this section we are going to discuss many ways to get attention for your business or organization by renting a booth and inviting the public to visit.

If done correctly, low cost trade shows are a powerful chutzpah tool. Examples of trade shows are:

- Health fairs
- Job fairs
- Garden and home shows
- Gun shows
- Specific business oriented trade shows, i.e., computer, auto, boat, motor home or health industry fairs
- Psychic fairs
- Renaissance fairs
- Community fairs
- Craft fairs
- Open air markets
- Octoberfest
- Heritage fairs
- Harvest festival
- Pumpkin festival
- Honey festival

Many companies (non profit and for profit) hold community events, for example:

- In my area there is a two day craft fair that transforms a large park into merriment, and raises money for local charities.
- A local hospital does a health fair in their parking area with lots of booths extolling the virtues of using the hospital, along with free health screenings.
- The local cancer association chapter has a weekend walk-a-thon that is well attended. Lots of fun and health information.

This partial list is just a taste of all the ways you can get your name out. Depending on your needs, any of the above events can be used to generate customers and good will.

A dummy example of getting attention.

How valuable would it be to your company if you were given two minutes on CNN to talk about your service and how you advertise it? That is what happened to Kenny Tessel the owner of KT's Barbecue in Redding, Ohio. When business slowed down, Kenny told CNN, "I needed to get these people who are driving by to stop in my store … and they have been, and it's thanks to Bar Be."

Bar Be Que is a busty mannequin who stands out in front of KT's Barbecue. In three weeks, Bar Be has brought in 70 new customers, an increase in sales of 30%. Kenny says, "Let Bar Be bring them in, and let my food bring 'em back." In addition to new business, Bar Be and Kenny got a lot of local and national free media attention.

Bar Be Que is a busty mannequin

I'm uncomfortable with an information booth...

The main purpose of a booth is to get attention for your product or services. This attention is often uncomfortable for many business owners. But, and this is a big but, without attention, no one will know of your services. So, what is more fear provoking, not being known, or being known? Later in this chapter I will show you ways for your booth and your message to get attention. Often this takes a lot of the lime light off of you, and puts it where it belongs, on your customers' needs and how your services can help them with their needs.

Chutzpah booth design

Below is a photograph of a typical booth that you might see at a local trade show or health fair:

Typical booth presentation

This booth has all the basics. Sign of product, product literature, and examples of product. Behind the table you have 3 nice people, willing to assist any and all.

This is a basic booth, but it is basically uninviting. As we discussed earlier when discussing print ads and brochures, you need to grab the passersby's eyes and get their attention. I do not know anything about the Mystery Writers of America, and at first glance I would assume I know all I need to know about the subject. Are they selling books? Are they encouraging me to become a mystery writer? Can I meet a real live mystery writer at this booth? This basic booth makes the passerby work too hard to figure out what the booth is all about and invite themselves in.

Booth space tends to be rented in allotments of 10' x 10'. Corner booths and high traffic area booths are prized, and demand a much steeper fee.

For the purpose of this section, we will assume you will rent a 10' x 10' booth space at an indoor health fair.

10' x 10' x 10"

Your booth space is three dimensional so as you think about how to use it, you need to picture it in three dimensions. When you are standing in front of your booth, you notice the booth is 10 feet wide. It is also 10 feet deep. And it is ten feet tall. (Some fairs limit you to 8 feet tall.)

Front view of trade show booth

When you stand in front of the booth area it may seem large, because it is 10 feet wide after all. But this size is deceiving. In actuality, the viewable space of your booth is more likely only 2 feet tall by ten feet wide. Please let me explain. When the event is going, lots of people will be milling around. As people walk by your booth, others just feet away will have their view of your booth blocked by moving people traffic. Because of this, your chutzpah attention getting, eye grabbing, all controlling "hook" needs to be above the human traffic. Like your brochure headline, this hook needs to be about your potential customer.

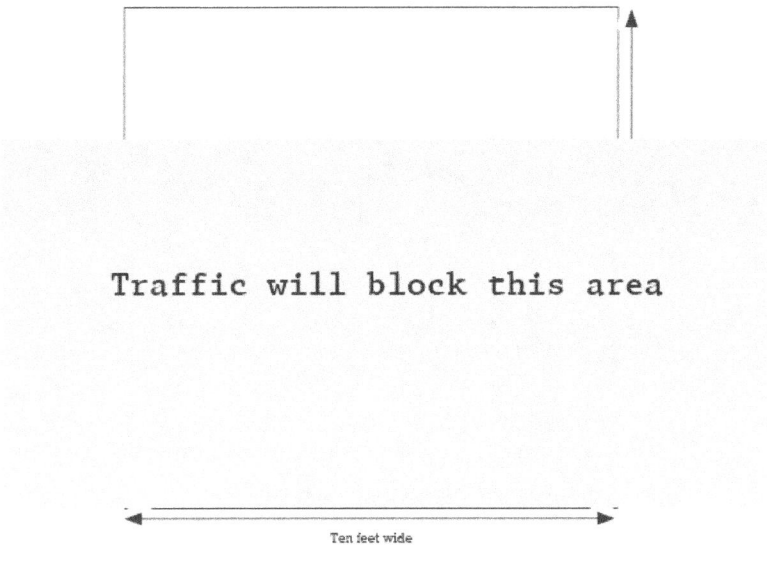

Traffic will block this area

Ten feet wide

Blocked view of booth

Your chutzpah hook needs to grab the attention of attendees. Just as with your brochure, Yellow Page ad, and your postcard campaign, your hook line should be the first of at least 4 steps:

All chutzpah booths have four major components.

1. Chutzpah headline
2. Chutzpah supporting information
3. Chutzpah supporting secondary benefits
      ------Name and address
4. Chutzpah call to action

Plus a 5th, if possible— save/stick/pass-ability.

As someone moves towards your booth, from any direction, your chutzpah headline should capture their interest. As they get closer, through the pedestrian traffic, more of your message should help pull them in. Your supporting information should be legible from at least 6 feet away (10 feet is better). The overall colors of your backdrop should be inviting, and informative words. Graphics should encourage the passerby to stop and allow eye contact with your booth personnel.

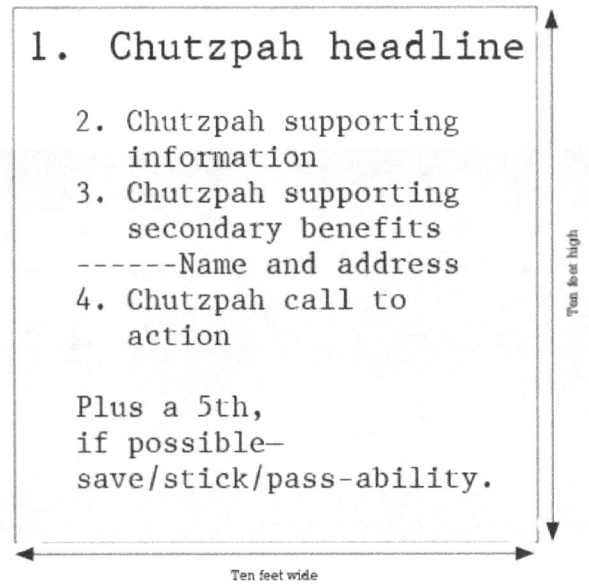

Capturing the public's attention

In addition to interference from pedestrian traffic, you and your staff, and your display table are occupying the 10' by 10' space. More on booth design later in this chapter.

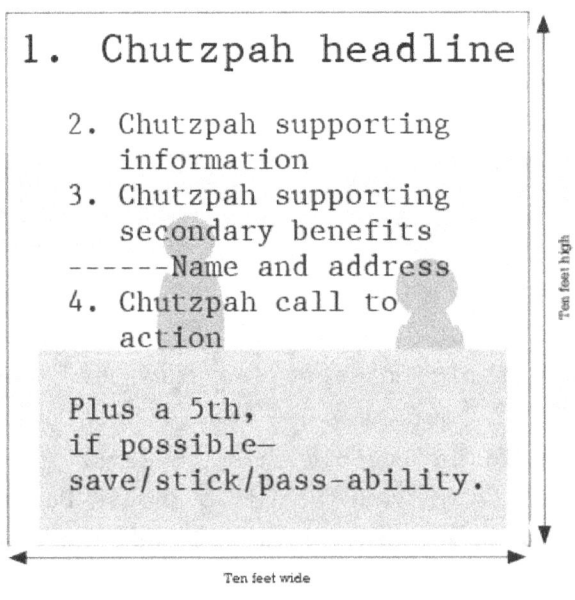

Using your space carefully

Types of booth signage

Due to the explosion of digital printing, it is possible to get fantastic, eye candy, color banners at reasonable prices. 2' by 10' full color custom banners can be ordered for around $100.

Empire Banners has an informative price list available at:
www.empirebanners.com/pricing.cfm

I have found my local digital sign store very competitive.

Rectangular vinyl banners tend to be up to four feet high and as long as you would like. They tend to be offered in 13 ounce (economy) weight or 15 ounce (heavy) weight. Banners can be printed on one or both sides. A 3' x 10', custom designed, full color banner can dress up the back of your booth. (For more information concerning banners see: Chapter 7: **Advertising Part D: Your Office, Store, and Vehicles Are Chutzpah Marketing Tools: Banners**)

This next photo shows a powerful backdrop banner that was eye catching even in this large area.

Large area banner

If you look carefully at this banner you can see that the four sides are hemmed and that the grommets are placed every two feet. The hemming and grommets are important, allowing you to hang and re-hang your banner. Most reputable banner printers incorporate the cost of the hemming and grommets into the banner's basic cost, if your printer does not, I advise you to look for a different printer. Grommets or hemming should not be an additional fee.

Another consideration should be floor banners and signs. Banners have been used for centuries to bring participants to the correct area. The following example shows a banner dating back to the 14th century. It is the rallying banner of the Corporation of the United Boot and Shoe Makers of Issoudun.[21]

Realtors have learned that rafters on the Sacramento River, CA are potential home buyers. As you leisurely float by the boat launches and palatial back yards, colorful signs invite you to dream about home ownership on the river.

14th century banner

In modern times we still use the banner to garner attention and to direct groups. Below you will find a basic welcome floor banner.

21 Project Gutenberg EBook of Manners, Custom and Dress During the Middle Ages and During the Renaissance Period, by Paul Lacroix www.gutenberg.org/files/10940/10940-h/10940-h.htm

This type of banner can add a lot of color and professionalism to your booth. It is inexpensive costing about $200 for a double sided sign and stand. Most sign companies have a selection of pre-made general purpose banners, or you can custom make you own. I recommend you custom make your banner, your area is small, and it is best to control every quarter inch with your message.

Below is an excellent example of how Rutgers University customized a floor banner. This banner is a nice example of general self promotion. If you look at the bottom of the banner you will notice that this is a spring loaded pull-up banner. It is like an upside down window blind that is pulled upward for display. This type of banner housing is a little pricier, $300 plus, but it makes for easy transport and safe storage of your banner between uses.

A custom banner

For about $1000.00 you can get very fancy with a hanging scrolling banner as shown next. This is really three banners in one. The banner slowly scrolls revealing each banner. This eye catching signage will get people to stop and look.

Hanging scrolling banner

At a recent trade show I found a free standing scrolling banner placed strategically 5 feet across from the bottom of an escalator. The descending escalator riders were a captured audience for all three of the scrolling posters. That was chutzpah placement. Next we see a floor sign ($100 - $300 depending on size.) These vinyl signs stick to the floor and slow pedestrians down as they read them.

Floor signage

 A homemade version of this type of sign was done by a pre-school and Head Start program. They took hundreds of black silhouettes of little feet and had them tracking the floor to their display.

The footprints directed folks from all directions to the center of the booth where there was a kiddie pool filled with sand and seashore toys. The theme of the booth was Summer Enrichment and Fun.

Tear drop banners are becoming very popular. They are an eye catching change from the standard rectangular banner.

Tear drop banners

Tear drop banners are usually 3 to 16 feet high and are easy to install, usually by poking them into the ground or placing them into a weighted stand. They are made to quiver in a breeze adding to their eye catching appeal. The collapsible spine makes them easy to transport and store. (Over the last few months I have had a few friends despair that their tear drop banners have been pilfered. One friend said, "I last saw it waving from the back of a pickup as it sped off." My friend is the manager of a Sprint cellphone store and for the life of him couldn't imagine that he needed to guard a large yellow sign that boldly read "Sprint". I assume it became a rally banner for the "hoodlum" element of a local high school track team.)

The overall look of your booth

Earlier in this chapter we looked at the typical local booth. Now let's get a little bit picky and look at how, with a little bit of chutzpah, and a tiny budget, your booth can stand out.

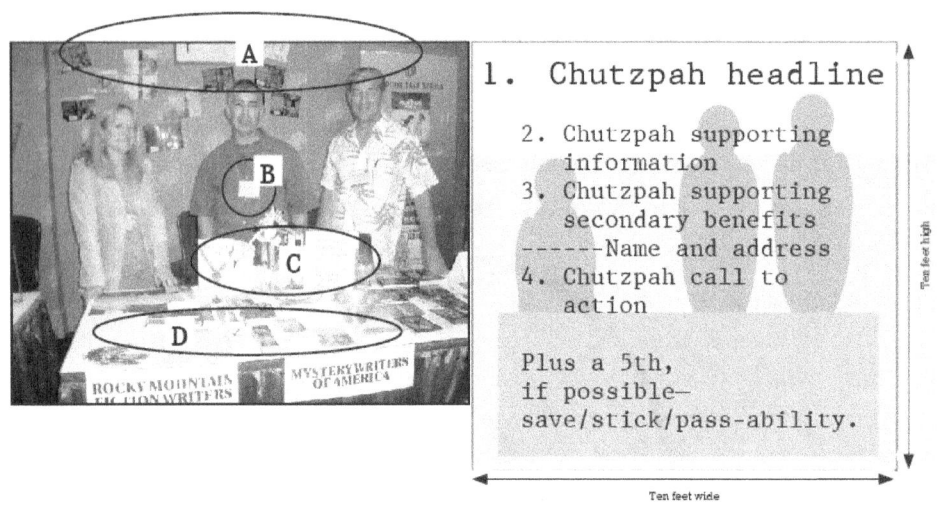

Compare and contrast a typical booth

Most booths at a local event will look like the one above. The vantage point of the camera is where your booth visitor will be standing. Take a second, and study this picture. What is this booth all about? What message or tone catches your attention? The three smiling people seem nice, but are they inviting you to ask questions? If so, questions about what? People do not like to feel even a little stupid. People avoid feeling even the tiniest bit stupid. Often, if your message is not clear and easily understandable, people will simply walk on by, avoiding the minor discomfort.

Helping the passerby into the role of visitor to your booth is very important. This is where your Chutzpah Headline comes in. Your headline starts the conversation from a calm, non threatening place. Just like with your company brochure headline, your booth headline needs to get the passerby contemplating their needs.

Let's play for a second. What would you suggest the mystery writers' booth chutzpah headline be:

_____

_____

_____

_____

_____

_____

My suggestion:

Any unsolved, questionable or lascivious secrets...
you would like to tell a mystery writer?

From the vantage point of the passerby, the pictures on the backdrop are too small to be useful. Your goal should be large, colorful, and powerful graphics that capture the passerby's eye.

Moving our attention to the people in the picture, we see three nice individuals. Many trade shows give badges to the participants making it easy for them to come and go through the exhibit doors. These tags are not enough identification for your booth worker. Booth workers need to present as professional members of your team. Professionally made name tags, and/or silk screened shirts, go a long way to making your workers look the part.

At one health fair I attended, the Herbalife independent dealer had all her people wearing the following button on their green tee-shirts.These three inch buttons were nice ice breakers.

We will talk more about ice breakers later in this chapter.

The table stand-ups (see, Compare and contrast a typical booth, above) are there to help keep the initial conversation going. Once the pedestrian has stopped at your booth, you want to focus them towards your offerings. Again, signage is important, you do not want to make the visitor have to figure out the correct next step. If the visitor is supposed to touch, let them know.

I use this sign when I exhibit my books.

All of Dr. Copitch's books
have an extensive index

Please browse

Questions Welcome

When you put out brochures it is a good idea to put out a small sign, "Free information" or "Please take one" or "Please take two".

If you are doing a raffle, this is the area that the capture bowl goes. Have it well labeled. Have the rules of the raffle printed large and easy to find. You do not want to wear out your booth staff by having them say, "Please put your raffle ticket in the bowl," eighteen-hundred times. (The sign will help them say it only 600 times.)

You ingratiate and welcome visitors with clear mid-level signs.

The tabletop is where you present your chutzpah call to action, and if possible— save/stick/pass-ability.

Your chutzpah call to action and if possible—save/stick/pass-ability

In reality, a trade show booth is a one trick pony. If you try to do too much, you're going to lose your impact. The hard truth is that you get one call to action, one suitable to your booth. Most professionals do not believe this truth. These people are greedy and do not understand that capturing the public's attention is hard and fleeting.

When you plan your booth, have a single purpose, a singular goal that you want to achieve. Such as:

- Get the names and address of potential customer. A raffle will do this well.
- Get name recognition for your company. Giveaways will do this well: pens, magnets, scratch pads, calendars, balloons, or a free, or very low cost, mini service.
- Sell books. Show discount will help.
- Sell services. Show discount will help.

If, for example, you want to do all four of the above, I am afraid you will be disappointed. By not focusing on a single goal, your presentation will be scattered. Your booth staff will be overworked trying to figure out which goal to promote with which visitor. You will lose your audience. As discussed earlier, multitasking does not work well.

Table bunting

Table bunting is the colorful curtain that covers the front and sides of your table. As with a clean coat of paint in an old kitchen, bunting hides many a secret. Bunting allows you to "hide" the mess that inevitably ends up under the booth table.

Many events offer bunting as part of the event's overall coordinated look. If not, you will need to provide your own. Customized bunting is an extravagant expense and since it will mostly be blocked by visitors' legs and baby strollers, an expense that is easily skipped.

If you opt for a large table cloth or blanket, make sure your table cover is secured to the table. Inevitably some little tyke will grab it and run, accidentally pulling your display onto the ground.

Dealing with the great outdoors

Many valuable and low cost booth opportunities will be outdoors. A health fair at a local hospital has become a fun and healthful community event, transacted in the hospital's parking lot.

All the rules we have already discussed concerning booth presentation count for indoor as well as outdoor booths, but outdoor booths have some added considerations.

You will have to prepare for weather conditions. It is best not to plan for the perfect day. Plan for hot or cold. Plan for too much sun or drizzle. Plan for wind. Encourage your staff to dress in layers and bring clothing of differing weights. Demand shade hats and sun screen. Discourage sun glasses because eye contact counts, even on sunny days. Provide lots of iced drinks or hot drinks. I bring my own, it costs a fortune to buy food and drinks at most events.

Because of wind, you will need extra weights to hold down signs and brochures.

I advise you to invest in a booth canopy of some sort. Protection from the sun or occasional drizzle has to be planned for. Also, a canopy defines your space. On a warm day, a little shade is inviting to visitors and booth workers. The best price I have seen for canopies has been at Costco. They have a white aluminum framed 10' x 10' canvass canopy for $149.00. It weighs 68 pounds and comes with four removable walls. Costco also has a Shade Logic Quick Clamp Canopy that is 7' x 10'. It clamps directly onto the table. (30 pounds, $95.00) See www.Costco.com.

Outdoors your 10' x 10' booth will look smaller. With the expanse of sky above your booth, signage doesn't show up as well as it does indoors.

One way to combat the shrinking booth phenomenon is to think tall. Helium filled balloons are an inexpensive way to float a second story over your booth. By adding a few colorful paper streamers to each balloon, the wave of color will get you noticed.

Sixteen foot tear drop banners at the corners of your outdoor booth will help get your real estate noticed.

As you can imagine, it can get very expensive to doll up a booth. So it is important to stay focused on the message you are teaching the public, much more so than the expensive esthetics of the booth.

Educate your booth staff

Events are usually at least a day (8-12 hours) or longer. Some can last over a week. Working with the public, answering similar questions all day long tends to wear booth workers out. Workers will be drained after events.

It is imperative that booth workers be well trained. This means lots of 9-second speeches. The focus of the 9-second speech is to "talk-up" the major goal of the booth.

During the event, supervision is important. You want to make sure your people are staying on message. A friend of mine, a veteran of trade shows, told me of a problem he had with an overly enthusiastic booth worker. "Carl was so excited about helping people that he made our 15% Fair Discount on future services 50%. I couldn't really get mad at him when he told me, 'They seemed so happy to be getting 50% off.'" It is important to supervise even the enthusiastic worker.

Chutzpah tricks for garnering attention

If people do not stop at your booth, you have wasted your time and effort attending the event. In this section we will look at chutzpah tricks to get people to stop and look, interact and learn about your offerings.

Candy

By offering wrapped candy in a bowl, people will stop to graze. Many other booths will be offering candy, so you will have to up your offerings. Wrapped hard candies are passé, the mini "fun size" candy bars are the entry level sugar bribe of choice. Use a deep glass/plastic bowl that is always kept partially full. Have the visitor reach deep into the bowl, leaving the impression that lots of visitors have already gotten candy.

One high school counseling department wanted to hand out community health information to parents. They were aware that their information was important, but boring. The community health fair was over Father's Day weekend. They asked the cheerleading squad for help in livening up their dull, no frills booth.

At the back of their relatively drab booth they put up a blanket wall with a sign, "Happy Fathers Day! Free kisses from a cheerleader."

The bubbly cheerleaders asked "dads" as they approached the table, "Do you want a kiss?" Then one of them would drag the dad behind the curtain, give him a Hershey's kiss and say, "Please tell everyone that you have never been kissed like this before," and she gave him a sticker that read, "Kissed by a cheerleader." On the way out of the kissing booth a high school counselor gave each dad a plastic bag of information. The "dads" played along with the whole thing. Some swooning and gasping as they left the kissing booth. Throughout the day, hundreds of men wore "Kissed by a cheerleader" stickers. The drab, low cost booth got a lot of buzz.

As the day went on, the counselors fielded lots of questions concerning the information in the bags. It seemed that after being kissed, lots of moms and dads were encouraged to look into the information bag.

Smile and make eye contact

As people approach your booth, a smile is very important. It may not seem like much, but a smile is inviting.

It is best to have your booth staff verbalize an invite. "Welcome, look around… let me know if you have any questions." It is important to ingratiate.

Being upbeat is hard to do for the duration of an event, so it is best to look for naturally upbeat and hyperactive individuals to help out at your booth.

Police your booth

It is good policy to constantly police your booth, keeping it neat and tidy. A trade show or fair is an active, noisy and messy event. Keeping your area as nice as when you started the day, will calm your visitors and offer a few minutes of solace in a very chaotic day.

Think tactile

Whenever possible, offer tactile things for your booth visitors to touch and interact with. People feel more trustworthy of things they can touch. Offer items to hold such as display books, or examples of your business equipment.

One entrepreneur displayed a photo album of her staff's commitment to the Think Pink Walk in her area. The album was full of about 100 photos of happy people doing good things for the community.

Another entrepreneur showed a computer slide presentation of his staff, family, and himself landscaping for Habitat for Humanity. Again, lots of happy faces doing nice things for others.

Avoid being a bump on a log.

Don't just sit behind your booth table. Events are long, so sitting is a must, but use tall chairs, allowing for easier and more natural eye contact. Feel free to mingle in front of your booth. Schmooze or lose.

Interact with the other exhibitors

Make sure you meet every other exhibitor on your breaks from your booth. These people tend to be active people in your community. Interact with them. Teach them about your services.

When I work a charity booth, my chutzpah goal is to get a donation from every booth owner. Some write a check, while others give products. It is not unusual on the last day of a show, for another exhibitor to donate their exhibit to my charity, lock stock and barrel. What charity doesn't need extra chairs, tables, lights and 3000 pens that say, Wells Fargo or Apple. The charity gets the donation, while the company gets the write off and a great thank you letter. For years we did not need Post-it notes, because we had 10 cases that read, "Ford."

Dancing Chewbacca

I once participated in a 14 day booth event at the Santa Clara County Fair. KLOK radio donated the booth and thousands of KLOK tee-shirts to be given away as prizes. The booth was a simple coin toss, anyone who tossed a quarter into a glass on the table six feet away, won a tee-shirt. The radio station wanted everyone to win a tee shirt, and my charity got all the tossed quarters. The on air radio personalities helped out throughout the 14 days and signed autographs. The bulk of the volunteer power came from the Fremont Optimist club, an energetic group of caring people.

KLOK radio gave us lots of free radio time for weeks before and straight through the county fair.

The rental of a Chewbacca costume was a lot of fun and a lot of work. The suit is made for tall people, but over the course of the county fair, lots of volunteers wore the outfit. We had baby chewy one afternoon when a 4'9" woman took her turn.

During the afternoons, the suit was hot. So I made a rule that no one could wear the costume for more than an hour. Being Chewy was so much fun, I had to force volunteers to stop dancing and greeting and to get rehydrated.

 Steve Goldstein, then president of the Optimist Club of Fremont, came up with the idea of having Chewbacca, of Star Wars fame, stand out in front of our booth and greet people. What an idea! The county fair was huge, and it was easy for a booth to get lost in all the excitement. Having Chewbacca dancing around, hugging, and posing for pictures generated a lot of energy and buzz. By the third day, Chewbacca was making hourly appearances on the grandstand, getting lots of cheers from the crowd, while the announcer spoke highly of our charity and directing everyone towards our booth.

Promotional giveaways

It is common for exhibitors to give things to booth visitors. My local waste disposal service handed out 4 inch green waste receptacles at a recent event. I don't know what you were supposed to do with them, and when I asked a booth worker he said, "I keep paperclips in it on my desk."

There is a whole industry dedicated to making promotional items. There are the common things like pens, scratch pads, and mugs, that can be emblazoned with your name and logo. And there are interesting promotional items such as custom printed condoms, fortune cookies, or Sanitizer on a Clip.

The idea is to give someone a free gift with your name on it. Later, when they use the free gift, they think highly of you and may decide to frequent your establishment. In theory this is a good idea, but what you don't know until you try it, is if it will work for you.

Promotional items tend to cost real money because you have to buy in quantity. And, they won't work unless you hand out lots of them. The question for you is, "Is there a return on your investment?"

I use promotional pens because I figure I am going to use lots of pens at my office, so when they walk out of my reception area, I don't care. However, I have never recorded a new patient because of my promotional pens. When I teach CEU seminars, I give out pens, hoping participants will use the pen in the future and say to themselves, "Oh, yeah… I need to get my CEUs!" I use the Bic Clic because it works well and costs less than 50¢ each when I buy in quantities of 500.

Promotional pen

Mr. Berg, the attorney, gives away a great black mug with gold lettering, it is quite striking. He is a defense attorney, so his custom mug gets attention.

Stolen from the Law Offices of
Berg & Associates
Criminal Defense & Divorce
(530) 223-5100

Mr. Berg's mug art, both sides.

Dr. Hanson, the dentist, used a promotional pen, "Extracted from the Office of Kenneth Hanson, DDS." Patients seemed to love the joke.

Dr. Hanson also used a refrigerator magnet as a promotional gift. I really like this idea because it gets placed on a family's refrigerator, getting noticed throughout the year.

Frequently Called Numbers

Doctor
_____

Hospital
_____
Dr. Hanson 223-0441

Dentist
_____

Pizza

Hanson Dental Group

Kenneth Hanson, DDS
2809 Bechelli Lane • Mission Square
Call: 223-0441

Refrigerator magnet as a promotional item.

Mugs and magnets are relatively inexpensive. Many promotional items are not. When you think about promotional items, make sure you keep in mind your return on investment. A chutzpah marketer does not spend a dime if 9 cents will do.

Over the last few years, the promotional give-away industry has become very aware of "green" products. You may want to keep this in mind, many people see give-aways as landfill fillers. By going green you may be able to keep everyone happy.

My favorite free giveaways are very low cost, fridge art handouts as discussed in Chapter 7: **Advertising Part D: Your Office, Store, and Vehicles Are Chutzpah Marketing Tools: Fridge Art.** These giveaways give you enough room to print your chutzpah advertisement. Most promotional items only have room for your company name and maybe a little ad copy.

To start your search for your perfect promotional give-away, Google: promotional items. As of today I got 11,400,000 hits. The big players are on the first few pages.

Be creative

When it comes to promotional giveaways, your creativity is a big plus. Feel free to let your personality shine.

The picture below is an example of low cost creativity that "talks" to the potential customer. Attorney Amy Spencer-Martyn was giving away Anti-Stress Kits at the county fair. These little gems were getting a lot of attention. What a wonderful ice breaker for someone who might need her services.

The card inside a small baggy of goodies:

SPENCER-MARTYN LAW OFFICES

Knock Out Debt!

2201 Court Street
Redding, CA 96001

Phone: (530)244-0300
Fax: (530)244-0302
Web: www.Redding-Lawyer.com
Email: info@redding-lawyer.com

Anti-Stress Kit

Contains the following:

1.) An eraser - so you can make all your mistakes disappear.
2.) A penny - so you will never have to say, "I'm broke!"
3.) Marbles - in case someone says,"You've lost your marbles!"
4.) A rubber band - to stretch yourself beyond your limits.
5.) String - to tie things together when everything falls apart.
6.) A hug and a kiss - to remind you someone cares about you!

Amy Spencer-Martyn
Attorney

WITH COMPLIMENTS

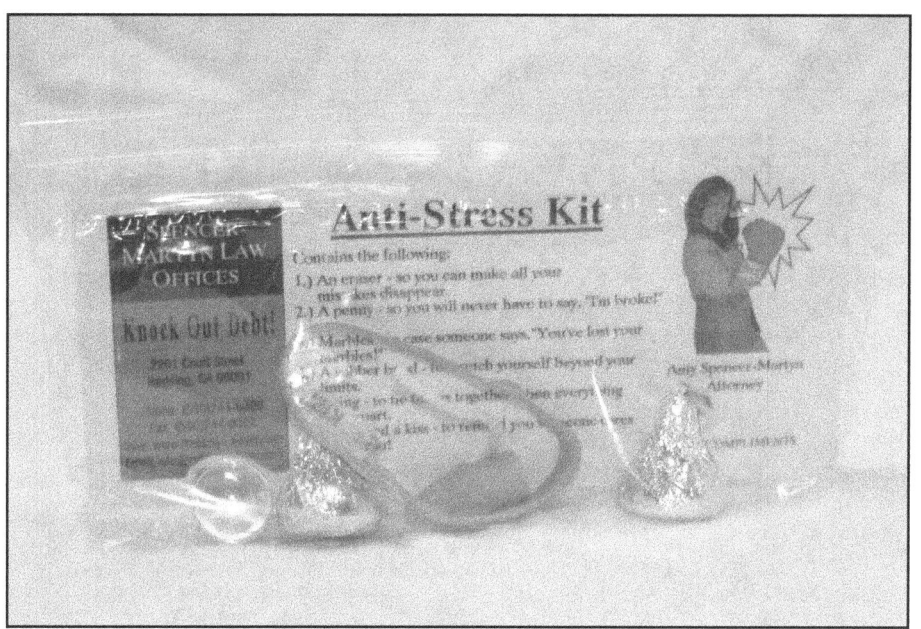

Anti-Stress kit giveaway

By allowing your personality to come through, your chutzpah giveaways will show the *feelings* of your company. When a customer is touched by your feelings, your company will be able to build a relationship with that individual. Be creative and allow your creativity to show!

IN CLOSING

Life and business can be overwhelming when we don't feel in control. By controlling ourselves - through planners and calendars; and encouraging others to be accountable, we feel safer, calmer, and get our needs met. A chutzpah marketer has goals. Chutzpah marketers take control of the 86,400 seconds of their day, every day.

Please allow me to quote Mark Cuban:

> It doesn't matter how many times you fail. It doesn't matter how many times you almost get it right. No one is going to know or care about your failures, and neither should you. All you have to do is learn from them and those around you because… All that matters in business is that you get it right once. Then everyone can tell you how lucky you are.

Be well,

www.ingramcontent.com/pod-product-compliance
Lightning Source LLC
Chambersburg PA
CBHW081109170526
45165CB00008B/2380